The
Marriage
Problem

The
Marriage
Problem

HOW OUR CULTURE
HAS WEAKENED FAMILIES

James Q. Wilson

HarperCollins*Publishers*

HarperCollins books may be purchased for educational, business, or sales promotional use. For information, please write: Special Markets Department, HarperCollins Publishers Inc., 10 East 53rd Street, New York, NY 10022.

FIRST EDITION

Printed on acid-free paper

Library of Congress Cataloging-in-Publication Data

Wilson, James Q.
    The marriage problem / James Q. Wilson.
        p. cm.
    ISBN 0-06-620983-8 (hardcover)
    1. Marriage—United States. 2. Family—United States. 3. United States—Social conditions—1980- I. Title.

HQ536 .W555 2002
306.85—dc21

2001024495

01   02   03   04   05   WB/RRD   10   9   8   7   6   5   4   3   2   1

To Matt and Becky,
Annie and Bob . . .
together forevermore.

Contents

Acknowledgments

The research for this book, like that of so many of my earlier ones, was supported by the Alfred P. Sloan Foundation. That donor has by its generosity helped shape my intellectual life and I remain immensely in its debt.

Livia Besharat, Russell Burgos, and Melissa Knauer provided skilled assistance on this project. My work would have taken twice as long had it not been for them.

Peter B. Clark, Richard T. Gill, Linda Waite, Roberta Wilson, and Christopher Wolfe read the entire manuscript and gave me their most helpful views. Individual chapters were read by Jay Belsky, David Buss, Mary Ann Glendon, Alan MacFarlane, Gertrude Himmelfarb, Charles Murray, Orlando Patterson, Peter Skerry, Scott Smith, Donald Symons, and John Witte. I received some valuable advice on Swedish policies from Elisabeth Langby and Rebecca Popenoe. All of these friends shared with me their vast knowledge of the puzzle I have been trying to unravel. Naturally, I take responsibility for the errors I made by recklessly choosing to ignore some parts of their advice.

Some paragraphs from chapter 1 are drawn from the Boyer Lecture I delivered to the American Enterprise Institute that was later published in *The Public Interest* under the title, "Human Remedies for Social Disorders" (number 131, spring, 1998). A few pages from chapter 9 first appeared in *The Public Interest* under the title, "Crime and American Culture" (number 70, winter 1983).

But my greatest obligation is to my friends who have been married to the same spouses all of their lives. I realize I have lived among what are by contemporary standards some unusual people: though the nation seems to believe in divorce, the great majority of my friends do not. Are we just too old to know better? I think not, and this book tries to explain why.

And five more people have had a vastly greater impact on me: my wife, Roberta, our son Matthew and his wife, Becky, and our daughter Annie and her husband Bob. From family and friends, I have learned a great deal.

The
Marriage
Problem

Chapter 1
Two Nations

Americans live in a nation confident of its wealth and proud of its power, yet convinced that this wealth cannot prevent and this power cannot touch a profound corrosion of our cultural soul. We are materially better off than our parents but spiritually worse off.

The poorest Americans today live a better life than all but the richest persons a hundred years ago. But despite this great wealth, we inhabit, as Benjamin Disraeli said a century ago, "two nations, between whom there is no intercourse and no sympathy; who are as ignorant of each other's habits, thoughts, and feelings, as if they were dwellers in different zones, or inhabitants of different planets." The two nations of which he wrote were the rich and the poor. But the great production and more even distribution of wealth that we achieved have altered the principle on which our nation is divided. Our money, our generosity, and our public spending have left us still with two nations, but separated by law and custom more than by wealth or favor. As Disraeli put it, these worlds are "ordered by different manners, and are not governed by the same laws."[1]

The American sociologist, Elijah Anderson, describes the matter more bluntly: "In our big cities, the middle-class, both white and black, thinks of itself as the outcome of the great tradition of Western culture, but nearby, there is a second culture of young, marginally employed, sexually adventuresome, socially aggressive young men who reject the idea of hard work and social conformity that made their elders successful. For some, decent jobs are hard to find, but for at least as many the effort to find and hold such jobs as exist has disappeared."[2]

In one nation, a child, raised by two parents, acquires an education, a job, a spouse, and a home kept separate from crime and disorder by distance, fences, or guards. In the other nation, a child is raised by an unwed girl, lives in a neighborhood filled with many sexual men but few committed fathers, and finds gang life to be necessary for self-protection and valuable for self-advancement. In the first nation, children look to the future and believe that they control what place they will occupy in it; in the second, they live for the moment and think that fate, not plans, will shape their lives. In both nations, harms occur, but in the second they proliferate—child abuse and drug abuse, gang violence and personal criminality, economic dependency and continued illegitimacy.

The facts about children raised in the second world—the world without fathers, without safety, without a decent life or reasonable prospects for the future—are well known to everybody. What once was a political argument has now become conventional wisdom, and like most such bits of wisdom, it is based on real facts.

In 1960 one-fifth of all black American children under the age of eighteen lived with a mother and no father. When Daniel Patrick Moynihan said that this was an important social problem, he was reviled.[3] By 1996, nearly one-fifth of all *white* children were living without a father, and now everybody said it was a problem and Moynihan was hailed as a prophet. When fatherless white children fell into the same plight once occupied only by black ones, the country woke up. But meanwhile the family circumstances of black children continued to deteriorate. In 1996, more than half of all of them lived in a mother-only family.[4]

Matters were even worse for teenage mothers. By 1995, three out of every four births to all teenagers were to unmarried girls; for black girls, it was nine out of every ten. In Washington, D.C., virtually every birth (to be exact, 97 percent of them) to a teenage girl was to an unmarried adolescent.[5]

The number of children born into these families has been falling because the birthrate of women, including teenagers, has been declining for the last several years. But for women who do have children, the illegitimacy rate remains high, and for teenage women, unimaginably so. Children are having children. And to these grim totals must be added the number of children who live with a divorced parent. There were fewer than a half million such kids in 1960; by 1995, there were well over a million.

Of course, some of these children go on to live with a stepparent, usually a stepfather, after the divorced parent remarries, but second marriages are even more vulnerable to breakup than the first ones. More than half of all stepfamilies were disrupted after ten years.[6] What is worse, stepparents—and again, especially stepfathers—are much more likely to abuse or murder their own stepchildren. The homicide rate for children in stepfamilies is seventy times higher than it is for those living with both biological parents.[7] The old family legends about evil stepparents were literary expressions of a grim fact: people care for their own children more than they care for those of others.

Why Not Just Live Together?

Some children born to an unwed mother will live with her and the father, who stay together without being married. The polite modern term for this is *cohabitation;* the Census Bureau calls it Persons of the Opposite Sex Sharing Living Quarters (POSSLQ). When I was a boy, it was called shacking up. Cohabitation has become common throughout the Western world. In England, France, and the United

States, cohabitation between a man and woman precedes marriage in roughly half or more of all cases. In Sweden, cohabitation is on its way to becoming the norm; roughly one-third of all couples cohabit instead of marry.

Scholars are divided about what this means. To some, cohabitation is an alternative to marriage; to others, it is an alternative to being single. For the first group, living together is like being married without the fuss and bother of licenses and ceremonies. If marriages are becoming rarer and living together more common, then men and women are just working out their lives as they see fit. For the second group, living together beats dating; after all, now you can pay one rent rather than two, share all of your meals instead of just dinners together, get rid of unnecessary roommates, and have sex in your own bedroom instead of in a motel. For the first group, cohabitation is the end of the story; for the second, it is a nice way to live before you decide to get married, usually to the person with whom you have been living.

Americans seem to have adjusted rather nicely to this new world. Nearly 60 percent of all high school seniors agreed or mostly agreed with the statement that "it is usually a good idea for a couple to live together before getting married in order to find out whether they really get along."[8] Public opinion polls taken by the Roper Center for Public Opinion Research show a big increase in the tolerance Americans have for unmarried life. In 1974 about one-third of us thought that "there is no reason why single women shouldn't have children"; by 1985, that proportion had risen to nearly half. Or so it would seem. In the same Roper poll, these people were then asked whether it was "acceptable for a daughter of yours to have a child outside of marriage," and suddenly the answers changed. In 1974 hardly anyone agreed; even in 1985 only about one-eighth would agree.[9] Something is going on here. Half us approve of *other* people's daughters having children out of wedlock, but hardly any of us approve of that for *our* daughters.

I suspect that we are displaying a widening tension between tolerance and belief. We have come to tolerate how other people live, but we have higher standards for how we ought to live. Tolerance is a virtue, but one with fuzzy edges. We don't wish to be "judgmental," unless what is being judged is something we care about.

What is at stake, when we do care about it, is the well-being of people we cherish. We suspect, rightly, that marriage differs from cohabitation. Cohabitation means that two people agree to live together, sharing rooms, meals, and sex. Marriage means that two people promise to live together until they die, sharing rooms, meals, sex, and a permanent obligation to care for one's spouse. The promise is the heart of the matter. Compare two business transactions. In one, two people agree to work together, selling some product. In the other, two people sign a contract saying that they will sell something, and that if one fails to do his or her share of the selling, or decides to run off and sell a similar product with another partner, then the abandoned partner can sue. In the first transaction, people will cooperate, at least until cooperation becomes bothersome. In the second, people will not only cooperate, they will invest heavily in the enterprise knowing that their investment is protected.

Marriage, unlike cohabitation, produces investments. Even though many marriages end in divorce (just as many businesses fall apart), the heightened costs of exit induce one person to count on the other. That may explain why cohabitation tends to be, in the United States and much of Europe, relatively short-lived. Here, the typical (more exactly, the median) cohabitation lasts 1.3 years.[10] Most Americans who do cohabit get married, sensing, I think, that the marital contract not only will please their parents, it will heighten their investments. Cohabitation may be fun when you are twenty-one and attractive; it looks a lot less inviting when you are fifty-one and drab.

High school students may be so tolerant of cohabitation because they suppose it is a good way to find out if they will get along for the long haul. But in fact it is not so helpful. People who cohabit before they get married are much more likely to get divorced than those who get married without cohabiting.[11] In Sweden, women who cohabit before marriage have a divorce rate that is 80 percent higher than that of married women who have not cohabited.[12] Similar differences were found in Canada and the Netherlands.[13]

Well, fine, say the students, that shows that the men and women learned they could not get along with each other. There is some truth in this. The higher divorce rates among couples who cohabit before marrying is in part the result of self-selection. That is, people who do not value marriage and don't mind having children out of wedlock are more likely to cohabit than those who want long-term commitments and think every baby should have two married parents.[14]

But cohabitation is a two-way street. Cohabitation may attract people with certain views, but it also changes the view of people who do cohabit. Living together without getting married makes people more willing to accept divorce. As two scholars put it, "cohabitation may change the way individuals view marriage and divorce" by, for example, persuading them that "intimate relationships are fragile and temporary in today's world."[15] Barbara Dafoe Whitehead said it more bluntly: "cohabitation is not to marriage what spring training is to baseball."[16] Living together may be better than dating, but it is not as good as commitment. But young people act as if this were not the case, and so the number of cohabiting couples rose from about one million in 1977 to nearly five million in 1997.[17] As a result, nearly half of all American men and women aged thirty-five to thirty-nine have cohabited at some point.[18] One study showed that only one-quarter of all American children born to cohabiting couples would go through their adolescent years living with both parents.[19]

A lot of children, perhaps more than two million, live with cohabiting rather than single or married parents. But that does not necessarily make them better off. In general, the education, employment, and earnings of a cohabiting couple with children are not much better than that of single parents. Children are as likely to be poor living with cohabiting parents as are those living with a single mom.[20] Those born to cohabiting parents will spend about one quarter of their childhood years with only one parent.[21] And when they grow up, these youngsters will be more likely to live in unsatisfactory marriages and to experience a divorce than is the case with children who grow up in two-parent families.[22] In England children living with cohabiting rather than married parents are twenty times more likely to become the victims of child abuse. This makes them worse off than even children living with an unmarried mother (they are only fourteen times more likely than are children in two-parent families to be abused).[23]

Cohabitation in America is different in at least one important way from living together in Europe. Here, people with a lot of schooling are more likely to marry than to cohabit, while less educated people are more likely to cohabit. In Europe, matters are reversed. There, the better-schooled people are *more* likely to cohabit, while the less schooled are more likely to marry.[24] I do not know quite how to explain this difference.

Families and Children

The family problem lies at the heart of the emergence of two nations. We wish people to work and to learn more in school. There have been times in our history when unemployment was high and public schools barely existed. Yet in those days we were not two culturally opposed nations. Boys did not carry guns on the street, people were not shot to get expensive sneakers, drugs did not dominate our urban life, and students who had gone to school could actually read and write. Today, we are vastly richer, but the money has not purchased public safety, racial comity, or educational achievement.

The reason, I think, is clear: it is not money but the family that is the foundation of public life. As that foundation has become weaker, every structure built upon it has become weaker. When our cultural framework is sagging, the foundation must first be fixed.

The evidence as to the powerful effect of this familial foundation is now so strong that even some sociologists believe it. Children in one-parent families, compared to those in two-parent ones, are twice as likely to drop out of school. Boys in one-parent families are much more likely than those in two-parent ones to be both out of school and out of work. Girls in one-parent families are twice as likely as those in two-parent ones to have an out-of-wedlock birth. These differences are not explained by income. Children in one-parent families are much worse off than those in two-parent families even when both families have the same earnings.[25]

When the Department of Health and Human Services (HHS) studied some thirty thousand American households, it found that for
whites, blacks, and Hispanics and for every income level save the very
highest, children raised in single-parent homes were more likely to be
suspended from school, to have emotional problems, and to behave
badly. Another study showed that white children of an unmarried
woman were much more likely than those in a two-parent family to
become delinquent, even after controlling for income.[26]

The children of single moms are more likely than those of two-
parent families,* to be abused, to drop out of or be expelled from
school, to become juvenile delinquents, to take drugs, and to commit
adult crimes.[27] Now, single-parent families are generally much poorer
than two-parent ones, and so some of these consequences may flow
from poverty, not family structure. Two scholars, Sara McLanahan
and Gary Sandefur, have painstakingly sorted out the independent
effects of income and father absence. They concluded that poverty by
itself accounts for about half of the differences in how children
behave; the rest is explained by living in a one-parent family.[28]

Take, for example, the chances that a child will wind up in jail or
prison. Perhaps it happens because he or she comes from a poor family, perhaps because he or she did not live with a father. There is a way
to sort out these and other competing explanations. Every year since
1979, the National Longitudinal Study of Youth (NLSY) has interviewed the same group of young people. The NLSY interviewers
notice when they talk to a young person who is incarcerated. This
makes it possible to figure out what factors earlier in the youngster's
life are associated with being locked up. When Cynthia Harper and
Sara McLanahan analyzed the results, they found that, holding
income constant, young people in father-absent families were twice as
likely to be incarcerated as those in two-parent families. They did not

---

*Throughout this book, the phrase "two-parent family" refers to the biological
mother and the biological father of the child living together. In the great majority of
cases, these parents will be married. When they are not married, the word "cohabiting" will be used; when one adult is a stepparent, the word "stepfamilies" will be
used.

do any better if they had acquired a stepfather.[29] In one study, boys born to unmarried teenage mothers were eleven times more likely to become chronic delinquents than were those born to married mothers who were age twenty or older. Money makes a difference, but family structure makes one that is about as big.

Even the health of children is at greater risk if they are raised by a single mother. Nicholas Eberstadt studied infant mortality in Washington, D.C., where the rate is more than twice as high as in the rest of the country. Of course, most Washingtonians are black, but being black does not answer the question, for blacks in Washington have a higher infant mortality rate than blacks in many other cities. Some of this difference might be linked to lower incomes, less education, and less health care, but not much. On all of these measures, African Americans in Washington are better off than those elsewhere. What really explains the difference is that babies born to African Americans in Washington are much more likely to have low birth weights than those born to blacks elsewhere. Low-birth-weight infants are at greater risk to die when young than are normal-weight ones. A good predictor of producing a low-birth-weight baby was the mother being unmarried when the child was born. And in Washington, unmarried births are much more common than they are elsewhere, even in comparison to African Americans, and they became much more common in the 1990s than they had been two or three decades earlier. No one is quite certain why blacks have more low-birth-weight babies than do whites, but we do understand a little about why young, unmarried black women do a poorer job of raising them than do married black women. In part it is because the former are much less likely to get good prenatal care than are the latter even after you control for income. There may be other behavioral differences between married and unmarried mothers as well (perhaps the former smoke or do drugs more than the latter), but lowering the unemployment rate or providing more money will not change matters nearly as much as getting them married.[30]

Absent fathers also create problems outside the family. Imagine growing up in a neighborhood in which most children live with an unmarried mother. What are children to think of their prospects when they have no father earning a living but see all about them unmarried men who are either unemployed, stealing, or selling drugs? It is not likely that such children, especially such boys, will think that school and work will pay off. What pays off, if anything, is idleness or crime. The idlers have a lot of free time, the criminals a lot of money.

And then ask who will protect that child. Fathers are part of the first line of defense of a family, guarding their wives and children from unsavory lures and dangerous predators. The police are a backup force when adult protection is inadequate. But without a father, the family is less safe and the streets more threatening. Energetic, sexually active, unsupervised males fill the streets; many have impregnated women but few have married them. In that world, a child's safety is at risk. Going to and from school becomes a perilous adventure. Gangs exist; they threaten strangers. To become safer, the boys (and increasingly the girls) join a gang. It may or may not sell drugs; it may or may not commit serious crimes. But it protects its members against rival gangs. Now the only forces on the street are outnumbered police officers and ever-present gangs, and so life is more dangerous and choices more limited.

In single-parent families, even the mothers are less likely to have meals with the child, to impose chores, to read to their children, or to enforce rules governing watching television than would be the case in two-parent families.[31]

Some careful studies of neighborhoods suggest that family disruption is more important than race in explaining violent crime. African Americans are much more likely than whites to commit violent crimes, but when one looks at poor neighborhoods where blacks live, the rate of violent crime is much more strongly correlated with family structure than with race. Female-headed families seem to make a bigger difference than race or poverty.[32]

Both poverty and father absence produce these effects, but these two forces are really not as independent as we might imagine. A mother forfeits a chance to become affluent by having a child and not marrying; a mother, once affluent, loses income as a result of being divorced. Avoiding poverty in the United States is not as difficult today as it once was. William Galston, formerly an assistant to President Clinton and now a professor at the University of Maryland, has pointed out that you need only do three things to avoid poverty in this country—finish high school, marry before having a child, and produce the child after the age of twenty. Only 8 percent of families who do this are poor; 79 percent of those who fail to do this are poor.[33]

There is little point in dwelling on these facts; almost every American already understands them. Perhaps because of this understanding, the 1996 Welfare Reform Act is popular. But it is not obvious why our fears about families should make that law seem a solution. If implemented as intended, it will enforce a work requirement on women seeking welfare. In short, it will tell young mothers to be employed, away from their children for much of each week. These children, already fatherless, will now become partially motherless. They will be raised by somebody else. A grandmother? A neighbor? An overworked day care manager? Or they will be left alone.

Everything we have learned in the past few decades about the future of children suggests that the course is largely set in the earliest years. I doubt that many parents would disagree. If you wish to make a lasting difference in a child's life, start very early and work very hard. Children are not raised by programs, governments, or (in this country) villages; they are raised by two parents who are fervently, even irrationally, devoted to their children's well-being.

Problems in the First Nation

The problems of marriage are not limited to the second nation, the world of poor, unmarried mothers. Two-parent families in an age of affluence can have their own problems. The stories are frequently told: working mothers and fathers who leave their children unsupervised at home or on the street. When the parents travel, drunken teenage parties occur at home. All-night rave parties take place in empty warehouses or vacant lots, with drugs, especially Ecstasy, in heavy use. Schoolteachers are told by angry parents that their unruly child should not be punished. Unhappy adolescents take to alcohol and drugs either to cope with their distress or to make friends with other kids.

When young people pass puberty, they are much less likely to date and much more likely to "hook up." Tom Wolfe describes hooking up as a sexual experience that occurs outside of that old-fashioned notion, the date. A date occurs when a boy asks a girl out for a meal, a dance, or the movies; hooking up occurs when a bunch of boys and a bunch of girls head out in packs; if a boy from his pack likes a girl from hers, they hook up, which means have sex, chiefly oral sex, and as a recent president has explained that isn't really sex at all.[34]

How prosperous families are formed has also changed. Once a woman went to college and got married shortly after graduation; now she is likely to leave college for a career. The career may be in law or medicine or investment banking, or it may be in one of the low-paid but presumably glamorous jobs in publishing or entertainment. The longer in those jobs, the lower the chances of finding a husband, not only because more and more men are already married but because, as we shall see in chapter 3, men tend, as they get older, to marry women much younger than they. Older women lose out in the marriage race much faster than do men. It may be unfair, but that is the way the world works. These career women acquire boyfriends, but many of these have wives or girlfriends or odd habits. Some male companions are found as a result of what one unhappy woman called the "bantering dive-bar pickup" followed by "drunken sex, a rushed exchange of phone numbers afterward on a subway platform, then other nights of dive-bar bantering and drunken sex."[35] A relationship might ensue, but it is often followed, as Barbara Dafoe Whitehead puts it, by one or more of the following male remarks: "We should cool it for a while," "I've been doing a lot of thinking," "This week has been terrible," or "It's not you, it's me."[36] And so the relationship ends. Or sometimes marriage occurs, but then, in many cases, a divorce follows. As one popular movie made clear, there is no such thing as a happy divorce.

Being single has acquired a certain cachet. A popular magazine ran a lengthy essay on how single women, once treated after a certain age as social outcasts, are now a central part of our social life. They figure prominently in the television series *Sex and the City*, where the female characters acquire and discard boyfriends at a furious pace, all the while maintaining their glamour.[37]

In 1963, 83 percent of women aged twenty-five to fifty-five were married; by 1997 that number had dropped to 65 percent. Many of them, of course, cohabit with lovers, but we already know that cohabitation, at least in this country, tends to be a short-term arrangement. In the magazine article, almost all of the pictures of these single women were of attractive, obviously middle-class persons. The magazine left out poor single women who do not run a business, practice law, or appear on TV. But it did make clear what the preferences were of the people they displayed. When asked by a pollster, 61 percent of single women aged eighteen to forty-nine said they would consider raising a child on their own.[38]

Both poverty and affluence create problems, but the poverty problem, or more accurately, the problems of poor single-parent families, are easier to measure and harder for society to endure. Crime, drug abuse, educational failure, and teenage gangs create greater problems for most of us than the enthusiasm some women have for the single life, the conflict between careers and babies faced by well-educated women, or by the problems caused by upper-middle-class degeneration. Because the marital problems of the poor nation are more painful for society than those of the affluent one, this book will focus on the former.

Is Marriage Dispensable?

There have been countless essays by critics of marriage who have tried to describe it as a disposable convenience, but not many people believe this. The great British anthropologist Edmund Leach said that "far from being the basis of a good society," the family, "with its narrow privacy and tawdry secrets, is the source of all our discontents." He predicted that the nuclear family is "only a transient phase in our society."[39] Stephanie Coontz goes even further: Any call for a return to family relations or to "family moralism" leads "easily to scapegoating and victim blaming" in ways that coincide with an outburst of nativism and racism.[40] Judith Stacey, a sociologist, has argued that the alleged value of a two-parent family was merely a "widely shared prejudice"; people holding that prejudice were displaying a "misguided nostalgia for 'Ozzie-and-Harriet'-land."[41] Marriage might persist, wrote Jesse Bernard, but it could only do so adequately if it were able to mitigate "its hazards for women." For it to do this, the "family" would have to include new forms—communes, group marriages, the ménage à trois, marital "swinging," unmarried cohabitation, and limited-commitment marriages.[42]

Many of the criticisms of the family rest on the argument that marriage as conventionally defined has harmed women by restricting their talents, narrowing their opportunities, and reducing their rewards. The enemy, in this view, is the Ozzie-and-Harriet family of a bygone television era or the even worse threat of a Victorian marriage. There is merit in this criticism that cannot be wished away. Women have in fact been held back by the culture of almost every society and are still kept in a wholly subordinate status in many large nations. Everywhere there have been times—and such times still exist in many places— where women could be confined to harems, covered with veils, denied much schooling, refused any property, deprived of the vote, excluded from professions, and beaten with impunity. In a few places, ghastly operations were performed on the vagina of unmarried females in order to ensure their virginity when they wed.

In view of all of this, no one should be surprised that women will be intuitively suspicious of any call for a return to some undefined "traditional family." But the significance of the family does not depend on it being embedded in a traditional culture. The family is as important for the well-being of its members and the prospects of its children today when women have been emancipated from many ancient burdens as it was when they still suffered under them. The family is found in every culture, from the most sexist to the most emancipated, and its value depends more in its existence than on its cultural location. The one indispensable link between family and culture is that the latter supports the former, not that the latter supports it on the basis of some traditional orientation.

In every family system, the women will face some hard choices. In traditional families dominated by privileged males, the wives had to

worry about retaining affection and support. In modern families operating in a world of broadened female opportunities, they have to
worry about managing the conflicts between careers and children.
Every family no matter how it is organized implies some inconsistent
alternatives. As Christopher Lasch put it, even the "the bourgeois
family simultaneously degraded and exalted women" by requiring of
them, as Jane Austen put it, that they choose sense over sensibility,
that is, prefer marriage to opportunity.[43] The degradation may have
been oppressive, but the exaltation was also real. What women once
lost because of the restrictive limits placed upon them they gained by
the assurance of home and hearth.

Today women must make these choices as they go along, without a
culture to tell them unequivocally what to do, and the balancing act
they try to perform as a way of reconciling opportunity and home is a
difficult feat that is often emotionally distressing. When our culture
changed from the Victorian to the modern, it required of each woman
that she decide for herself what to do on her own, in a few brief years
in her life. This is both a great opportunity and a terrible burden. Each
woman now must do for herself what once several generations of
women had learned to do and passed on to one another as the tested
choice.

In the magazine poll mentioned previously, two-thirds of the single
men and women said they would marry if they could find the right
partner, and a quarter said they definitely wanted to get married.[44] But
as we shall see in chapter 3, that is not so easily done, at least for
women. The chances of their marrying decline dramatically with
every passing year because the supply of available men dries up
rapidly. This fact is not absent in *Sex and the City*: single women
encounter some objectionable lovers and some pleasing ones, and for
many such women ending the relationship produces a painful ache.
The program conveys sexual freedom, but also much wistfulness.

Men think that they survived this cultural change in far better shape.
If the culture offers sexual access and does not require in exchange
personal commitment, a lot of men will take the sex every time. If
divorce becomes easier, a lot of prosperous men will leave their spouses
to marry a trophy wife. (Not as many women will leave their husbands

for a boy toy.) And when single-parent families become commonplace, it is overwhelmingly the mothers, not the fathers, who raise the children.

If Marriage Is Good, Why Is It in Trouble?

American society suffers from family problems despite the fact that marriage is good for people. In their remarkable book, Linda J. Waite and Maggie Gallagher make a case for marriage that is overpowering.[45] Married people are happier than unmarried ones of the same age, not only in the United States but in at least seventeen other countries where similar inquiries have been made.[46] And there seem to be good reasons for that happiness. People who are married not only have higher incomes and enjoy greater emotional support, they tend to be healthier. Married people live longer than unmarried ones, not only in the United States but abroad.[47]

Some of this difference may be the result of predisposition: healthier people are more likely to get married, perhaps because they find it easier to acquire a spouse. But even though healthy people are more likely than unhealthy ones to get married, this is not the whole story. Marriage itself improves health in several obvious ways. For example, all unmarried men do worse without a wife than do married ones, even if the unmarried ones got that way by having their wives die. Widowers die sooner than married men.[48]

Explaining this difference is not very hard. Most married men have wives who tell them what to eat, urge them to stay home instead of going to saloons, keep them away from rowdy gangs, and reduce the amount of alcohol they drink. The message is, stay home and stay alive. And for some reason, these wifely instructions are not offset by higher suicide rates. Married men are much less likely to kill themselves than either bachelors or widowers. When you are married, somebody else is always around, checking up on you. As a result, the early symptoms of disease are more likely to be detected. Wives and husbands tell each other that they "ought to go see the doctor" more frequently than do friends and neighbors, many of whom probably think that somebody else's health is none of their business. Married men are likely to have wives who urge them to stop smoking, cut back on drinking, and eat a more nutritious diet. But when a man loses his wife to divorce, he starts smoking and drinking more than he did when he was married. Waite and Gallagher describe this as "the virtues of nagging."[49] But women gain less from marriage than do men, probably because they are women; that is, when single, they don't drink, smoke, fight, and carouse as much as men, so marriage confers fewer health benefits on them.

But women, though they may not gain as much as men, still gain a lot. Married women live longer than unmarried ones, and the former are less likely to engage in risky behaviors, such as smoking and drinking, than are the latter. When they get older, married women are less likely to become disabled or to enter a nursing home than unmarried ones. And married women tend to have more money than unmarried ones, and for that money they are more likely to live in safe neighborhoods and to obtain better medical help.[50]

Men seem to benefit more than women from this solicitude for reasons that many married man will readily understand. Left alone, a lot of men eat hamburgers and steaks, go out with their buddies to the bar, smoke cigars, and play poker through half the night. When they are married, the wives cut back on all of these things, and so men, more than women, experience a reduction in those things that contribute to cancer, cirrhosis of the liver, and general debilitation.[51]

Even the mental health of married couples is better. Despite all of the jokes about stupid husbands, battle-ax wives, and irritating kids, the mental health of those who marry improves over what it was before they married. Again, some of this may be the result of nicer people getting married, but not all of it is. The best studies of this pattern take into account the psychological well-being of people before they marry and still find that marriage makes them better off.[52]

And married people have more money than unmarried ones, even after allowing for what they were earning just before they married. One study found that about half the increase in money earned by a married couple resulted from marriage and not from their prior earning power.[53] Since two people can live together more cheaply than each separately, the reduction in costs they must bear means that gains in income create real gains in wealth. But the reason each earns more is that both, but especially the man, are more productive: healthier men with a wife and children to support can and do work harder.

But there is another reason that married couples earn more, one that will not rest so comfortably in the minds of some feminists. In a family, there is more specialization of labor. The husband will do some of the household chores, but far fewer than when he lived alone.[54] The wife will do more of the household chores than the husband, even if she also is working. I doubt that anyone will be surprised to learn that there are very few families in which both the husband and wife share all efforts—earning an income, keeping up the house, and raising the children—equally. When men marry, they get more time for work because somebody else is helping run the home. When women marry, they get some help around the house, but less than men do. In part this is because mothers spend more time with their infants and children than do husbands. This reflects to some degree the powerful mother-infant bond, an attachment that is the biggest reason many married women earn less money than married men. But the difference may also reflect the fact that women worry more about how the house looks and how the cooking is done, and so they give it more attention than do their husbands. The reader may like or dislike this observation, but it accords with studies of how husbands and wives participate in household work. The safest generalization is that men ought to appreciate more than they do how much their earning power depends on the (unpaid) household labor of their wives, even in families where both men and women are employed.

Since marriage has so many benefits, especially for men, it is astonishing that it should be in so much trouble. If men on the average are going to live longer, be happier, and earn more money after they marry, why do so many men reject it? Of course, a few men have no interest in marriage because they are gay, or confirmed bachelors, but for many decades an increasing fraction of them have rejected marriage to women whom they have impregnated. It is as if something good were offered to people, and, preoccupied with what is in their immediate interest, they reject it in favor of the pleasures of unmarried sex, brief cohabitations, unmarried parenthood, and frequent divorce.

It is a bit like asking people why they abuse drugs or tobacco when they know in advance that they will be better off by avoiding these temptations. The immediate temptation overcomes long-run judgment. A martini now, cocaine now, a cigarette now are all more appealing than hangovers, addiction, or cancer later on. So with marriage: sex now is more fun than sex always with the same woman, especially if with the same woman comes children and duties. A man may notice happily married men, but he does not link the happiness to the marriage.

Put this way, what is hard to understand is why marriage occurs at all. Some way must be found to persuade men that marriage makes sense in the long run. In the next chapter we shall consider the difficulty society has had in trying to make the persuasion compelling or even compulsory.

There is, of course, an easy way to explain why marriage is in trouble. We can bring out the sovereign explanation of all cultural ills, "the sixties." No doubt our life today was affected by that period of self-emancipation, cultural rebellion, and expanding freedom. We know, for example, that no-fault divorce laws were passed in the United States and many European countries during the sixties, and as we shall see, those laws helped increase the divorce rate. And we also know that though welfare payments to unwed mothers have been American law since 1935, it was not until the sixties that there was a dramatic increase in the number of women who took advantage of this subsidy.

But it would be remarkable if an institution as old and as universal as marriage could prove so vulnerable to one decade of cultural change. If people could be so easily talked out of marrying, surely they would have cut back on marriage in some places many decades— indeed, many centuries—earlier. As we look about the world, we do not find marriage in trouble in every nation. Marriage remains the goal of every couple desiring children in much of Africa, the Middle East, and the Far East and in some parts of Europe. But in much of the Western and Caribbean worlds, marriage is in trouble. This trouble is not an American oddity. In the late 1990s, one-fourth or more of all births occurred to unmarried mothers in Australia, Canada, Denmark, France, New Zealand, Sweden, the United Kingdom, and the United States. This rate was, on the average, more than six times higher than it had been in 1960. In most Caribbean nations, such as Barbados and Jamaica, and in some Central American countries unmarried births are even more common.

But the illegitimacy ratio was much lower in Italy, the Netherlands, and Germany[55] and vastly lower in Belgium, Israel, Greece, Hong Kong, Japan, Korea, Spain, and Switzerland and among white South Africans.[56]

Immigrants to the United States have brought with them a strong or weak attachment to families. That attachment was powerful among Asians, Italians, Latinos, and Jews and tentative among Africans and the Irish.[57]

Something affected parts of the West and the Caribbean that did not affect other parts of the world. I will suggest two causes: slavery and the Enlightenment. Slavery weakened families, the Enlightenment made many people think families were unimportant. Families are weak where terrible things were done to some people, as in slavery, and when wonderful things happened to others, as under the Enlightenment. Recall the immigrants to this country: those that came from areas where enslavement occurred and the Enlightenment was powerful had weaker family attachments; those that came from places where both forces were less important had stronger attachments. These arguments are controversial, and so much of the book will be devoted to defending them. The sixties made a difference, but it was a development that was, in my view, merely one more change added to those that had been accumulating for several centuries. Though the fraction of teenage girls who had out-of-wedlock births rose in the 1960s, for African American females it was already more than one-third in 1950.[58]

In America, we live where both historical forces collided. We suffer from the legacy of three centuries of slavery and enjoy the advantages of three centuries of political and intellectual emancipation. The costs of slavery are obvious, but even the Enlightenment came at a price. Most of us do not feel that price because we have transformed the teachings of the Enlightenment into personal wealth, political power, social advantage, and intellectual accomplishment. Those who have done so are part of one nation, proud of what freedom has allowed us to achieve.

But there is a second nation, growing more rapidly than the first. It is the nation that has paid heavily the high price of freedom. It is armed to the teeth, excited by drugs, preoccupied with respect, and indifferent to the future. Its children crowd our schools and fill our streets, unruly and dangerous. The first nation tries to hide from the second behind guarded gates or in protected apartments. In a modern society you can run, but you can't hide.

Chapter 2
Why Do Families Exist?

The family is a remarkable and fragile combination of nature and nurture, of social pressures operating within biological imperatives. There is a rich and growing account of how our biological heritage affects the kinds of lives we lead. The central element in human relations, the bond between a mother and her child, is the result of powerful natural forces that only extreme circumstances, if any at all, can completely set aside. The vast majority of mothers care deeply for their children. But that bond, driven by the biological needs of the infant and shaped by the natural expectations of the mother, needs help. And it only gets a little from human evolution. Nature leaves the mother in need, but nature does not supply that need automatically. Each society must devise and enforce the obligations on which the life of the mother and her infant depend.

Sometimes what a society enforces is a long way from what we today would call a marriage. The formal marriage, with a bride in a white gown, a member of the clergy, a group of witnesses, and important promises of fidelity and support, is a modern invention. At many times in the past, marriage existed when a man and a woman said it did. At other times and in other places, a marriage existed when the parents of the man and woman agreed that it should. And in still other times and other places, a marriage did not exist until a child was born.

That marriage can take so many forms will confuse some readers, worry others, and delight a few. To the distress of many and the excitement of some, the notion that the forms of marriage were an invention suggests that what was created can be destroyed. Today, when marriages are declining, divorces are routine, and cohabitation commonplace, the act of marriage seems dispensable. We can have a family—or something we choose to call a family—without bothering with white gowns, clergymen, judges, witnesses, or even the ancient pattern of one man marrying one woman. In this view, we may call any pattern of sexual cohabitation a family, however informal or short lived, and get on with our lives.

But the purpose of marriage, however it was defined, has always been to make the family secure, not to redefine what constitutes a family. The family is a more fundamental social reality than a marriage, and so pretending that anything we call a marriage can create a family is misleading. In every community and for as far back in time as we can probe, the family exists and children are expected, without exception, to be raised in one.[1] By a family I mean a lasting, socially enforced obligation between a man and a woman that authorizes sexual congress and the supervision of children. Its style and habits will vary greatly, of course, but nowhere do we find a place where children are regularly raised by a mother who has no claims on the father. A marriage is a ceremony that makes, or at least symbolizes, the legitimacy of the family. But in some places the obligation of a father to support his children can be enforced without a ceremony. In these cases, informal marriages are more easily tolerated. But when that social obligation weakens, marriage formalities become more important, a matter that will be discussed in chapter 4.

In nineteenth-century Brazil, marriage was the exception, not the rule. In one region, more than half of all the male-female unions were informal, and less than a third of the free—that is, nonslave—children were born from married parents. Among slaves, almost all of the children were born out of wedlock.[2] But in that region, other forces ensured that the child would be cared for.

Families in many other countries have at times rested on little more than the individual consent of man and woman and their habit of living together for a long period. Today we sometimes call these common-law unions, but they are neither recent inventions nor uniquely American arrangements. Children are raised by their parents, who sometimes are married and sometimes are not. But these arrangements existed because other forces required that the father and mother raise the child. Those forces may not have been called a marriage, but they were powerful nonetheless.

Biology and Culture

Biology explains why the infant is utterly dependent on its mother, but it does not go very far in explaining why a father is part of the family. Narrowly read, it argues that humans, like all species, have evolved from distant ancestors. This development ensured that during the hundred thousand years or so during which humans have lived, certain attributes were selected that enhanced the ability of people to survive. People who lacked those valued traits were less likely to produce descendants.

An evolutionary explanation depends on selection. Selection occurs when some genes that make a creature more fit for a particular environment are passed on to the next generation. Passing on such genes that help people cope with their environment makes them more fit. Long ago, humans who had the eyesight, coordination, and bravery that made them good hunters produced more offspring than did people who were nearsighted, all thumbs, and fearful cowards. Since hunting was an important way of acquiring food, skill at hunting was adaptive. The hunters maximized their fitness by producing children who were also good at hunting. Over the long run and as long as skill at hunting was important, one kind of man increased in number and the other kind dwindled. Or another example: Suppose at some time in the past a community existed in which women felt no particular desire to nurture their infants. Their children would die, taking with them whatever antinurture instinct they had, and so we would not find such people around (at least in any significant number) today. Increasing the progeny of skilled male hunters made them more fit; increasing the progeny of antinurturing women made them less fit.

When you read books about evolution and adaptation, you will learn a great deal about how selection affects fitness and how females are likely to be most attracted to males that have the physical or behavioral features that make them appear more fit than their rivals. But you will not read much about how families are formed or about what sustains them. In some of the best texts on evolution, the word *family* in the index usually refers to families as classifications of species or genera ("genera" is the plural of "genus"). There is not much discussion of permanent or enduring pair bonding of the sort we encounter among people.

Suppose we were to try to give a narrowly evolutionary explanation for the existence of the family. By "narrowly evolutionary" I mean an account based on the view that people are fitness maximizers. This account will face some difficult facts. Men value sex, something that women can offer both to conceive a child and to retain male interest. But men can have sex with lots of women. Men who maximize their fitness are those who have the most children no matter who their mother may be. Some of these children may die because, without a husband, the mother may not be able to raise them. But if men sire enough children, a lot will survive; more, in all likelihood, than will survive if the man confines his sexual activities to one woman, his wife, who can only have a dozen or so children.

Evolution, narrowly defined, rewards men who inseminate many women. These men are maximizing their fitness if they have more children that are endowed with whatever innate attributes permit them to do well in their environment. If evolution had produced on its own the family, few men would have sex with only one woman, and they would rarely, if ever, have sex with prostitutes or with women too old to have children. Why waste your sperm on a woman too protected or too old to produce a child?

If a man and woman do get married and then find that they are unable to have children of their own, a narrow evolutionary account of their behavior would give them no incentive to adopt a child. Raising children produced by some other man and woman would do nothing to maximize the fitness of the adoptive parents, since despite all of their child-care efforts, none of their genes would be carried into the next generation.

Evolution, as we understand it so far, does not help mothers very much. If mothers did not get some male help, the human species would have died out tens of thousands of years ago. What we know about evolution has supplied a ready explanation for sex, but only a partial one for families. If families depended wholly on evolution, men would not behave as we know they do. Donald Symons, who has devoted much of his professional life to thinking about these matters, has remarked that the family, if it had been selected for in the same way breast-feeding an infant were selected for, would have features that are quite different from what we see all about us.[3] If families were entirely the product of evolutionary development, men would always regard their wives as sexually more attractive than other females, even younger ones. As a result, there would be very little prostitution or concubinage, and scarcely any man would divorce his spouse and marry a trophy wife. In choosing a wife, men would not assign as high a value to physical attractiveness as they would to skill at child care. As a man's wife got older, his sexual interest in her would persist. Pornography would have little appeal for men; instead, they would read romance novels or, at worst, books on sports. Polygyny—that is, the right of a man to have several wives—would be rare (in fact, it is quite common around the world). By contrast, polyandry—that is, the right of a woman to have several husbands—might be commonplace (in fact, it scarcely exists). Having several husbands would help the wife get even more nurture and protection. In short, the lure of the wife would be so powerful that whatever aid a man, or several men, might supply would be supplied to her and to her alone.

Actual families are composed of men who (most of the time) stick with their wives even when younger, more attractive women are about. Actual families who cannot produce their own children will adopt the children of other women. Actual families that are destroyed by the death or desertion of the woman leave the man free to consider (social rules permitting) joining up with a new sexual partner. Men tend to favor women younger than they as that partner, just as evolution would predict, but a surprisingly large number will join with a woman too old to have children. Something has curbed the biological male's sexual interests.

What is curbed may well be explained in evolutionary terms once we learn more about evolution. Perhaps the desire of women for commitment (in order to acquire support for themselves and their children) would lead men who were prepared to offer commitment an evolutionary advantage. Over many generations, dads would come to outnumber cads. But until we understand this matter more fully, we are left with a catchall category called "culture." As a concept, *culture* does not explain very much; the word is often used as if it were some mighty force that organizes human societies without much reference to the kinds of people who live there. But all it really means is a collection of habits and beliefs that are shared among individuals.[4] If we knew more about how the sharing emerged, we would probably discover it grew up out of a complicated linkage among human biology, material resources, and historical experiences. Perhaps it would be better to substitute the word *customs* for culture. But this lively intellectual problem cannot be explored here. I shall use culture and customs interchangeably, worried by my inability to explain their origin but convinced that until that origin is known, these words suffice to describe how groups of people differ.

We know that every society has created families because each finds them useful. It looks about and notes that a mother with no husband will have a hard time raising her child and feeding herself, and so it decides it must arrange matters so as to help the mother-child bond survive. It can do this in several ways. It might create a mother-aid society in which people pool their labor to help each mother get through the infant-rearing years. It might organize other women to do this work in turn. Or it might create work groups of men and women who go out to find food for the mother and her child.

In some primitive hunter-gatherer societies, we can see reasons for thinking that mothers might be able to work things out without having a husband around. In these places, they are often able to gather enough food to care for themselves and their children.[5] Fruits and vegetables are available from trees and plants so that a woman without a husband might sustain life. Even in cattle-herding societies, a mother could plant and harvest a garden. Everywhere in Africa, and probably everywhere in much of the world at one time, women have worked the fields, sometimes while carrying their babies. This might be difficult or impossible at the time of giving birth, but there will be other women and children living nearby who can be called upon to help support the mother and her newborn infant by sharing the food they gather. In return, the mother who benefits from this will help other women when they experience childbirth. Reciprocal altruism will sustain a culture organized around and supported by women. When Gloria Steinem said that women need men like a fish needs a bicycle, perhaps she had some world such as this in mind.

But no such world exists. There is no society where women alone care for each other and their children; there is none where fathers are not obligated to support their children and the mothers to whom they were born. There never has been anything remotely approaching a matriarchal society governed exclusively by women. Some other force is operating that makes marriage of decisive importance. Not only do men need women, women need men.

But though a narrowly evolutionary view of the family leaves a lot unexplained, no explanation of it can fail to take into account what evolution has produced: women, for whom childbirth is a long, often painful, and time-consuming process; mothers, for whom suckling their child is a rewarding experience; children, who are born in a primitive state unable to care for themselves for many years; and men, who value sex, wish to be certain of the paternity of their children, and have the physical strength to dominate women. A mother values her children, the children depend on adults, and the man wants to be certain that a child born to a woman he has impregnated is really his, and he can find incentives necessary to produce that certainty. These facts have very different implications. Women wish to nurse their young and men wish to be certain of their paternity, but the former desire leads to a strong attachment between mother and child whereas the latter produces no equally powerful wish to feed the mother and child. The mother-infant bond will be tighter than the mother-father bond.

Somehow the family must reconcile these two somewhat incompatible linkages. It does so, I think, by embedding marriage in an elaborate set of rules designed to protect the fragile parts of marriage from the interests of a wandering male. Those rules are largely part of another universal feature of all human societies, the kinship system. As Lionel Tiger and Robin Fox have put it, the chief function of kinship systems is to "protect the mother-infant bond from the relative fragility and volatility of the male-female bond."[6]

Every society, they point out, finds it necessary to surround the mother-father bond with a host of customary rules and legal provisions. These constraints are essential because copulation can be the result of a chance encounter or an adolescent attachment, either of which *may*, but neither of which *will*, produce a lasting commitment between two people who are about to become a mother and father. Leaving the future of the child to what may be a passing emotional tie would be too risky. Moreover, the man's sexual interest will continue to be aroused by the sight of other young, attractive women, any of whom could lure him away from his obligation to the mother and the child that he has helped produce. To deal with these contingencies, every society imposes rules of courtship, provides for some kind of definition of marriage, restricts a man's access to other women, and in many instances requires that the marriage be arranged in advance by older family members. Sometimes the arrangements occur before those who are to wed have even reached puberty. In addition, the society bans sex between close blood kin.

In short, marriage may have been invented to make up for what narrow evolution has not by itself produced. In a small village where everyone knows everyone else—and humans have lived in such villages for most of the time people have existed on Earth—the marriage may rest on informal understandings or odd customs and be deferred until a child is produced. It may be linked to the exchange of property as when the husband's family pays a bride price to the woman's or when the woman's family pays a dowry to the husband's.

The marital union may depend in part on men other than the child's biological father. These may include the mother's brother. "In some human societies," Tiger and Fox note, "the weight of responsibility for a woman and her children rests with her brothers."[7] In such a world, a child grows up learning to have special regard for his or her uncle, a man who oversees the child's development even though the rule against incest forbids him from having sex with its mother.[8]

The forms of marital life are quite diverse. Mother and father may live in the same house, or the mother may live with her child in the house while the father sleeps elsewhere. In some societies several families band together so that overseeing children is shared by this group. In a few, many husbands have several wives, though the practice of polygyny is rarer than the rule that permits it. Children may be loaned from one family to another to perform certain chores. In much of Europe until rather recently, children not needed for farmwork were sent out as servants or apprentices.[9] All of these variations have led some to conclude that the family is simply a reflection of local culture. It is not. What is a reflection of culture is marriage. Marriage and families are linked, but they are not the same thing. They both depend on a few central facts: women have children, men impregnate women, men (usually) control the society, and close kin cannot mate.[10] But these facts permit a variety of marital arrangements, including ones that involve either elaborate ceremonies or any ceremonies at all. And each definition of marriage that is accepted by and endures in a particular society is that culture's way of protecting family life against the threats that it confronts. Since the threats vary, marriage varies, but the goal does not: marriage is designed to guarantee what biological drives cannot.

Marriage is in part a way of reinforcing a desirable relationship against the tendency of men to depart from it. The reinforcement may come from the kin of the wives or the customs of the people. But more than a useful connection is produced by marriage, for the family, when it lasts, does for people what no other institution can quite manage. Every person wishes to form deep and lasting bonds with other people, bonds that will endure beyond the first blush of romance or the early urgings of sexual desire. The family is our most important way of creating intimacy and commitment.[11]

But a marriage is not entirely dependent on cultural sanctions. One human disposition, natural to almost every man and woman, also tends to hold mother and father together: jealousy.

Jealousy

Men and women have their own ways of enforcing a family bond. Each fears the loss of a sexual partner to someone else, and acts on that fear. To a person with a wholly materialistic view of humankind, sexual jealousy may be hard to understand. Sex, after all, is nothing more than intimate contact accompanied by a certain amount of friction. In purely mechanistic terms, it is not that different from a handshake. But to lose a valued sexual partner to another is much more—vastly more—significant than seeing one's partner shake hands with somebody else. The real or imagined loss of sexual exclusivity is one of the leading causes of quarrels, murders, romantic poetry, songs, dramas, and dynastic wars.

Jealousy can, like all human emotions, be shaped in part by culture. There are a few societies in which marriage does not require sexual exclusivity, and some people have learned—up to a point—to live with that. These societies are often very poor ones in which a woman's need for economic support outweighs her desire for sexual fidelity, or ones governed by a powerful religious code that requires polygyny. Every society that allows men to have more than one wife is a society that expects some married women to live with the fact that their husbands have sex with other women, right in their own home. Opinions differ about the effect of this shared sexuality on the women; many studies find the several wives of one man to be quarrelsome and jealous, while others find that the women benefit by being part of a socially successful family (only affluent men ordinarily have several wives).[12]

Since men tend to dominate the politics of most cultures, one must wonder why polygyny ever ended. Why shouldn't rich and powerful males always insist on having marital access to more than one wife? They still do in many African and Islamic cultures. The reason that view is in retreat, I suspect, is that in cultures that have embraced the egalitarian code, monogamy turns out to be the only way of ensuring that every woman has a chance at finding a mate. A culture will adopt this view, I think, because doing so helps make men less dangerous. Unmarried men are more likely to become thieves, murderers, and soldiers; they become, in short, what Martin Daly and Margot Wilson called a "wellspring of disgruntlement and revolutionary potential."[13] This is not merely a theoretical possibility when one observes the behavior of unmarried young fathers today: many of them think it very important that they impregnate women and earn street-corner respect.

Even in the United States, where the requirement of sexual exclusivity is powerfully endorsed by public opinion, there are groups—homosexual males, married "swingers"—for whom jealousy is less important. Less important, but not absent. Among gay men, promiscuity is common. Despite this, gays are still likely to be jealous, though not as much as heterosexual men.[14] Among swingers, jealousy is, of course, less common than among ordinary married couples, but even for them there are important limits on how far sexual freedom can proceed. Swinging is ordinarily initiated by the husband over the wife's objections. If the wife goes along with this form of promiscuity, as sometimes happens, jealousy still remains a problem. To contain it, swingers adopt certain rules, such as not allowing their spouses to have sexual contact with others outside of organized sex parties in which both spouses are present and the other attendees are married couples.[15]

But though there are a few people in every society who can accept some degree of sexual infidelity, the notion that society should adopt "open marriages" has never caught on. In 1972 a book by that name appeared, arguing that "sexual fidelity is the false god of a closed marriage." The authors did not explicitly recommend extramarital sex, they simply said it was "up to you."[16] They suggested that since jealousy was less common among Eskimos, Marquesans, the Lobi of

West Africa, and the Sirions of Bolivia than among Americans, the demand for sexual exclusivity was probably nothing more than an outmoded Western culture rule that could be easily replaced to everyone's advantage.[17] Unfortunately for the advocates of open marriage, their facts were wrong. It turns out that the Eskimos and the Marquesans are quite jealous, a fact known to scholars before open-marriage advocates wrote their 1972 book.[18]

While surveys of the few people who live in open marriages sometimes find that they are at ease with their partner's infidelity,[19] the number of such marriages has not grown very much. Jealousy remains a powerful passion in almost every society. It is the leading cause of men attacking women and of spousal homicide, not only in advanced societies but in many primitive ones as well.[20] It even enjoys in some places special justification. Law and custom sometimes allow, without penalty, a husband to kill his unfaithful wife while giving a wife no similar recourse against an unfaithful husband. Until 1974, a Texas law explicitly permitted a man to kill an unfaithful wife and her lover if he found them engaged in intercourse. These unpleasant rules are now in abeyance, but they reveal how powerfully sexual jealousy shapes our lives.

The persistence of jealousy has occurred despite the efforts of many intellectuals to talk us out of it. In the 1930s, Margaret Mead said that jealousy is "undesirable, a festering spot in every personality so affected," and Kingsley Davis remarked that jealousy "shows on the lover's part a mistrust inimical to the harmony of perfect intimacy." Mrs. Havelock Ellis, the wife of the English physician who denounced Victorian attitudes toward sex, urged people to "subjugate" the jealousies of sex. In the 1940s, manuals aimed at high school girls described jealousy as "the most common of all unhelpful attitudes" and explained it as the result of our failure to outgrow "the selfishness of early childhood." As Peter N. Stearns later put it, for sixty years virtually all of the academic attitudes toward jealousy condemned it because it was inimical to "true love."[21] But people by and large ignored this advice. Love inspires jealousy, and the latter helps reinforce the former.

Both men and women exhibit jealousy. They are jealous when their partner has sex with someone else and when he or she becomes emotionally attached to a rival. But when they are asked which activity it would be more difficult for them to forgive—that is, when they are asked to make a hard choice between two behaviors that produce jealousy—it is clear that men experience jealousy differently from women. For men, it is the sexual contact that is most upsetting, while for women it is the loss of emotional attachment. These differences exist in many cultures—the United States, China, Japan, Korea, Sweden, and the Netherlands.[22] Neither men nor women want their mates to cheat on them, but men worry more about sex and women more about attachment.

Much jealousy can be explained by the desire of men to be certain of the paternity of their wives' children. But that cannot be the whole story, for childless couples, homosexual couples, and couples too old to even consider having children also display jealousy when infidelity is detected. Moreover, killing an unfaithful wife does nothing to ensure the husband's paternity, for now her child-rearing days are over.[23]

Evolution by selection, though of great importance to human life, is an incomplete explanation unless we first understand that what it produced were not robots that acted automatically on biological instincts but thinking, feeling people equipped by nature with a complex psychology that predisposed but did not compel them to act in certain ways. In another book, I tried to explain why humans are sometimes altruistic.[24] Part of the reason we help others at some sacrifice to ourselves is that they are our children; by helping them we perpetuate our genes. And another part is that we help people who are not our children in order to impress these people with our dependability and win from them some reciprocal help in the future. But these two explanations, inclusive fitness and reciprocal altruism, while quite powerful, do not clarify everything. They do not explain why people make sacrifices for their pets, grandmothers, or adopted children (their genes do not get passed on by these actions) or why people unobserved by others make sacrifices for others or make anonymous financial contributions. To explain all of altruism, it is necessary to first understand that what evolution has given to us is not a fixed mechanism to achieve a specific goal, but an emotion that not only serves that goal but achieves related ones as well. Let us call that emotion a desire for affiliation or, in simple language, a desire to be part of a social group.

Jealousy may well work in much the same way. Men and women marry under whatever arrangements may prevail in a society. The marriage may be arranged by parents or flow entirely from romantic love; it may occur within one culture or across cultures; the spouses may live with the wife's family, the husband's, or by themselves; and it may be either a monogamous or polygynous union. But the man and the woman are together.

We sometimes suppose, especially with respect to marriages that are distant in time or part of a remote and strange culture, that human affection is something that is more common today, or among Westerners, or when parents have played no role in selecting a spouse. Love is sometimes thought to be an invention of recent centuries and perhaps unique to the West. Several scholars have explicitly argued that affection was of little importance in the past or outside of Europe. Lawrence Stone, until his death one of the main figures in studying the history of marriage, wrote that "romantic love . . . is culturally conditioned, and therefore common only in certain societies at certain times, or even in certain social groups within those societies—usually the elite, with the leisure to cultivate such feelings."[25]

But there is remarkably little evidence that non-European or ancient marriages were loveless. William Jankowiak and Edward Fischer combed anthropological reports on 166 cultures. These societies include some of the most non-Western imaginable, such as the Sung dynasty of ancient China and the !Kung Bushmen of the Kalahari desert. Romantic love, defined as an intense erotic attraction between a man and a woman such that each idealizes the other and each hopes will endure into the future, was explicitly found to exist in nearly nine out of every ten of these societies.[26] (In fact it probably existed in even more, but the records were sometimes incomplete.) Thomas Gregor has described love in detail in one of the least Western societies in the world, the Mehinaku, a Xingu tribe of Brazil. Promiscuous sex is commonplace, but despite that, sex prompted by love is highly regarded—it is "salty," "spicy," "delicious,"—while sex without love is tasteless, like water. The Mehinaku have a lot of both kinds of sex, but it is clearly the latter they prefer, whether it is with a lover or a spouse. And like people everywhere, when a spouse dies, the partner mourns. Mourning expresses a loss of love and companionship.[27] Helen Harris has found it alive and well on a remote Pacific island where anthropologists once said it did not exist and has shown that love is important in forty-two hunter-gatherer societies, even those in which parents arrange marriages.[28] We should scarcely be surprised. Do we really imagine that in the past, or today in remote or unknown places, young men and women can live together without some passion and a bit of frenzy? Can anyone really believe that Western troubadours invented love? They may have idealized the notion of romantic love, but they did not create it.

If love operates in every society, then jealousy is a violation of a lover's expectations. A man is jealous if he thinks a male rival will inseminate his wife, or even if the rival simply kisses her (except on the cheek) in his presence where no sex is likely to occur. A man does not ordinarily stop loving his wife just because she is beyond child-bearing years, nor does an older man who marries a postmenopausal woman decide that he need not be jealous because she is infertile. The great majority of marriages involve affection, ranging from a comfortable and fulfilling relationship to a compulsive erotic preoccupation. We are jealous when a rival challenges any of those connections and threatens to cut them short. Jealousy, a broad emotion that involves much more than privileged sexual access, is the force that helps hold marriages together. Among men, it often produces rage, violence, and hiding wives under veils or behind harem walls; among women, it often produces crying, denunciation, and withdrawal.[29]

Jealousy, like love and altruism, are complex emotions that affect many more aspects of our lives than can be explained simply by asking whether they helped our genes reappear in later generations. But it is a mistake not to ask that latter question as well. Men everywhere are more jealous than women of sexual infidelity and have gone to great— often savage, sometimes horrible—lengths to prevent and punish it, whereas women everywhere seem to be jealous as much at the loss of commitment as about the sex. But though these general evolutionary tendencies operate, the emotion—jealousy—operates far more generally, so that it affects many circumstances in which no evolutionary link has yet been found.

When Jennifer Roback Morse, a noted libertarian economist, wrote a book about the family, she immediately realized that it could never be understood as a contract, because it cannot be thought of as an arrangement that has a monetary value: "love cannot be bought and sold."[30] Sex can and so can property. But not love. Jealousy is a way in which we enforce an arrangement that cannot be priced.

Cohabitation Instead of Marriage

If marriage is designed to help solve a society's need to maintain family, and if modern societies, such as ours, have created ways of raising children that are independent of family life, then family life ought not to be very important. If a child can be raised by a nanny or a day-care center, if its education can be left in the hands of public and private schools, if its physical well-being can be entrusted to police officers and social workers, then marriage does not offer much to the father and mother. And if the couple has no wish for children, then marriage offers nothing at all. Perhaps men and women can simply decide to live together—to cohabit—without any formalities that define a "legal" marriage.

But cohabitation creates a problem that most people will find hard to solve. If people are free to leave cohabitation (and they must be, or it would be called a marriage instead), then in many cases, neither the man nor the woman has any strong incentive to invest heavily in the union.[31] Marriage is a way of making such investments plausible by telling each party that they are united forever, and if they wish to dissolve this union that they will have to go through an elaborate and possibly costly legal ritual called divorce. Marriage is a way of restricting the freedom of people so that investing emotionally and financially in the union makes sense. I can join my money with yours because, should we ever wish to separate, we would have to go through a difficult process of settling our accounts. That process, divorce, makes merged accounts less risky. If a cohabiting couple has a child, its custody can be decided by one parent taking it. If we marry, however, the custody of the child will be determined by a judge, and so each of our interests in its custody will get official recognition. This fact makes it easier for us to have a child.

And love itself is helped by marriage. If we cohabit and I stop loving you, I walk away. This means that you have less of an incentive to love me, since your affection may not be returned by me for as long as you would like and hence your love might be wasted. But if we promise to live together forevermore (even though we know that we can get a divorce if we are willing to put up with its costs), each of us is saying that since you have promised to love me, I can afford to love you.

Cohabiting couples in the United States tend to keep separate bank accounts and divide up the expenses of their life together. And this financial practice signals a potential social burden. While married couples with unequal incomes are less likely to get a divorce than those with more equal ones, cohabiting ones with unequal incomes are likely to split apart.[32] If our money is kept in separate accounts, then your having more (or less) money than I makes a difference. If it is kept in merged accounts, then nobody observes differences in income.

Cohabitation ordinarily does not last very long; most such unions in America break up (sometimes with a split, sometimes with a marriage) within two years.[33] Scholars increasingly regard cohabitation as a substitute to being single, not an alternative to marriage. And a good thing, since people seem to bring different expectations to the former than to the latter. When high school seniors were followed into their early thirties, women who highly valued having a career and men who greatly valued leisure were more likely to cohabit than were people with the opposite views. Women seemed to think that cohabitation helps their careers, men to think it helps them spend more time with "the boys."[34] Neither view makes much sense, since cohabitation not only does not last very long, most people think cohabiting couples are doing something odd. Like it or not, the couple living together will discover in countless ways that society thinks they should either get married or split apart. And society's opinion makes sense. As Linda Waite and Maggie Gallagher put it, marriage makes you better off, because marriage makes you very important to someone. When you are married you know that someone else not only loves you, but needs you and depends on you. This makes marriage a contract like no other.[35]

Marriage and Society

Until recently, cultures set rules for marriage that were not only designed to protect the child but to achieve a variety of other goals as well. A family was a political, economic, and educational unit as well as a child-rearing one. It participated in deciding who would rule the community and (except in wandering hunter-gatherer groups) control or have privileged access to land that supplied food and cattle. Until the modern advent of schools, families educated their children, not with books, but by demonstrating how to care for other children, perform certain crafts, and mind cattle and agricultural fields.[36] These demonstrations sometimes took the form of games and sometimes depended simply on show-and-tell, but a child's life in either event was governed by the need to demonstrate, year by year, that it had learned how to watch, carry, feed, hunt, fish, and build. These tutorial, educational, and economic families were linked together in kinship groupings that constituted the whole of the small society—often no more than two hundred people, and sometimes even fewer—that lived together in a settlement.

These social functions did not prevent married men and women from caring for each other, even in arranged marriages. Affection existed, though of course it was sometimes interrupted by quarrels and beatings. This affection and the companionship it entailed were valuable supports to family life, but they were not until recently the chief, much less the sole, grounds for maintaining the union.

Today, the family has lost many of these functions. Politically, the family has been replaced by the voting booth and the interest group, economically by the office and the factory, and educationally by the school and the Internet. Modernity did not simply produce these changes: capitalism did not change the family (the family first changed in ways that made capitalism possible), and schools did not make families less relevant (families changed in ways that made schools more valuable). In later chapters we shall see how these complex alterations occurred.

But for now it is important to observe that the family now rests almost entirely on affection and child care. These are powerful forces, but the history of the family suggests that almost every culture has found them to be inadequate to producing child support. If we ask why the family is, for many people, a weaker institution today than it once was, it is pointless to look for the answer in recent events. Our desire for sexual unions and romantic attachments is as old as humankind, and they will continue forever. But our ability to fashion a marriage that will make the union last even longer than the romance that inspired it depends on cultural, religious, and legal doctrines that have slowly changed. Today people may be facing a challenge for which they are utterly unprepared: a vast, urban world of personal freedom, bureaucratized services, cheap sex, and easy divorce.

Marriage is a socially arranged solution for the problem of getting people to stay together and care for children that the mere desire for children, and the sex that makes children possible, does not solve. The problem of marriage today is that we imagine that its benefits have been offset by social arrangements, such as welfare payments, community tolerance, and professional help for children, that make marriage unnecessary. But as we have already seen, the advantages of marriage—personal health, longer lives, and better children—remain great. The advantages of cohabitation are mostly illusory, but it is an illusion that is growing in its appeal.

Chapter 3
Sex and the Marriage Market

For there to be a marriage, a man and a woman must be available. This is so obvious that we sometimes forget what might happen in a society if there were many more marriageable men than women, or vice versa. Imagine a society in which the number of men aged twenty-three is vastly greater than the number of women of roughly the same age. Because there are too few women to marry all men, the competition among men for women will become stronger. Men will have to work harder and promise more to find a wife or a sexual partner. This competition will raise the bargaining power of women. Women, within the limits set down by custom and biology, will be able to demand more from prospective mates.

In such a world, consider Amy. If a man wishes only to have sex with her, Amy can, if she wishes, easily reject him for a man who is willing to marry her. And if the man wishing to marry her is less handsome, less intelligent, or less likely to be financially successful than a

Of course Amy might not search the market at all, marrying instead her school sweetheart or the man she just met at the office, not wondering whether there are enough men to go around for all the women wishing to marry. But though Amy and her husband-to-be may not be affected, the total supply of available men and women will powerfully affect the marriage market. For all women taken together, the marriage market will make a difference.

When there are more marriageable men than women, women tend to marry men who are economically and educationally as well off—or, in many cases, much better off—than the women. Scholars call this tendency "hypergamy," an ugly word that suggests a serious disease rather than a connubial opportunity. But *hypergamy* (a word I will try not to use again) is valuable for women if they plan to have children, since it helps them support their offspring when they are unable or unwilling to let a job interfere with child care.

But if there are fewer marriageable men than women, a woman's prospects change. If the society is monogamous, there will be too few sexual or marital partners available, and so women, on the average, will have to accept what the man offers. It may be a one-night stand, or a few dates, or living together; it may even be marriage, but if the marriage does not work out and a divorce follows, there will not be a lot of unmarried men available to be her next husband. If the woman wants a baby, the father may have so many other sexual opportunities that he cannot be counted on to marry and become an effective father. With too few men, and men able to drive a hard bargain for their sexual favors, a lot of women may remain unmarried or even renounce marriage in favor of careers. And if a woman does marry in this tight market, it might not be to a man who is her equal or superior in financial or educational resources. As a result, the woman will marry down, and that will hurt her ability to care well for the children.

The Sex Ratio

The number of men per hundred women in a society is called the sex ratio. When there are more men than women, we have a high sex ratio; when there are fewer men than women, there is a low sex ratio. Societies differ in their sex ratios, and any given society may have a sex ratio that changes over time. In most societies unaffected by any disturbances, the sex ratio will be a bit over a hundred, as more male than female children are born.*

But this ratio can be vastly greater or lower than one hundred. A war will result in the death of many men. In Great Britain and many other European nations, the sex ratio dropped dramatically between 1911 and 1921 as a result of the carnage of the First World War.[1] Immigration usually means that more men than women will move to another county or country. In the seventeenth and early eighteenth centuries, men moved out of the English town of Coylton to find jobs elsewhere or abroad, leaving behind many women destined to become spinsters.[2] Prisons are disproportionately filled with male convicts, and so a high crime rate can take a lot of men off the street. Infant mortality affects boys more than girls. Men, especially unmarried ones, are more likely than women to die from murders, auto accidents, alcoholism, drug abuse, and many common illnesses. All of these factors would produce a low sex ratio—that is, an oversupply of women.

There is, of course, one obvious way to deal with too many women: allow each man to have more than one wife. As previously mentioned, this practice, called polygyny, has been widespread in the world and today still occurs among some cultures; among Muslims, it is authorized by the Koran. It is not hard to imagine why polygyny might be popular. Having many wives gives to each man a taste of

---

*There are some societies in which the number of male infants greatly exceeds the number of female ones. In Russia during the nineteenth century, the sex ratio for Jews ranged between 127 and 146, whereas for non-Jews that ratio was at its normal level, around 105. For this fact and an effort to explain it, see Marcia Guttentag and Paul F. Secord, *Too Many Women? The Sex Ratio Question* (Newbury Park, Calif.: Sage Publications, 1983), 85 and chapter 4 generally.

sexual variety, a chance to ensure that he has a large number of progeny, and, if he has more wives than other men, a reputation for status and power. All of these things are easier to gain if there exists an oversupply of women, something that is quite likely in any culture where men are regularly engaged in war, raiding, and dangerous occupations.

Edward Westermarck, in his magisterial study of marriage, asserts that among the Eskimos, some North American Indian tribes, and most African societies, the excess of women over men was a major factor in explaining polygyny. In the late nineteenth century, in Tanganyika, Madagascar, and the Congo and among the Kafirs and some Bantus and Kalahari Bushmen there were many more women than men, and polygyny was the rule. But among people in similar economic and cultural circumstances where men and women were present in roughly equal numbers, polygyny was rarer (though not absent).[3]

But our society, like every other Western one, does not allow polygyny, and so the problem created for the marriage market by having too few men may be acute. In a monogamous culture, a low sex ratio means that women must either struggle hard to find a husband, abandon marriage, or settle for some substitute form of sexuality, such as promiscuity, or raising children without a father.

An undersupply of women—a high sex ratio—has often occurred because in the past, and in some places still today, many women die in childbirth, leaving behind more men. That ratio can also be high when infanticide or sex-selective child neglect occurs, since in those countries where it happens, female children are more likely than male ones to be the victims. This has been true in several ancient societies, including Athens, and continues to be true in modern China.[4] In a country or region newly settled by immigrants, men are likely to outnumber women by a large margin. The American colonies were at first settled by more men than women, there were more men than women imported as slaves, the frontier territories were heavily masculine, and the California gold camps were overwhelmingly made up of men.

If men can adjust to an oversupply of women by having more than one wife, why can't women handle an excess number of men by having several? But no: with a few trivial exceptions, this practice—polyandry—is never found among humans. Westermarck found hardly any cases of it, and subsequent scholars have done no better. The striking difference between the number of polygynous and the number of polyandrous societies suggests that something important involving culture and biology is dictating marriage patterns, a matter to which I shall return in a moment.

Scholars have studied the effect of different sex ratios on a host of arrangements, including crime, promiscuity, adultery, feminism, cohabitation, births out of wedlock, labor force participation, the rise of the troubadour, and the prevalence of mysticism. Here we shall look at what has been learned about the connection between sex ratios and two things—how likely it is that a child will be born out of wedlock or raised in a single-parent family.

Sex Ratios, Marriage, and Births

The most ambitious and influential study of sex ratios was by Marcia Guttentag and Paul F. Secord.[5] Their argument is this: When there is a high sex ratio—that is, when there are many more men than women—marriage will be commonplace and cohabitation will be rare, women will play more traditional roles, and children will be raised in two-parent families. When there is a low sex ratio—that is, when there are many more women than men—marriages will be less common and more fragile, cohabitation will become more general, divorce will be more frequent, and children will be more likely to be raised in one-parent families. In the first case, women have a lot of bargaining power and so find it easier to get men to marry and stay with them; in the second case, women have less bargaining power and so must settle for what they can get.

From 1790 to about 1910, the United States had a relatively high sex ratio—around 104 or 105. After the First World War it fell, and by 1940 it was about 100. It continued to drop in the 1950s and 1960s until in 1970 it was 95.

But as Guttentag and Secord point out, these total numbers do not tell the whole story. To understand marriage, what is important is the sex ratio among unmarried people who are at a marriageable age and of the same race. (Even though the number of interracial marriages has grown in recent years, it is still the case that the vast majority of marriages for whites and blacks are among people of the same race.) Men and women only marry if they are unmarried, and most marry in their twenties, with a woman usually marrying a man who is two or three years older.

Since most men marry a younger woman, let us compare the number of unmarried white men between the ages of twenty-three and twenty-seven with that of unmarried white women between the ages of twenty and twenty-four. The sex ratio in those age ranges in America in 1970 was only sixty-seven.[6] That gap, or something like it, persisted for these women as they got older because there was no increase—and almost surely was a decrease—in the number of unmarried men who were at the right age. Another study came to much the same conclusion. In 1980 unmarried white women under the age of twenty-four had an ample number of males from which to choose, but for such women over the age of twenty-five the number of men shrank rapidly. What the author calls the "availability ratio" was cut in half as women left the twenty-to-twenty-four age group and entered the thirty-five-to-thirty-nine group.[7]

But in addition to age and race, education matters. If women want to marry up, they must find a man who has at least their level of education. That has become much harder. In 1950, there were twice as many men as women in American colleges; by 1997, there were only 79 men for every 100 women. Getting married to a college sweetheart had become much more difficult for women. For white women who have graduated from college, the marriage market deteriorates rapidly after age twenty-five. By the time they reach the age of thirty, there are only half as many unmarried men of the same age and education available for marriage. Today young women are urged not to marry early; instead, they should get an education and start a career. This may or may not be good advice, but if the goal is marriage, the suggestion creates some problems. As one study put it, in 1980 unmarried female college graduates between the ages of twenty-five and twenty-nine faced five female competitors for every comparable man.[8] Not very good odds. And the odds get worse depending on where you live. New York City has a shortage of men, but San Diego has a lot of them, and Rock Springs, Wyoming, even more.[9]

And for African Americans, matters are much worse. For a century or more, they have had a lower sex ratio than whites. By 1970, there were almost two young black women for every young black man.[10] The sex ratio was especially low in big cities; in New York City, for example, the sex ratio has been seventy-three or lower since 1940.[11] Of course, we know that the census does not count blacks accurately; many avoid enumeration by having no settled address or by staying away from government enumerators. This undercount is greater for black men than for black women, a fact that would make the sex ratio look lower than it really is.[12] But if so, the black men who avoid being counted are probably not likely to appear to black women as especially attractive spouses (they have no real address or may be in trouble with the law), and so in fact the sex ratio may appear to be as low to these women as the census count suggests. One study found that making adjustments for a census undercount did not much alter the proportion of available mates.[13]

Young black men are scarce because they are in prison or overseas in the armed forces and because black men die at a higher rate than black women from disease, alcoholism, drug abuse, auto accidents, homicide, and suicide.[14] There is even some evidence that illegitimate children in the United States who survive infancy are more likely to be female than male.[15]

If African American women had access to more potential marriage partners, more would get married. This conclusion comes from a careful study by Daniel Lichter and his colleagues in which they combined interviews with young people with measures of local marriage markets. Assuming that black women had as many marriage partners as white women of the same age, the chances of the former getting married would increase by almost one-fourth.[16] Since marriage is generally good for women, black or white, the shortage of mates for the former adds another reason to find ways of saving young black males from premature death. And since many of those deaths are caused by murders, we can begin to see how strong the link may be between high homicide rates and low marriage rates. But even allowing for the low sex ratio, black women are still less likely to marry than whites ones. In chapter 5 I shall suggest a reason for this.

The Sex Ratio and Family Life

The sex ratio, I think, makes a difference in family life, but it does not explain by itself the pattern of single-parent homes and out-of-wedlock births, nor does the sex ratio affect whites and African Americans equally. To show all of the reasons for my judgment would require a long and tedious tour through many studies, a trip that not many readers would enjoy taking. Let me summarize what I think scholars have learned.

A simple way to find how the sex ratio affects marriage is to correlate the two numbers across the states. When Guttentag and Secord did this using 1970 numbers, they found that the correlation between the sex ratios of black Americans and the proportion of black births that were illegitimate was −0.87. This meant that the proportion of African American children who were born out of wedlock was highest—by a substantial margin—in states where African American women outnumbered African American men. Making the same calculation for the white sex ratio and the white illegitimacy rate, the result was −0.27.[17] For both racial groups, the sex ratio made a difference, but for blacks a much greater one. In a later chapter I will try to suggest some reasons that might explain this difference. A child born out of wedlock might nevertheless be raised by a husband and father if its parents marry, or at least live regularly together, after its birth. But when Guttentag and Secord correlated black sex ratios with the percentage of female-headed black families, it was −.83 in 1970.[18] Where black women outnumber black men, children tend to lack a father.

But these correlations may be a bit misleading, for the total sex ratio (males per hundred females) leaves out of account the number of people who are unmarried but of marriageable age. I (or more accurately, my research assistant) made a similar calculation using 1990 census data, and we did it by using the sex ratio of unmarried men and women in the age group fifteen to twenty-four. We used two different measures of births: the number of illegitimate births for every one thousand women aged fifteen through twenty-four (call this the "illegitimacy rate") and the proportion of all births to women aged fifteen through twenty-four that are illegitimate (call this the "illegitimacy ratio").* The lower the proportion of men to women in a state, the more likely it is for there to be more out-of-wedlock births however measured, as rate or ratio. This link was strongest for the illegitimacy rate of African Americans.[19]

Similar results were produced by Mark Fossett and Jill Kiecolt, who found that the higher the sex ratio of African Americans in the parishes of Louisiana, the greater the chances that a child will live in a two-parent family and the lower the chances that the child would be born out of wedlock.[20] When they enlarged their study to look at African Americans in metropolitan areas, they found the same pattern. Even after holding constant economic status, in metropolitan areas with higher sex ratios marriage among African American women was more common and children were more likely to live in two-parent families. And they discovered that, other things being equal, higher levels of welfare payments were associated with lower rates of marriage and fewer children living in two-parent families.[21] Scott South and Kim Lloyd found much the same thing. In metropolitan areas, low sex ratios—that is, too few men for every hundred women—produced higher rates of out-of-wedlock births.[22]

In fact, the sex ratio may even influence divorce rates. Among non-Hispanic whites, marriages were more likely to break up when either wives or husbands found a lot of potential spouses outside their

---

*Be clear about the difference between illegitimacy *rate* and illegitimacy *ratio*. The rate—the number of illegitimate births per thousand women—can go up just because women are having more babies or go down just because they are having fewer. The ratio is what is interesting because it tells you what fraction of all births are out of wedlock. The rate measures both how fertile women are and how careful they are to acquire a husband; the ratio measures only the latter. For a good discussion of this, see Charles Murray, "Does Welfare Bring More Babies?" *The Public Interest*, no. 115 (1994): 3–30.

marriage. If a husband found a big supply of unmarried women where he lived, he was more likely to leave his wife, and a comparable pattern was true for wives who discovered a big supply of unmarried men.[23]

To check out these correlations, some scholars have looked at facts about individual behavior by examining marriage rates among black Americans who had been interviewed, comparing their marital status with the sex ratios in the communities where they were interviewed. The higher the sex ratio—that is, the more men available—the more likely it was for black women to be married and the less likely it was for them to be divorced.[24]

Daniel Lichter and his colleagues looked at individuals that have been part of the National Longitudinal Survey of Youth (NLSY), a massive study of several thousand young people who have been repeatedly interviewed since 1979, and compared their marriage decisions with the sex ratios in the communities where they lived. They found that an unfavorable marriage market—too few men—cut the number of marriages made and reduced the chances of a woman marrying up.

All of these results may remind the reader of the well-known argument of William Julius Wilson, a distinguished analyst of race and urban problems, who has suggested that the central family problem of African Americans is the shortage of employed black men of marriageable age. It is indeed true that the availability of such men (whom Wilson defines as those who were employed and in the age range sixteen to twenty-four) fell sharply after 1950 in comparison with the number of women of the same race and age. In 1950, there were about seventy employed nonwhite men aged twenty to twenty-four for every one hundred nonwhite women; by 1980, there were fewer than fifty such men for every one hundred women.[25] But though joblessness may be a factor in the plight of urban black families, it cannot be the whole story for two reasons. First, as we have seen, the shortage of unmarried black men—*whether they are employed or not*—is associated with high levels of illegitimate births and single-parent families. Second, Latino male immigrants, who have higher unemployment rates than black men, are much less likely to sire children out of wedlock or to abandon children whom they have fathered.[26] Something else is going on. Culture? History?

It is quite likely that ethnic culture, American history, and the sex ratio all affect the rate at which intact families are formed. Daniel Lichter, a sociologist who has been studying marriage rates for more than a decade, concluded that the sex ratio and employment make a difference, but not one large enough to explain why black and white marriage rates diverge so sharply.[27]

Culture and Biology

Whether there are too many or too few women seems to have an effect on the marriage market, but the effect is not easy to understand. If there are too many women, they are at a disadvantage, but what disadvantage? If there are too few, they have the upper hand, but the upper hand to do what?

If there are a lot of men and not many women (that is, if there is a high sex ratio), the women are in principle free to do whatever they would like in order to advance their sexual interests. Having a lot of bargaining power, they could either offer sex to men only on condition that the men marry them or decide instead to have sex with as many men as they want and ignore marriage. In the latter case, they might even create male brothels run by female pimps and start pornography shops that cater exclusively to women. They could even require men to raise their babies while the wives play cards, watch women's soccer games on television, and go to bars and drink with other women. They could do these things in theory. But mostly they don't.

If there are not many men and a lot of women (that is, there is a low sex ratio), the women will have to work hard to find sexual partners. They could decide to become prostitutes, enter a nunnery, or become unmarried members of various professions. If they want to have a child, they might have to live unmarried with several men (who are, in effect, trying them out) or settle for having a baby without being married. In short, women with little bargaining power could either go along with whatever the men wanted or renounce men and motherhood and view marriage as a useless, outmoded invention.

But, as Guttentag and Secord point out, some of these alternatives rarely, if ever, exist. Women could renounce marriage, but few do. Marriage, broadly defined, is a universal feature of all societies and apparently has been since records first were kept. Women could become more promiscuous than men, but that rarely happens. And no matter how few women may exist in a society, we do not hear of many women patronizing pornography stores or requiring men to abandon their careers, be virgins before they are married, and stay home and raise the babies while their wives drink at bars or watch football on television.

Why are some of these alternatives never found? Guttentag and Secord offer two suggestions, culture and biology, but they develop only the first. Their cultural explanation is that in every society the men dominate. They have "structural power" based on their high degree of control over the economy and their overrepresentation in government and the legal system. This means that when there are a lot of men competing for relatively few women, the women can become choosy, but only up to a point determined in large part by a male-dominated culture. Most will choose to be wives and live within the slowly changing definition of wifeliness; that is to say, they will spend more time at home with their children than will their husbands, thereby conforming to male expectations. Depending on the economic status of women, men may take on more household chores, but women will still do most of them. If women enter the labor force, they will usually have somewhat lower professional incomes than males of the same age and education because they will have less seniority. The lack of seniority is largely explained by motherhood. Women who are not mothers earn 95 percent of what men earn, but those who are mothers earn only 75 percent of the corresponding male wage.[28]

When women have relatively few men from whom to pick a sexual partner or husband, they cannot be too choosy. They will have more female rivals and hence less bargaining power. But though they now must act as men want them to act, they still, in the majority of cases, prefer marriage to cohabitation (though many will, of course, cohabit with male partners), and few will denounce marriage or argue in favor of some less settled way of living.

I think Guttentag and Secord are right to argue that culture shapes women's (and men's) choices, and that every culture in the world encourages or sometimes insists that men be in the front rank. And we know that cultures can change. One study looked at the effect of the sex ratio on the economic power of women and found that in nations with a high level of women in the paid work force the influence of that ratio on the percentage of women who are married and their fertility rate was much less than was the case in less developed countries where women had fewer paid jobs.[29] Economic advancement gave women more choices.

Moreover, there are some important differences in how the sex ratio affects behavior, differences that have a large cultural component. Consider the case of very high sex ratios—lots of men, few women. They have existed in old California gold mining towns, among Chinese laborers brought to this country to build the railroads, and in the southern colonies of seventeenth- and eighteenth-century America. Southern and gold rush Americans elevated decent women onto a pedestal, defending their honor and attacking their detractors with grim determination. In Yellowstone City, the law once imposed the death sentence on anyone insulting a respectable woman. Some cowboys were even afraid to talk to decent women for fear of getting into trouble. As late as the 1910s, David Courtwright reports, Wyoming ranch hands would call out, "Church time!" when a married woman approached and then lapse into an awkwardly respectful silence.[30] In the violent mining town of Bodie, California, respect for married women was enforced by a resort to sudden death for any detractor.[31] Frontier women often had good jobs at relatively high pay and attended school more regularly than did their eastern counterparts. Side by side with male deference to decent women one found, of course, the men's rowdy preoccupation with prostitutes and an attachment to alcohol, violence, and (often) a sordid lifestyle.

These circumstances may help us understand an otherwise puzzling fact. Though the political movement for women's suffrage was based in the East, the eleven states that had, by the end of 1914, granted women the vote were all in the West. Indeed, wild, boisterous Wyoming led the pack by extending the suffrage in 1890.[32] Sophisticated easterners argued for female suffrage, but primitive westerners did it. The reason, in most cases, was the belief that if women could vote they would help civilize the territory. As Alan Grimes put it, "Men conquered the wilderness, women made it habitable."[33]

The Chinese laborers who came to the West in the nineteenth century also had a high sex ratio—in 1890, there were twenty-seven Chinese men for every Chinese woman—but they managed to put most of the few women who arrived into servitude as prostitutes.[34] A few became the brides of rich men who kept them in a state of nearly complete isolation. Almost none went to school, and except as prostitutes, few worked. Culture explains why Chinese women were treated as property at the very time that Caucasian women were the objects of deference. The Triad, the secret societies that celebrated fraternity and encouraged criminality, dominated the early Chinese social life. They helped keep women under centralized control.[35] It was not until 1970 that the Chinese sex ratio fell to 110 (still much higher than the Caucasian one); as recently as 1940 it was 285.[36] By contrast, Caucasian frontier life was open, loose, and barely under any central direction.[37] For the Chinese immigrants, powerful male organizations controlled what happened to women; for the Caucasian frontiersmen, female bargaining power was so high that any respectable woman received extraordinary deference.

The absence of such powerful organizations is evident in the history of slavery. Usually more men than women were kidnapped and imported, producing a very high sex ratio. But the male slaves had no opportunity to form anything like the Chinese secret societies in order to enforce servility on women, and they lacked any opportunity to define, as frontiersmen did, the difference between respectable and not-so-respectable women. Given the limits imposed by slavery, the abundant African American males took advantage of their opportunities and had many sexual liaisons with relatively few marriages (see chapter 5).

But these cultural considerations cannot be the whole story. Biology sets important limits on how far culture can change things. Nowhere do we find any society, whatever its sex ratio, in which women dominate the government, are the principal consumers of

pornography and prostitution, or make men do most of the child rearing. In even the most egalitarian societies, such as Sweden, single-
parent homes are headed, in the great majority of cases, by women.[38]
Culture and biology interact in powerful ways, especially with respect
to those social arrangements that are especially important and
durable. Guttentag and Secord acknowledge that, in general, men are
physically stronger than women and only women have babies—two
important biological facts—but they argue that male strength in a
modern economy is much less important than it was in a hunter-
gatherer society and that, even though only women can give birth,
anyone can care for the infants.

If that were all there was to biology, we might be inclined to dis-
miss its significance. But there is much more to it, enough to set the
outer limits within which cultures can vary. At this point some readers
will groan that I am beginning another "nature versus nurture"
debate, but they are wrong. Virtually every important human characteristic is the joint and complex result of the interaction between biology and culture. It is impossible to speak of almost any
trait—personality, intelligence, athleticism, beauty, strength, or navi-
gational skills—without taking into account both nature and nurture.
The only writers who insist on "nature *versus* nurture" are those who
believe that everything about humans is the result of learning—that is,
nurture or culture. And that is wrong.

Everywhere men are more violent than women. They commit
more violent crimes, are more likely to get into auto accidents and
street fights, and are more likely to make violent threats. This is not
because men are driven by a "violence gene," but probably because
their evolutionary past has led them to compete vigorously for social
rewards, including access to the most desirable women.[39] We are the
descendants of the most successful competitors. Wars are fought in
many primitive societies in order to increase access to women.[40] And
if they obtain those rewards, including the women, they will struggle
hard to maintain them. Men may be physically stronger than
women, but what is just as important is that they are more willing to
use that strength—or in modern times, that energy—to get what
they value.

Men almost everywhere tend to prefer women who are younger than they and who conform most closely to what appears, in a study of many cultures, to be a nearly universal standard of beauty. In every culture where it has been studied, men and women agree that symmetrical faces with wide-set eyes are ideal. This finding comes from merging hundreds of photographs of women taken in almost every culture in the world. People who look at the composite photograph—the computer-linked average of scores of pictures—like this *average* better than almost any single face.[41] This preference is neither Western nor simply learned. It exists among Asian, African, Indian, and American respondents and it appears among infants as young as three months of age.[42]

Men also like slender waists; to be exact, a waist-to-hip ratio of roughly 0.7.[43] (To put that ratio into everyday language, if a woman has a hip measurement of thirty-six inches, men want her waist to be twenty-four to twenty-five inches. Recall the old phrase, "36–24–36," once made at beauty pageants in the ancient and now lost days when referring to measurements was still politically possible.) This preference for narrow-waisted women is not simply a male attitude. Women have the same view, as is evident by glancing at any magazine offering to them advice on style and clothing. Nor is it an easily changeable cultural preference, because it exists in all of the many different cultures where the matter has been studied. Of course, men and women may differ on some aspects of beauty. Men are more likely than women to value large breasts. Women know this, and so some seek out the services of plastic surgeons. Women value broad shoulders, and so many men go to gyms. But on waist size, both sexes think alike.

And there may be good reasons for it. Several studies have found that narrow waists are associated with a greater ability to become pregnant. In two studies of women seeking artificial insemination, those with a waist-to-hip ratio below .8 were almost twice as likely to become pregnant as were women with thicker waists, and this was true even after controlling for the women's age and weight.[44] Even heavy women are regarded as attractive if their waist is narrower than their hips.

Consider what this preference for youth and beauty means for women. On the average, a young man will marry a woman about two or three years younger than he, but this preference for youth will continue as the man gets older. By the time he is sixty he will marry a woman who is forty-five. Think, for a moment, what that does to the sex ratio. As women get older, their chances of marrying fall dramatically, since (again, on the average) men prefer younger women. In Canada, for every one hundred women aged forty there are only sixty men available, and that number would be even smaller if you deducted from the total gays, perennial bachelors, and those cohabiting with another woman.[45]

Based on studies done in many different cultures, David Buss has shown that while both men and women chiefly value intelligence and kindness in prospective mates, men greatly value physical attractiveness while women heavily value status and earning power. It was evident in American studies done in 1939 and persists in studies done in the 1980s, long after the sexual revolution had occurred.[46] On the average, both men and women want a pleasant mate, but to this men add beauty while women add financial capacity. Given the male orientation to beauty, no one should be surprised that sexual fantasies are likely to be more common among men than among women and to be oriented to having sex with several women or some unknown but beautiful one. "Numbers and novelty are key ingredients of men's fantasy lives."[47]

All of these differences can be explained—though not proved—by understanding the fundamental sexual difference between men and women. A man can impregnate countless women but without DNA tests he cannot be certain a child produced by some woman is his offspring. A woman can raise only a few children, but she will be certain that they are her offspring. If the man wishes to devote his scarce resources to caring for his own children—and the overwhelming majority of men do—then he has to be certain of his paternity. For him, marriage is one answer. He obtains exclusive sexual access to his wife and thus knows that the children he supports are really his. To become married, he must pick a woman who can readily bear a child, and her age and physical appearance are important clues to that ability. For the woman, marriage is also the answer. It commits the man to providing her with financial and emotional support during the long and sometimes painful process of reproduction and child rearing. For her, the best marriage is to a man able to supply these resources, and one sign of that ability is his present economic situation and prospects.

Marriage has become a nearly universal institution because society has figured out that this bond will reinforce a man's willingness to support a mother. But it is also a fragile institution that requires constant efforts to keep it intact. Men have roving eyes, and so once having contracted a marriage they may nevertheless look lustfully at other attractive women. Women have commitments to child care, and so once they have entered into a marriage they will worry that the husbands will desert them for other women and take their economic resources with them. And a woman may also be attracted to another man, especially if she thinks her husband is inadequate to his emotional duties. Men and women must work hard to maintain a marriage, and society—since it sees the value of marriage as a way of managing property and child care—will impose upon this institution many rules designed to keep it intact whatever the wandering eye of a husband or wife may settle upon.

Much of what we observe about human behavior today follows from these simple requirements. Men want to have children, and so they prefer young and attractive wives. Women want to manage child care, and so they choose husbands who seem to have good economic prospects. Men want to guarantee that the children they support will be theirs, and so they become enraged at the sexual infidelity of their wives. Women want to keep their husband's necessary child support, and so they worry about his lack of an emotional commitment. Men, if they can afford it, are tempted to acquire more wives, and so many societies tolerate or even endorse polygyny. And when polygyny is illegal, as it is in most industrialized nations, a man may be tempted to acquire new wives illegally or serially—first a wife who is his children's mother and, when she ages, divorce her and marry a new, younger, trophy wife to provide him with sexual excitement and social status or, in lieu of divorce, acquire a mistress. Women are keenly aware of this possibility, which is probably another reason they worry more about emotional commitment than about sexual regularity. And though an economically successful woman could abandon her first husband for a new boy toy, that happens much less frequently than men abandoning the first wife for a trophy version.

In many primitive societies, male aggressiveness is physical and even brutal, but though modernity has found important alternatives to war and pillage it has only sublimated the motives that produce aggression into a contest for status, wealth, and political power. A great achievement of modern times has not been to weaken male aggressiveness but to convert the struggle for physical superiority into one for monetary or political advantage. Samuel Johnson once remarked that every meeting and every conversation is a contest in which the man of superior parts was the victor.[48] That aggressiveness helps explain why men dominate in so many professions in which climbing an organizational hierarchy is important. Men are more likely than women to be focused on occupational achievement and to value it as much or more than they value family attachments, and so men are more likely to work longer hours and take greater risks than are women.

But culture also contributes to this in just the way we would expect of any nature-nurture interaction. To reduce competition, men will often exclude women from certain professions or the higher ranks in any profession. They will create glass ceilings and enforce a home-maker ethos. That cultural component can, of course, be changed, as we have seen in the last few decades. American women now make up a large proportion—sometimes the majority—of people studying to become lawyers, physicians, architects, and veterinarians, and they have taken jobs in all kinds of civilian and military occupations. This transformation has helped women, moderated male aggressiveness, and had mixed effects on marriage by reducing the wife's financial dependence on men while at the same time making it easier for child rearing to be given to outside parties of uncertain talents.

But biology, though it is not destiny, will place limits on how far this cultural change can proceed. Most women want children; to give birth to and nurse infants, they will drop out of the seniority rat race, thereby yielding space to their male rivals. Some will discover that being a mother is more rewarding than being an investment banker.

And even if they do not give ground in order to acquire children, male aggressiveness, now channeled into bureaucratic infighting and political struggles, will give men an edge—not a decisive advantage, but an edge—in the struggle for success.

These biological differences also help us understand why women are more likely than men to read romance novels and men more likely than women to read pornography. The emotional fantasies of each group are differently focused, with women more concerned about attachment and men more about sex. Most women read magazines that display beautiful women and offer secrets about improving one's own appearance; they rarely read magazines displaying beautiful men. By contrast, most men do not read magazines that feature handsome men and offer tips about how to become more handsome; instead, they read magazines about sports or ones containing pictures of cars, gadgets, or beautiful naked women.

It should also make it clear why prostitutes are overwhelmingly female and their customers overwhelmingly male. For men, sex is an activity only occasionally connected to reproduction, whereas for women, sex, though a greatly enjoyable experience, is closely linked to reproduction, especially when, having forgotten to stay on the pill, sex leads to an unwanted pregnancy.

Because men are more interested in activities and women more in commitments, the conversations between men and women are shot through with misunderstandings. If a woman has a problem, a man may try to solve it when in fact what the woman wants is a sounding board. When a woman expects her husband or lover to constantly reassure her that she is loved and wanted, the man is puzzled because, having said that once or twice, the matter should now be settled and not need further elaboration. Cartoon strips and television sitcoms regularly feature married men who find it hard to say, "I love you."

But the simplest argument for the extent to which biology influences, albeit without controlling, the effects of the sex ratio on men and women is easily stated. Forget tastes in beauty or differences in physical strength, important though those are. The central fact of family life is that when the father and the mother do not live together for whatever the reason, the women in the vast majority of cases wind up with the children. The sacrifices women make for their children are much greater than the ones men make,[49] and these commitments explain why, whenever a choice must be made between sex or careerism on the one hand and parenthood on the other, women will choose the latter much more often than will men.

The Marriage Market

The market for marriage is defined by the presence of young men and women whose numbers may vary in ways that affect the chances of having a marriage. Those chances are in part culturally influenced (our parents either tell us, "You ought to get married!" or "You ought to have a career!"), but they are also in part driven by powerful biological urges. You can talk some women out of wanting a baby and some others will come to that conclusion on their own, but you can't talk most of them out of wanting them. You can talk men into being kind to women and tolerating their aspirations, but you can't persuade men to have no sexual interest in women to whom they are not married.

When the sex ratio changes, the way men and women pursue their sexual interests must also change. The magnitude of that change will vary because of the culture of the society and the degree of its economic development, but neither culture nor the economy will prevent any change from occurring at all. The evidence so far suggests that when there is a shortage of young females, most men will devote themselves to finding and marrying a woman because, unless they offer a serious commitment, any desirable woman will turn to a rival who will make that commitment. And when there is a shortage of men, many women will settle for less than what they had hoped for by never marrying, accepting casual offers of sex from men who offer no marital prospects, or producing babies without being married to their fathers.

Chapter 4
The Rise of the Modern Marriage

A common view of families is that once upon a time marriages were arranged by parents who decided what boy should marry what girl. Though the contemporary mind usually finds such arrangements distasteful, at least they produced large, extended families in which many grandparents, aunts, and uncles lived under one roof with the married couple so that every person could help care for everyone else. Romance and love were less important then, but those days are now gone. Now men and women marry out of romantic attachment and, for better or worse, live in small, nuclear families. Such families are nice, but some of us miss the old days of extended families and the social support they provided.

Unfortunately, every one of these views is either wrong or seriously misleading. In the West, and especially in England and the lands settled by English people, marriages, except among the aristocrats, were usually not arranged since at least the thirteenth century. Men and women have for hundreds of years chosen for themselves whom to marry or at least with whom to live, since a formal marriage was sometimes ignored. In much of medieval England, no public ceremony was required to make a marriage valid, and so a lot of these unions were conducted privately, at home, before few or even no witnesses, and sometimes done in bed, a garden, a tavern, or a field. Many of these unions were later solemnized in a church, but many were not.[1] And these families—the ones that first settled this country—were nuclear from the beginning. Occasionally, of course, several generations of relatives might live with the husband and wife, but scholars have learned that for many centuries the average size of a household changed only slightly, if at all. In family size and personal consent, Western families today are pretty much what they have been for centuries.

It is remarkable that this family system should be so old. Considering how much is often at stake, letting people decide for themselves whom to marry needs to be explained. How can property be managed and the elderly cared for if we let a couple of young people decide for themselves, and sometimes only after the girl has gotten pregnant, that they would live together in their own home? The farm might be neglected, the children badly raised, and their parents ignored when they needed help.

Since the beginning of history, a marriage has always meant more than merely a lasting sexual union confirmed by some social custom or religious liturgy. Marriages involved more than sex; they involved the identity and custody of children, the management and often the ownership of property, and the history of one or more families that extended through the generations, an enduring legacy of social identity and personal history that implied status, obligations, and expectations. The family is not only a universal practice, it is the fundamental social unit of any society, and on its foundation there is erected the essential structure of social order—who can be preferred to whom, who must care for whom, who can exchange what with whom. The family not only created the basis for this vast array of social habits, it has also been the arena in which children learn how to act in the larger world. Surely one would expect that creating a family, with so vast an array of social roles, would rarely, if ever, be left merely to the romantic passions of two young people.

The Chinese have long thought that filial piety requires that no one acting alone can arrange his or her marriage. Instead, the family must do this. Edward Westermarck has summarized this and countless other examples of parent-arranged marriages.[2] Among the ancient Hebrews the father had the absolute right to give his daughters in marriage and to choose wives for his sons, a right that forms an important part of the motion picture *Fiddler on the Roof*. The ancient Romans made the wife as well as all the children the personal property of the husband, and his consent was essential to his children's marriage. Few other civilizations gave to the father the absolute authority conferred by Roman law, but ancient Greek fathers could give their daughters in marriage to a man she might not know, and the authority of Hindu fathers has always been very strong. In contemporary India, though the opinions of the man and woman are sometimes consulted, most marriages are arranged. These unions usually lead to affection between husband and wife, but many Indians assume that this fondness will be the result and not the precondition of marriage.[3] For many centuries in Eastern Europe and elsewhere, land was owned by clans—that is, by extended families—and it was hard for marriage to occur except by the consent of the elders.

In addition to these European and Asian examples, there have been very different kinds of family life found in much of Africa. In Europe monogamy was almost always the ideal, a new family required property, brides were accompanied by dowries paid to their husbands, and concubines were common. By contrast, in much of Africa polygyny was frequent, a new family might require cattle but rarely property, husbands paid bridewealth to their brides' families, and concubines were rare.

Ester Boserup and Jack Goody, two anthropologists, explain these differences largely in terms of the modes of economic production.[4] In Europe, where animal-drawn plows were used to farm rich land, intensive agriculture made monogamy important. Somebody or some family had to own the land from which virtually all human support was derived. There had to be a certain heir if land was to be preserved by a family. In these places, men did much of the agricultural work and women were confined to household duties. Intensive farming meant land was the chief source of wealth; the richest man or family owned the most land. Because land was unequally owned, large differences in wealth (and through wealth, power) arose, and government was preoccupied with defending or acquiring land and managing the relationships among its owners. As commerce among landowners increased, cities arose to which aspiring tradesmen and servants would move in search of employment.

In much of Africa, by contrast, farming was done by handheld hoes used to work small plots of land that were often rather infertile. Women were widely used to do the hoeing and carry in the produce. Many husbands found that they could use extra wives to wield even more hoes, and so marrying several women made sense economically. Land was abundant—in some communities, almost unlimited—and so land ownership was less important. What counted was having the ability, that is, the labor, with which to scratch something out of whatever piece of land lay nearby. Because land was both abundant and relatively unyielding, land ownership was not an important route to wealth. And because land-based wealth was unusual, political power tended to rest more on personal skills and tribal alliances than on marketable goods or vast estates. "Poverty," Goody has written, "was related to labor rather than capital."[5] In these villages, family life was not organized around landlord-tenant relationships, sexual jealousy had to adapt to a family life in which many wives had a common husband, and child rearing was a shared activity that was carried on in a communal setting.

This view has been criticized for having neglected herding cattle (that is, pastoralism)[6] and for being unable to explain the absence of the European marriage system in India (where there is rich soil and some plowing), but the Boserup-Goody argument covers enough cases to serve as a useful starting point. As we shall see in a later chapter, the conditions they describe may have had important consequences for the kinds of families that had to endure the travails of slavery in the Western Hemisphere.

Property and Marriage

When a man and a woman acting alone can choose to marry, we have a modern marriage market. This market seems to have arisen in England and parts of northern Europe many centuries ago for reasons that are not altogether clear. To understand marriages today, we must first understand the long history that has produced them. If we think that today's marriage problems are merely the result of that all-powerful secular deity, "the sixties," we will not understand why so many nations do not have these problems even though youthful emancipation and the rise of individual self-expression have affected people everywhere.

For most of its history, marriage has not been simply about sex or reproduction, it has been about property. People live on land; they inherit land; they buy, sell, and bequeath land; and they have a stake in trades, licenses, economic activities, and other forms of personal property. In many cultures, valuable land is in short supply, and so rules must be designed to manage access to it. The best account of how property rules affect marriage has been given by Alan Macfarlane.[7]

There are chiefly two ways of managing land. The first is for a group—a clan, tribe, or a family—to own it and decide who would use it. The second is for an individual—a person or a married couple—to own and work it. I shall call the first method group control and the second individual control. Group control is characteristic of peasant societies. A plot of land has no individual owner; it is managed by a group, usually consisting of an extended family. One man might take the lead in this management, but he would not own the property or be able to sell it. Only the household, and through it a larger clan, could do this.

W. I. Thomas and Florin Znaniecki in their multivolume book, *The*

Polish Peasant in Europe and America, published between 1918 and 1920, make this clear.[8] In Poland—and, as we shall see, in much of Eastern Europe—few people could buy, sell, or inherit a farm. The farm stayed in the group even though the membership of the group changed over time. Family control also implied that no man could run it simply because he was the father. The father would have to yield managerial authority to a son who showed greater skill, and do so without recompense. "Land property," wrote Thomas and Znaniecki, "is essentially familial; the individual is its temporary manager."[9] When the son becomes more able than his father at agricultural direction, the former replaces the latter as head of the enterprise even though he has not inherited it.[10] Indeed, no one person inherited the farm at all; it belonged to a continuous flow of children, no one of which was ever an heir. In the twentieth century, of course, individual inheritance became possible, but it only replaced the older, peasant system with great difficulty, and it was quite late in arriving.

Much the same system existed in Russia, where for centuries before the Bolshevik revolution farmland belonged to a clan—indeed, one supremely powerful clan—and not to any individual.[11] Richard Pipes, in explaining the absence of any historical commitment to personal liberties in Russia, has suggested that it is due in great part to the lack of individual property. The grand duke of Moscow, the great power that by the fifteenth century had conquered Russia, imposed on the country a regime under which the ruler owned all of the land. From then until the end of the eighteenth century, title to land was vested in the monarch whose income came in the form of rents paid by his subjects.[12] This not only meant that political liberties had no sure footing in individually owned land, it also helped ensure that marriages would be arranged. Few people could start a new household on land they had acquired. There was nothing to acquire; it all belonged to the prince.

Near the end of the eighteenth century, Catherine the Great granted to the landed gentry the right to own property, including the right to sell or bequeath it, but the property they owned included the serfs who lived on it. What the gentry gained, ordinary people lost. Landlords could now do what once only the czar could do—sell, exploit, punish, exile into Siberia, and force into marriage against their will all of the ordinary people who lived on their property. There were, to be sure, some restraints on the landlords' powers—the absence of any market economy that gave them an incentive to maximize what the serfs produced and the presence of communes that helped them collect taxes—but until the serfs were liberated in the middle of the nineteenth century they were at their landlords' mercy. Their marriages could be arranged for them by their landlords and they had little chance of acquiring property that could provide the economic basis for a new family.

In peasant societies, marriages were planned with group interests in mind, the two most important of which were food production and social harmony. Both goals required marriages when the bride and groom were quite young: the family needed children who would add to the supply of household labor and believed that every person of decent character must be married. Marriage supplied "a steadiness of life which is necessary for [a family's] interior harmony," and that steadiness and harmony was either made manifest or directly caused by marriage.[13] As a result of these expectations, there were rarely many bachelors or spinsters about. By the time they reached the age of forty-five, nearly all of the women would have been married. Given the great importance of family-managed marriages, matchmakers were important. They supplied the information on the basis of which the family could choose a spouse for a son or daughter.

Because married families were part of a subsistence economy, there were not many chances to leave the village or even the household and start a new enterprise. Few crops were sold for cash, few family members went off in search of employment elsewhere. There were scarcely any organized markets for Polish peasants or Russian serfs.

These group marriages could not be found in England or in the colonies settled by Englishmen. No peasant society existed there because property rights were established on an individual basis. This individualism was evident, Macfarlane suggests, as early as the thirteenth century in England, and something like it probably existed in some parts of northwestern Europe. Contrary to what many historians have suggested, social life in England was not a more or less steady progression from a peasant world of family-controlled land to a modern world of individual choice because, in fact, there never had been a peasant world.

From as far back as historical records go, property in England (but not in much of Europe) was vested in individuals. One owner—typically a man, but on occasion a woman—could buy, sell, inherit, or bequeath land. This fact made group control of marriages very difficult in England because there was not much of a group to exercise control. Macfarlane shows that in many villages in the seventeenth century there was scarcely any record of two married couples living under one roof.[14] The extended family, one of several generations living under the same roof, has often been held up by modern writers as an ideal away from which contemporary society has drifted, but the reality is quite different. In America, England, and other English-speaking lands, we cannot find extended families no matter how far back we go. From at least the sixteenth century down to the present (and in reality probably from an even earlier period), the average size of a household has not changed.[15] Peter Laslett has shown that in 1650 the average English household had just under five people in it; in 1921, it had about the same number. Since 1921 it has become smaller, but the change occurred long after people had been writing, wrongly, about how much bigger (and presumably better) nineteenth- or eighteenth-century families had been. During most of the period Laslett has analyzed, the sex ratio was about ninety-one, a fact suggesting, as we have seen, that men were competing hard for scarce women.

Without land, a man could not easily marry, and so he had to work to obtain land: "No land, no marriage." He might acquire land by first hiring himself out as a laborer or servant. Happily for many men, this employment did not have to last indefinitely. Because life spans were so short, men died in their forties or fifties, leaving land for distribution by bequest or sale. Still, getting the money took time, and so marriages in England occurred at much older ages than was true in peasant societies. And not just for the affluent: property ownership was quite common in England. In 1600, owners of property made up between half and two-thirds of the entire population of the country.[16]

Because of the need for property, marriages in England occurred at an older age than was true in feudal or African societies. The advanced age meant that there were far fewer married women in a country such as England, with its individualistic system, than in eastern or southern Europe, where clan control was powerful. In English communities around 1800, only about half of all the women aged twenty-five to twenty-nine were married; by contrast, in a Russian community at the same time, nearly all of the women of that age had married.[17] Sweden was similar to England, whereas Tuscany was akin to Russia.

When the new marriage had produced children, they were often fewer in number than in peasant societies; after all, the average age of an English mother might be ten years older than a Polish one, and so the former had fewer child-producing years than the latter. And producing for cash markets in England took less labor than producing for a large extended family in Poland. This meant that English families required fewer young workers, and the children they did have often had to be let go into the larger community in order to find a spouse and acquire some land of their own. As a result, English children were often apprenticed out as servants or workers.

The Requirement of Consent

When men and women were allowed to arrange their own marriage, it would have effect only if their consent was sufficient to make it binding. It was his land and her child-rearing capacities that were at stake. Relatives might urge a particular spouse on their kin, but they could not as easily command one. Jane Austen has left us some memorable accounts of how children and parents argued over suitable marriage partners, reminding us that the children usually won.

Macfarlane has argued, I think convincingly, that individualistic land ownership and the marriage system it sustained made England the natural place for the emergence of capitalism. The technological advances of the eighteenth and nineteenth centuries no doubt gave a powerful boost to capitalism, but these advances were available to many countries. What was distinctive about England was that, at least from the thirteenth century on, there had grown up a land-based, market-oriented, individualistic society that could take advantage of technology.

If individualism fostered capitalism, so also did it shape family life. What was distinctive about individualist as opposed to group control of land is that it created a more or less free market for marriage. By "market" I mean exactly what any economist would mean: a voluntary transaction between two independent people designed for their mutual benefit. Men and women had to save and invest if marriage was to be possible. Only the man and woman could consent to a marriage, and to arrange that consent a courtship would be necessary. Each side—the husband and the wife—would acquire rights because each could control land. The man, of course, was by far the dominant partner in any marriage, but because the widow could inherit land and then under some circumstances sell it, there were many women endowed with some capital.[18]

In theory, families could still try to control the marriages of their children, and certainly many tried, and a few, especially among the aristocracy, with some success. But individual property ownership made familial control difficult, and over the centuries both the church and the state worked hard to make it impossible. We do not know precisely why the English marriage market required the free consent of man and woman, but some plausible arguments can be advanced.

England had an early respect for individual rights, some loosely defined by the Magna Carta, and more flowing from the common law. When independent judges heard arguments about who owned what bit of land and who owed what fee to whom, they were setting in motion a way of thinking that gave to landowners, debtors, and creditors a set of expectations, and these expectations, sanctified by the passage of time and their repetition by ever more generations of judges, began to acquire the status of rights. A right is a claim that is endowed with authority, and the right to land or a fee must have affected how people thought about marriage. If I, the landowner, have rights, then surely I, the groom, must have them also.

This view of rights received, of course, a powerful reinforcement from political developments, such as the settlement in 1215 between the barons and King John as set forth in the Magna Carta. The document, read literally, is not about marriage at all and only a few parts of it are even about individual political freedom. Though the comparison is sometimes made, the Magna Carta was not at all like the American Bill of Rights. Much of the document was about taxes, debts, fines, licenses, and inheritances. It did contain memorable phrases about not delaying or denying justice and imprisoning offenders only after a trial by their peers, but most of it is only loosely connected to any declaration of human rights. But as Erwin Griswold, once the dean of the Harvard Law School, put it, the Magna Carta was less significant for what it was than for what it was to become. What it became was the basis for reconciling quarrels between the king and his followers, quarrels settled by announcing—on at least forty occasions between 1215 and modern times—that the king had "confirmed" the Magna Carta. Each confirmation heightened the notion that the English people had certain rights, ones that were part of whatever protest that led to the new confirmation of the document. The Magna Carta grew like a tree, and the rights it gave to the English people were in time far more numerous than the ones with which it began.

It would be comforting, I suppose, to imagine that the idea of individual rights arrived "with a clatter of drums and trumpets in some resounding pronouncement" like the Magna Carta or the American Declaration of Independence,[19] but in fact this view, one of the most powerful ever to affect human history, first grew into existence almost imperceptibly in the arguments of medieval theologians and in the actual ownership of property.

The growth of individual rights reinforced the English tradition of local government. Local courts would settle local grievances and adjust personal claims, and among these claims were the rights of men and women to choose their own marriage partners.

But at least as important as all of these were the changing views of
the church. No one has done a better job of sorting out the impact of
religion on marriage than John Witte, Jr., at Emory University. He
notes that both Catholics and Protestants came to believe that a marriage was not valid unless it reflected the free consent of the man and
woman, even if, as was true for many centuries, that consent could be
expressed by the couple without appearing in church. Marriage is a
union recognized by society in which a man and woman are allowed
to live together, required to raise children, and (often) to manage
property. Whether that union will be recognized by some solemn formality has varied over the centuries. What our British ancestors called
being married "over the broom" and we now call common-law marriages—that is, long-standing informal unions between man and
woman—have an ancient history. When organized religion began to
regulate the nature of these marriages, they did not always insist on a
church ceremony. In 1215, the same year the Magna Carta was signed,
the Fourth Lateran Council urged couples to publish their banns (that
is, their intention to marry) in the church and to solemnize the wedding with the aid of a priest and in the company of witnesses, but did
not make either of these requirements absolute. What the council
emphasized more than the formalities was the need for individual consent. Both the Catholic and Protestant churches have changed their
minds about marital formalities, often in response to arguments going
back at least to the fifth century that there was a "family crisis," but
they have never changed their views about the need for free consent.[20]

In the twelfth century, Pope Alexander III required the free consent
of the man and the woman before a marriage would be regarded as
proper and dismissed the idea that parental consent was the only necessary agreement. A marriage was a "voluntary union of two hearts."
Initially, both the betrothed and their parents must agree, but in time
parental consent fell by the wayside.[21]

Just why the church took this view is a matter of dispute. Some
scholars think that it was part of Rome's effort to enrich itself by
acquiring more control over the way property passed from one generation to the next. If a man died with no heirs, then his land might be

forfeited to the church. In this view, it was in the church's interest to reduce the number of heirs, and it could do this by making it a sin for marriages to occur between first cousins and even among in-laws, godparents, and godchildren, and to forbid polygamy, adultery, concubinage, and remarriage after divorce, all methods for producing more children.[22] (Priestly celibacy had the same effect.) Other scholars take a different view. Since many bishops rarely claimed any church authority over land and since there is little direct evidence that the church acted out of mercenary motives, their actions probably had, as the pope claimed, a religious origin.[23] The church was, after all, interested in improving the morals of people and had adopted the confessional and the sacrament as ways of doing this. If the faithful were required to confess their sins, the confession must be the spontaneous act of an individual, not a clan statement; if marriage was to be a sacrament, then it only had meaning if the persons receiving it—the man and woman—had voluntarily and individually accepted its obligations.[24]

Now, these church rules applied throughout Christendom, yet in many—indeed, in most—parts of it marriages continued to reflect family control. Obviously the pope's word was by itself not sufficient to produce an immediate change, but that word, heard by people who had already escaped familial control over land and were part of a political order that was beginning to discuss individual rights, was an important additional reason for accepting the rule of voluntary consent.

Until the Catholic Church tightened the rules, voluntary consent was the essence of a marriage. By the late thirteenth century, it was enough for the couple to exchange promises to enter into the marital sacrament, a bond that was inviolate and lifelong. When in 1215 a Church council urged that the promise be solemnized by the blessing of a priest in the presence of witnesses, it did not hold the marriage to be invalid if these steps were ignored.[25] To ensure that the consent was voluntary, the marriage could be dissolved if fear, fraud, compulsion, or extreme duress impinged on the couple's agreement.[26]

By the sixteenth century, the Church formalized marital arrangements in order to overcome certain abuses it had learned from experience. Now minor children had to have the consent of their parents, priests were required to announce the banns of marriage before the ceremony, and that ritual was to be performed by a priest in the presence of witnesses. But the Council of Trent that announced these tougher rules continued to insist that the marriage had to rest on individual consent.[27]

In the Protestant Reformation, marriage was a major issue. As part of his broad program of civic reform, Martin Luther took issue with the Church's views on marriage, not because they required free, mutual agreement, but because of the sexual immorality of priests and bishops. Their use of concubines and prostitutes, he felt, was encouraged by the requirement of priestly celibacy and the ban on remarriage after a divorce. He called for an end to both, arguing that adultery (and, in the eyes of some followers, desertion or abandonment) was grounds for a divorce, after which both man and wife could marry someone else.[28] To Luther, marriage was vitally important, but he did not agree with the Catholic Church that it was a sacrament. And since it was not a sacrament, it was not indissoluble.

Moreover, Protestants objected to the Church's willingness to recognize secret or informal marriages even though that willingness had a long philosophical history. To reformers, however, that recognition would encourage people to marry "on the basis of sexual desire alone." As historian Steven Ozment put it, the Protestants wanted to "tame the old Adam in human nature, not strengthen it."[29] Wherever the Protestants came to power, they challenged secret marriages by insisting, to the extent they could, that some public ceremony was necessary and by creating secular courts to oversee marital affairs. By 1563 the Catholics decided to agree, and the Council of Trent required that marriage vows be uttered before a priest and only after the couple's intention to wed (the banns) has been announced publicly three times.

In the early seventeenth century, England converted into a statute the requirements of the Anglican Prayer Book that marriages be preceded by publishing banns in advance and performed in a church, but added some loopholes. Publishing banns was costly and time consuming, and so some arrangement was necessary to handle the needs of poor people or those who had to travel because of military service. The English 1604 Canons allowed people in these circumstances to acquire a license to marry immediately, without announcing in advance what we call today an engagement.

The loophole, designed to handle special needs, soon became commonplace. Licensing officials proliferated, the requirements to get a license eroded, and many couples used these opportunities to marry secretly and quickly, just as they once had before the churches had made matters more formal. A century and a half later, England tried to reverse what one lord called the "underground marital industry" by toughening licensing requirements. The 1753 Act for the Better Preventing of Clandestine Marriage, produced by Lord Hardwicke, restated the requirement of formal banns, church ceremonies, and public witnesses and limited the opportunities for quick marriages based on buying a cheap license.[30] Needless to say, the law was condemned in some quarters by those who thought it created a burden on the poor.[31]

Throughout these arguments, one thing never changed: the requirement of free consent. To it was steadily added the view that the reason for free consent was less the fact that marriage was a sacrament (Protestantism had already denied marriage any sacramental status) than that such consent reflected the true love of the couple. Love was now being called the "necessary, even indispensable" ingredient in a marriage.[32] This love was not, as some historians have argued, an invention of modern times. The West did not discover romance after centuries of arranged marriages; in England, its colonies, and much of northwestern Europe, affection was always central to marriages based on free choice.[33] But if love was the central feature of marriage, what would happen to the ancient effort of society to shape and control it by law, custom, and religion? The answer was that the cultural context within which marriage could operate would start to evaporate.

That context, as a later chapter will suggest, rested on communal pressure to take responsibility for children even if they were conceived before marriage or born out of wedlock. Though marriages in the seventeenth century depended on the free consent of man and woman, they were also part of a "social drama involving family, peers, and neighbors in a collective process aimed at making things right economically, socially, and psychologically, as well as legally."[34] There often would not be a formal wedding ceremony, but the man and woman clearly knew from the expectations of their acquaintances that they had to take care of their children. The alternative was for the children to starve. And if a formal wedding did occur, it was accompanied by enough teasing, horseplay, and ritual to embarrass a modern couple. After the ceremony, the couple might be barred from leaving the church until the groom ransomed them by shoving coins out to the crowd. The groom (and sometimes the bride) had to jump over a stone, and the bride had to yield up her garter to the winner of a race. As John Gillis has observed, the older formal wedding was not designed, like modern ones, to permit participants to express their emotions; instead, it was carried out in a way that set forth the couple's relationship and responsibilities.[35] Among these relationships was the primacy of the man; central to these responsibilities was care for the children. It was a "gross breach of a man's honour to refuse to marry a woman with whom he has been 'keeping company' " and has caused her to become pregnant.[36] Not only a breach of honor but a major economic mistake: unless the child had become an orphan and was adopted by another family, it ran the risk of dying for lack of either parental or communal care.

The American Version

America was settled by people from England who brought with them the English marriage traditions but subjected them to revisions that accorded with the needs and preferences of frontier immigrants. The Puritan family of New England was like the English model, but even more so: religious doctrine led the Puritans to stress that marriages ought to be peaceful, permanent, and faithful.[37] For a marriage to occur, the bride and groom had to consent as individuals,[38] but New Englanders emphasized, perhaps more than was true in England, the Puritan ideal of patriarchy. Though men and women were equal before God, men were expected to rule in the family.

Patriarchy, however, had to adapt to the rigors of colonial life. In the harsh New England world, men often died from wars, accidents, and illnesses, and women had to be ready to carry on. Unlike earlier English tradition, as John Demos has observed, Puritan wives were often able to enter into legal contracts.[39] The Revolutionary War and the popular desire for a republican life intensified the acquisition by women of greater legal autonomy. When the American colonies asserted their republican rights to self-rule, people in them were inclined to assert the same rights for family life. A husband gone to fight against the British left behind a wife who had to supervise the farm; a husband killed in that war produced a widow who could marry again and who in the meantime had to run a farm on her own. Reinforcing this freedom were the growing views that men and women had rights, a tendency that gave to the changing Puritan family a role that Linda Kerber has called "republican motherhood."[40] With the passage of time, patriarchy as a principle weakened. Unlike in England, where primogeniture existed (that is, the rule that all land passed to the eldest son), no such laws ruled America, and so land was divided among several children in ways that, over time, weakened the power the father could exert over his children and grandchildren.[41]

So great was this change that Alexis de Tocqueville, when he visited America in the 1830s, was later to write that "the family, taking this word in its Roman and aristocratic sense, does not exist." That is because "from the moment when the young American approaches manhood, the bonds of filial obedience are loosened day by day" until he becomes, not simply master of this thoughts, but master of his conduct.[42] And not simply with sons: before the daughter has entirely left childhood "she already thinks for herself, speaks freely, and acts alone" until she is "full of confidence in her strength."[43] Unlike European girls, an American one rarely "shows a puerile timidity." She sees and knows the perils of the frontier; many have left large cities to go with their families to "share the innumerable perils and miseries" that abound in "leaky huts in the middle of the forest."[44] Because of that she "never falls into the bonds of marriage as into a trap set for her simplicity and ignorance."[45]

Southern families had a somewhat different history. These settlers were less likely to be Puritans and often had to adapt to large-scale agriculture instead of small family farms. Patriarchy lasted longer and was more powerful, coupled, as it was, with a culture of honor. Men ruled their families and defended their wives and their public reputations with fights and duels. The slave economy probably strengthened patriarchy, as the male head of the white family had, if he were at all prosperous, a large enterprise to manage that required the subjection of African Americans and offered the temptations of illicit sex.

Throughout most of America, the courts and later state statutes recognized common-law marriages. This helped put to rest on American terms a problem that had long afflicted English law. Though English tradition often allowed a man and woman to be regarded as married if they voluntarily lived together without any church service, it clearly preferred that the formalities be observed, especially after the passage in 1753 of the Marriage Act. Lord Hardwicke's law made religious ceremonies compulsory, excepting only Quakers and Jews. But as we have seen, many ordinary people were inclined to flout the law, if only to avoid paying for the ceremonies.

Early on, America decided to make any flouting unnecessary by conferring legal authority on informal unions. In a famous case decided in 1809, James Kent, the chief justice of the New York Court of Appeals, said that a couple living together continuously were married whether or not they asked the church's blessing. "No formal solemnization of marriage was required," he wrote, and later, in Kent's famous *Commentaries* on American law, he made his judgment universal: "No peculiar ceremonies are requisite by the common law to the valid celebration of the marriage. The consent of the parties is all that is required. . . ."[46] As Michael Grossberg notes, Kent's argument in favor of common-law marriages was widely accepted by lawyers, judges, and state legislators almost everywhere except in New England, where church formalities remained decisive.[47] The effect of this acceptance of common-law unions was to carry the notion of individual consent to its logical conclusion: two people, by their own actions, and by those alone, could decide whether they were married.

The Enlightenment and the New Meaning of Modernity

The expansion of human choice and the freedom people might acquire from dogma and tradition were given a powerful boost by the Enlightenment, but in the century or so leading up to that transformation several important English authors were already beginning to see marriage in purely secular terms.

John Milton, abandoned by his young wife within a month after his marriage in the mid-seventeenth century, sought to obtain a divorce, but none was forthcoming. He thereupon set out, in language that was glorious in any case but extravagant for the time, an argument for divorce that was akin to the civil argument for revolution: if either marriage or government failed to produce happiness, either could be set aside. When a married couple faces irreconcilable differences, their marriage should end. His plea went unheeded—for the time being.[48]

John Locke also wanted to liberalize divorce laws, but he wrote at a time when opinion had shifted in a more democratic direction and, to protect himself, confined his most striking remarks to his private diary. In the *Two Treatises*, published in 1689, Locke suggested that divorce ought to be readily arranged, even at the wife's request, and in his diary he suggested that any childless couple should be free to separate at will. Two centuries later his views were law.

These new demands, revolutionary for the seventeenth century, passed temporarily from view during the next century, when philosophical writings were focused neither on family matters nor on political rights, but instead on the nature of human knowledge and the

value of a market economy. The most important writers of the
Enlightenment, such as David Hume and Adam Smith, calmly went
about preparing the West to accept the proposition that human life
could be understood by human reason alone. The Enlightenment had
many faces, but its most important, perhaps, was the view that reason, not tradition or authority, would enable people to understand
themselves and their world. Reason, not religion or custom, would
permit us to know the truth.

But the family was an odd institution. It arose out of the natural
sexual appetite between men and women and was valuable in
enabling children to be reared, but one could in principle devise alternatives to it. A child might be raised by an unwed parent, or a marriage designed to bring children into being might be terminated when
they went off to become apprentices, or a man and woman might live
together without anything like a marriage agreement. Every human
union that one can now see about us could be devised and assessed by
reason alone. Perhaps any union that might exist in theory would turn
out to be valuable in practice.

Hume, Smith, and the other leading figures in the Scottish and
English Enlightenment did not think much about these possibilities.
Instead they took for granted the conventional marriage, a man and a
woman solemnly united for the purpose of raising children. Hume
observed that an organized society was valuable to its members but
that any would-be member might not be aware of the benefits it could
supply. Happily, he said, they will be made aware of these benefits by
entering naturally into a union whose existence will acquaint them
with the virtues of an orderly society, and that union is the family.
Children especially would learn why society is valuable as they are
reared by their parents. The family would be, thought Hume, "the
first and original principle of human society."[49]

Hume and Smith acknowledged that the family was of great
importance but assumed that its existence could be taken for granted.
Adam Smith understood that the need to care for the young was the
chief reason for marriage, but he took for granted that the affection
on which marriage was based would persist. He wrote that "the affec-

tion of the sexes is therefore constant and does not cease on any particular occasion."[50] Neither here nor elsewhere did he confront the question of the promiscuous male. He lectured at some length on polygamy and divorce, correctly understanding that monogamy had the advantage of avoiding the jealousy that would erupt among several polyandrous wives and that easy divorce laws might be a great mistake. Hume was in full agreement. Polygamy would produce jealousy and harems would educate children to be tyrants. The possibility of divorce, though it would accommodate the desire of people for new romantic experiences, would harm the children, reduce the chances of husband and wife becoming friends, and produce between them endless threats and quarrels.[51]

In *The Theory of Moral Sentiments* Smith said that if you wish to educate your children to be dutiful, kind, and affectionate, do so in your own home. They might attend public schools, but they should always live at home. He was opposed to educating boys at distant schools or colleges and sending girls to nunneries or boarding schools. "Domestic education," he wrote, "is the institution of nature; public education is the contrivance of man. It is surely unnecessary to say, which is likely to be best."[52]

He surely spoke for almost everyone when he said that a "parent without parental tenderness, a child devoid of filial reverence, appear monsters."[53] Then as now, everyone is appalled at the sight of a parents who care nothing for their children or of children who despise their parents. Of the two passions—that of a parent toward his child and of a child toward his parent—the former is, by nature, much stronger. There is no religious commandment ordering parents to love their children but there is one telling children to honor their parents. The former sentiment is natural, the latter must be encouraged.

"The world the Enlightenment inherited and critiqued was a man's world" Roy Porter was later to write, but it was also a world, he notes, in which women, despite being subject to their husbands, enjoyed a "Europe-wide fame—or notoriety—for their remarkable public independence."[54] The burdens against which women would labor in the nineteenth century cannot obscure the freedom, at least by the standards of the world, that they enjoyed in the eighteenth: "Urban women walked about freely, unveiled and for the most part unchaperoned," went to the theater, became members of mixed male and female debating societies, and published novels, histories, and literary criticism.[55] By the end of the eighteenth century Mary Wollstonecraft had written a vigorous denunciation of the common tendency to treat women as hopelessly innocent creatures put on Earth solely to please men; she called for a "revolution in female manners" but not yet (this was 1792, mind you) the right to vote.[56] These early feminists still expected women to be wives and mothers, but the foundation for broad new claims about legal and moral equality were being laid.

Laying foundations and slowly changing attitudes were what the English and Scottish Enlightenments were all about. But there was a very different version of how far any enlightenment could extend, and that was in France. Soon after the French Revolution, the government announced that marriage was no more than a civil contract, revocable on a month's notice, and bastards were given the same rights as the offspring of married couples. Edmund Burke denounced all of this in prose only he could produce. To him, manners were more important than laws because the former governs us daily while the latter touches us only rarely. The task of law is to uphold decent manners, but to Burke the very opposite happened in France. "When manners were corrupted," he wrote, "the laws were relaxed." The new French law of divorce was not, to Burke, for the purpose of relieving domestic unhappiness, but instead for "the total corruption of all morals." He was astonished to report that in the first three months of 1793, 562 divorces occurred in Paris, one-third of the number of marriages in that period.[57] We can only imagine what Burke would have said of contemporary America, where nearly one-half of all marriages end in divorce.

Many observers have commented on the difference between the Scottish and French Enlightenment. The differences are real. In Scotland, a constrained, cautious, and sober view of human nature was the basis for a prudent judgment about the reach of human reason. It pushed forward the view that ultimately would reduce dramatically social controls on marriage, but did so in a cautious way and on the basis of the happy assumption that marriage was secure unless it was directly attacked by the state. But in France an unconstrained, boundless, and wildly optimistic view of human nature supplied the grounds for recklessness about what reason could achieve. Hume and Smith wrote about the importance of sentiments; by contrast, Voltaire wrote about crushing the infamous church and Condorcet thought that all human behavior could be described mathematically. In Scotland, the prudence of the Enlightenment thinkers seems warranted, but France gave the clue that this assumption could and would be challenged.

But if France produced a more extreme version of the Enlightenment, why did England—and English-speaking colonies around the world—produce in the centuries ahead more single-parent families than France? It occurred, I suspect, because the doctrines of the Scottish Enlightenment, though initially more moderate and prudent than the ideological declarations of Voltaire and his colleagues, fell on more fertile soil. England and Scotland had been setting in place for hundreds of years concepts of human rights and limited government that were alien to France where the authoritarian rule of absolute kings was replaced by that of revolutionary parliaments. The Enlightenment took root in England and Scotland in ways that slowly but inevitably led to a redefinition of marriage as an agreement between two people with individual rights rather than as a partnership made sacred by law, custom, and God. In France that redefinition took generations longer and with less immediate effect.

The Victorian Interlude

When Victoria became queen, marriage in England was given its modern formalities: licenses, ceremony, and state regulation. When she left the throne sixty-four years later, marriage in England was under attack as a system that oppressed women and for some critics lacked social merit. In the nineteenth century marriage underwent its most striking redefinition, one that at first gave it greatly enhanced stature and then later subjected it to the most withering attacks.

The modern market for marriage, founded as far back as the thirteenth century, did not become a wholly secular, individualistic, and unconstrained arrangement until seven centuries had passed. In the intervening years, philosophers and religious leaders tested new theories of marriage while the ordinary people struggled to arrange marriages the most economical way. The full-dress, church-based white-gown wedding is a relatively recent invention, at least for everyone but the aristocracy. But when reason replaced religious conviction and a popular aversion to supporting out-of-wedlock children, marriage lost a large part of its social support, so that by the end of the twentieth century the full-dress, church-based white-gown wedding has become mostly a formality, moving to those who attend it but modest in its capacity to link together a man and a woman.

The Enlightenment laid the groundwork for replacing a sacrament with a contract and then a contract with an arrangement. Where marriages were once controlled either by local custom or religious tradition, they were now controlled by the married parties, and by them alone. And the Enlightenment did this for many good reasons. As Witte put it, these thinkers never doubted the value of marriage or its usefulness to society; they simply wished to purge it of paternalism and patriarchy. By the twentieth century, they had succeeded, and everything that Milton and Locke and other writers had argued for had become, not only law, but part of the religious tradition of many churches.[58] The price they paid was that marriage became weaker and the children more vulnerable.

But before that happened England and America regrouped their moral passions and for a century or so put in place an extraordinary—and so far, last-ditch—effort to maintain cultural control over marriage. It was the age of Queen Victoria, that period when the middle class imposed for what may be the last time its view of propriety. It was a time when science had tested religion and change had undercut tradition, but it was not yet a time to give up on the moral habits that religion or custom had once supported. They had a "duty to be moral," as Gertrude Himmelfarb has written, a duty that was "not God-given but man-made, and it was all the more 'peremptory and absolute' for that."[59]

We sometimes suppose that Victorian England (and, to a lesser extent, Victorian America) was all of a piece: a complete devotion to convention, an unquestioning acceptance of propriety, and an exasperating habit of referring to sex, body parts, and private habits by the most elaborate circumlocutions, all mixed together with a frequent dose, at least for affluent men, of discreet gambols with prostitutes. That is not quite right. It is true that there was both decency and lubricity, but throughout the nineteenth century there was a growing effort to challenge the grounds for decency and to question the label of lubricity. That challenge was led by people, many of them artists and intellectuals, who were the first to sense that England's extraordinary redefinition of the moral impulse from religion to habit meant the emancipation of habit from any external support save preference and freedom. Even the oldest of customs, marriage, could be questioned. What Milton had suggested and Locke had hinted at became fair public game for a later generation of writers. By the beginning of the twentieth century, and certainly by the time that everyone had awakened to the psychological disaster produced by the First World War, marriage, though for most people still an important goal, was for some writers a dispensable oddity.

Underlying the questioning of marriage was a single core event: the slow emancipation of women. Women in England (and matters were often much worse in other nations) lived under a variety of powerful legal constraints. A single woman had, given the times, a remarkable array of legal rights. She could sue and be sued, act as a trustee, administer a will, and own property; she had to pay the same taxes as a man. But a married woman yielded many of these rights to her husband. By common law, she and her husband were one person; she lived under his protection, and this protection, or cover, led to the word *coverture* to describe her status.[60] When she married, any real estate she owned remained hers, but the rest of her property—stocks, bonds, jewels, bank deposits, and the like—became her husband's. If she earned money, it became her husband's money; if she had children, they became her husband's children should they separate or be divorced. Once married she could neither sue nor be sued, execute a will, or administer a trustee save with her husband's permission.

But common law, administered by the common-law courts, was moderated by the rules of equity, administered by the chancery courts. As Joan Perkin notes in her history of Victorian women, equity rules—that is, rules laid down by the chancery courts to implement, and in so doing, to restrain, the common law—gave back to married women some things that the common law had taken away. A married woman might have property placed in a trust for her personal use, retain claim to land given to her in a will, and sell the property and keep the proceeds. She was able to write her own will and sue others (in some cases, even her husband) if she had a strong claim, and retain the profits of a business she ran.[61]

The different rules produced by equity courts compared to common-law courts have both puzzled foreign observers and frustrated English participants. The latter were divided along class lines by these differences, because private law—the law of the chancery or equity courts—cost money. Women in the aristocracy and the affluent middle class could more easily take advantage of looser equity rules, but there were limits even here. Private law could not be used to circumvent three areas where wives were at a disadvantage: child custody, control of earnings, and access to divorce.[62] The husband under every rule still had the right to the children, to his wife's earnings, and to any reasonable chance of getting a divorce. Meanwhile, the ordinary folk were usually left to struggle with the much more restrictive common law. By one estimate, only one in ten English women benefited from equity rules in the 1850s.[63] But whether puzzling or frustrating, English law governing women became a major issue for reformers. The feminist movement began not simply with a demand for the vote, but with an attack on coverture.

In America, the emancipation of women was already a bit more advanced. In many states, American women were allowed to own and operate businesses in their own names provided their husbands had approved this in writing or even when the husbands' support was tacit.[64] Some states, such as New York, Maryland, and Virginia, adopted the English system of allowing two different kinds of courts, those applying common law and those applying equity, to decide whether women could own property. The courts applying equity laws, what the English and Americans called chancery courts, often allowed women to own property. In New England, women obtained the right to initiate a divorce.[65]

Both the North and South had experienced the momentous impact on families of the Civil War and the discovery of gold in California. Both events had a powerful effect on the sex ratio: a quarter of the male population was killed or maimed by the war, and thousands of men fled without wives to Sutter's Creek.[66] The widows of the war and those abandoned by male gold-seekers had to manage on their own. The Victorian model of propriety—the "cult of domesticity"— helped maintain family life in the old model even when women greatly outnumbered men and thus, had they been in a less constrained culture, were vulnerable to exploitive sexual predation. Women's associations were formed to preach temperance, help put an end to slavery, and serve the masses of new immigrants that were flooding into American cities.[67] Women's associations in America were more broadly based than those in England and less reliant on the leadership of a few elite ladies. The absence of an American aristocracy meant a higher degree of citizen involvement in any effort to change society. Although there were many similarities between England and America in the campaign for woman suffrage, the women's movement in this country was more broadly based and its members more fully equipped with legal standing.

Moreover, the American version of feminism had a somewhat different view of marriage. Elizabeth Cady Stanton, a leading advocate of female suffrage, felt that common-law marriages ought to be abolished because they weakened the family by allowing informal unions, by which she meant those not supervised by the state. To her, a rational marital system would be one that required state oversight of the union coupled with a divorce law that would make it easier for unhappy couples to part.[68] She and other reformers had, by the end of the nineteenth century, made some inroads in limiting common-law marriages by, for example, requiring all couples to obtain a marriage license from the state. But these informal unions persisted. Many judges were determined to keep the state out of the business of certifying who was married. By so doing, they kept alive well into the twentieth century the view that marriage was essentially a private arrangement.

The Advent of Modernity

That attack in England on patriarchal authority was part of a great struggle in the nineteenth century between what marriage seemed to require and what some women wanted. The traditional individualistic marriage based on free consent was not in doubt, but the rise of big cities and the emergence of an enlarged view of human rights had created a problem, namely, how could a local culture any longer enforce a moral code on the somewhat informal nuptial habits of ordinary people? In small towns, a common-law marriage might be acceptable because everyone knew and recognized the arrangement, and the risks of premarital intercourse and out-of-wedlock children might be managed by using informal social controls to ensure that either a marriage followed the pregnancy or that the father supported the illegitimate child. But in a big city, especially in London, these natural cultural forces were weakened. At the beginning of the nineteenth century only about one-quarter of the English people lived in towns of any size; by the end of the century more than three-quarters did. Farmers were one-third of the English population in 1801, one-eighth in 1901.[69] Moving out of farming and into the towns helped people by freeing them from the oversight of "squire and parson" and opening up to them the opportunities of new friends and pubs, but it also had a cost: the controls on family life weakened and the men often found more benefits in city life than did the women.

The Industrial Revolution did not radically alter the inner life of families. Some people suppose that with the advent of big factories, densely populated cities, and the spread of commerce, family members became either (if you are an optimist) more individualistic or (if you are a Marxist) more alienated. But as we have seen, the individualistic family preceded the Industrial Revolution; in fact, the former helped accelerate the arrival of the latter. Moreover, industry did not immediately create a market for female employment that would pro-duce new tensions in the family. Friedrich Engels supposed that the modern factory broke up the family by driving women and children into the workforce. In fact, for at least the first century of the indus-trial revolution, female employment did not change much; women still worked, as they always had, in domestic service and garment making. There were, to be sure, more jobs as domestic servants, but most of these were taken by unmarried women, a practice that had existed, though at a lower rate, for centuries before industrialism.

To be sure, married women who did take jobs in the new factories were away from their families for many hours every day and this surely had some effect on how children were raised. But as Lawrence Stone pointed out, only a tiny minority of all married women worked in factories except, perhaps, in a few cotton-spinning towns.[70] Chil-dren did go out to work in mines and factories in large numbers, but almost always with the consent of their parents. This led to over-worked children and higher family incomes; the net effect on the emo-tional nature of family life is unknown.

The aristocracy had never been closely governed by local cultural forces because it already consisted of the most emancipated women in Europe.[71] They were endowed, through the aid of equity law and clever lawyers, with money and power to which they added their for-midable presence in society. Its members, along with ordinary folk, became the object of middle-class arguments.

But that middle class was divided. One part wanted to strengthen marriage even at the expense of the claims of women whereas the other wanted to emancipate women even at some cost to marriage. The first group drew heavily on religion. Respectability, G. M. Young observed, was the secular side of Evangelicalism.[72] This group embraced religion in part because of what it taught them and in part because of what it made them: it trained them to control their vices, notably the drinking habits of men, and it confirmed in them their social decency and personal dignity. The supporters of greater rights, by contrast, were motivated less by religion and more by the advanced teachings of the Enlightenment, especially as John Stuart Mill expressed them in his famous book, *The Subjection of Women*. It begins with a famous sentence: "That the principle which regulates the existing social relations between the two sexes—the legal subordination of one sex to another—is wrong in itself . . . and ought to be replaced by a principle of perfect equality, admitting no power or privilege on one side, nor disability on the other."[73] To Mill, female emancipation was the completion of the Enlightenment enterprise.* Having freed the market, ended monopolies, increased free choices, and reduced the privileges of caste and birth, how can anyone deny extending the same freedoms to women?[74] As Mill suggested, there was no logical incompatibility between strong marriages and emancipated women. Or at least that was true so long as one thought that both sexes should be legally equal. But as we shall see, the notion of equal freedom gave way in the minds of some to very different impulses: an argument either against marriage as an institution because perfect freedom required the absence of any institutional arrangement, or a claim that equality of condition was more important than equality of opportunity. By the end of the Victorian era, some activists attacked marriage head-on.

Female emancipation meant not simply getting the vote but allowing married women to share in the ownership of a family's property and earnings instead of permitting it to fall entirely under the control of the husband. Advocates pointed out that American states had already done this in the mid-nineteenth century. After a long struggle, they succeeded with a new law passed in 1870, but that law gave women the right to property only starting with the date of its enactment. By 1891, English women had overthrown the right of their husbands to confine them forcefully in their homes, and by the 1920s they had acquired a right to petition for divorce on terms that were more or less equal to those enjoyed by their husbands.

---

*One cannot help noting that in his marriage to Harriet Taylor, Mill acquired a wife who believed that she was superior to her husband in every way. Mill agreed. For him, the subjection of women was replaced by the subjection of Mill. On this see Gertrude Himmelfarb, *Marriage and Morals Among the Victorians* (New York: Random House, 1987), 10–11.

But alongside these reasonable improvements there came from a handful of people an attack on marriage itself. The early-nineteenth-century Utopian writer, Robert Owen, had condemned marriage along with religion and private property as enemies of a good society. The French writer George Sand was understood to have endorsed free love.[75] Vanessa Bell, sister of Virginia Woolf, wanted a society with sexual freedom for all. There were a few others, so-called new women, who wanted to choose a father for their child without entering into a marriage and then live in what was called "bachelor motherhood."[76] But this group was initially quite small and its arguments typically fell on deaf ears. But those arguments, though lacking in much influence at the time, were justified in pure Enlightenment language: a marriage was simply the right of private contract, and like most contracts it could be negotiated on any terms the parties wished. In time, the language would gain more and more adherents.

In 1929, Bertrand Russell created a great stir with his book *Marriage and Morals* in which he suggested that no marriage should be legally binding until the woman's first pregnancy. He claimed that he believed in the importance of the family, but argued that to ensure they would be as good as he hoped, trial marriages, dissolvable at will, should be allowed, jealousy should be avoided, and infidelity should be tolerated. In time, he thought, the state would replace the father. That change would not to him be a matter for rejoicing, but he thought it was likely to be inevitable, especially in poorer neighborhoods.[77] This prediction was, of course, quite accurate, but he seems not to have noticed that it became true in part because of a more general acceptance of trial marriages and marital infidelity that he had already applauded.

The antimarriage crusade was limited to a few highly visible writers and activists; most middle-class women valued marriage greatly even as they hoped to obtain better legal rights. Even most feminists were prepared to accept marriage once women had been given equal rights.[78] To them, a good marriage rested on equal rights even if husband and wife performed very different duties in the household. This view has not rested well with modern feminists, many of whom complain that legal rights are not enough; the sexual division of labor must itself be abolished.[79] So long as men and women do different things in the home, these activists argue, the notion of equal rights is insufficient because marriage is not just.[80] But of course this view rests on the premise that justice is the highest good for a family and that in its pursuit the differences between men and women—differences that could never have justified English coverture laws, but still important differences—should be obliterated or ignored. One can think of other things we may value as much as justice in a family—love, companionship, manliness, and femininity, to mention but four. And these other qualities depend to some extent on differences between men and women that cannot be easily wished away. But mentioning these matters will irritate some readers when my goal is not to arouse anger about feminism but to instruct them about history.

Even if Victorian feminists did not satisfy the expectations of some modern ones, they did set in motion changes that completed the shift to the individualistic family. By demanding more rights for women they were changing the conception of a family from a status (that is, a set of obligations enforced by law and tradition) to a contract (that is, a set of rights protected by law whatever the custom).[81] The family slowly stopped being a unit with its own social identity and became a relationship defined by the preferences of its members. The old social unit was patriarchal in theory (though sometimes much less so in practice); the new set of relationships was to be egalitarian in theory (but sometimes much less so in practice).

But marriage based on individual rights and personal contracts would have its own hazards. What rights were the children to have, and who would protect them? How was the procreation of children to be confined to the family that would raise them? For many decades these questions never became major issues. From the end of the nineteenth century to well into the twentieth, the assumption that families were valuable governed almost everyone. As Paula Fass points out in her study of American marriages, the family by the 1920s was becoming smaller, planned, and much more democratic, focused more on nurturance than on direction and allowing a wide latitude for childhood development.[82] This new family life emerged at the same time society recognized the labeling of adolescence, those intermediate years when the offspring were neither children nor workers and thus neither exposed to clear parental direction nor required to contribute important financial support. Once, a young child stayed home and helped; a bit older, and he or she worked the fields or ventured out as servants or apprentices. Now in the years between ten and eighteen they stayed at home but increasingly lived in and took guidance from a teenage world of youthful peers.

Moreover, young men were in short supply during the 1920s. Millions had been killed during the First World War. This produced a very low sex ratio among men aged twenty-five through thirty-nine in England, France, Germany, the Soviet Union, and the United States.[83] With so few available men, women had to compete more vigorously for sexual and romantic attention, a competition that did little to discourage flamboyant dress and exotic habits.

But the war changed more than just the sex ratio. It produced a profound reaction against the cultural verities of Victorian life. The emancipated views of a small aesthetic and philosophic elite at the end of the nineteenth century were converted by this terrible war into a massive and widely shared indictment of what a small number of writers and artists had been criticizing. When the war began, men volunteered for service in extraordinary numbers; it is claimed that two-thirds of all Oxford undergraduates enlisted. But the horrors of trench warfare, the blundering of incompetent generals, and the inability of statesmen to explain why men had to die meant that, when armistice came, Oxford undergraduates took an oath swearing never again to fight for king and country.

The impulse toward personal liberation evident in the arts, mores, and fashions among a few in 1900 was greatly enlarged by the war. The British tradition of duty and propriety persisted, but its foundation was profoundly shaken. Old habits had to sustain themselves without the support of ancient convictions or religious beliefs. The poet Stephen Spender put it this way: "The war knocked the ball-room floor out from under middle-class English life. People resembled dancers suspended in mid-air yet miraculously able to pretend they were still dancing."[84] And the younger people noticed that the floor was no longer there—or the walls or the ceiling—and began to express their cynicism about convention in all its forms.

The low sex ratio caused by the war was a problem in its own right, but now people, especially women, had to adapt to a culture that had shaken loose from its moorings. A more tolerant family life, the acceptance of adolescence as a privileged dominion, and the availability of new forms of entertainment helped create a decade with a name, the Roaring Twenties. But though young people (and people eager to appear young once again) took advantage of provocative clothing, cheap liquor, and exhibitionist dancing, these advantages did not yet change them very much. There was no significant increase in illegitimate children, no rush for the divorce courts, little new involvement in street gangs. The twenties were a kind of test run, a dabbling in exotic behaviors that put on display the freedom from traditional definitions of family life that had been slowly won at the end of the Victorian period, but a dabbling that did not yet reveal much commitment to pushing this new freedom to its limit. That commitment might have emerged had the sentiments of the Roaring Twenties lasted, but the era was suddenly and brutally cut short by the Great Depression.

This powerful economic shock brought families closer together.[85] If a family had to struggle to eat, everyone had to help with the struggle. Cheap gin, late parties, and fancy clothes were no substitute for bread on the table. As Glen Elder has reported, the depression pushed young people out into the labor market, or what there was of it, in ways that accelerated their movement into adulthood. Though we lack any systematic measure of crime from the early 1930s, such local studies as we have suggest that it declined.[86] But though the depression brought families together, it also removed the one remaining claim of the old order. The war had wounded Victorian cultural claims; the Great Depression ended its economic ones. The West's moral capital was weakened and now its economic capital was gone. All that prevented the emergence of a powerful commitment to radical individualism in these troubled times was another war, this one fought not because for some obscure reason Englishmen and Frenchmen did not like Germans, but specifically because they were now certain that Germans, the Nazis, had launched a brutal and sadistic attack on all of Europe.

After time out for the Great Depression and the Second World War, family matters returned to the course on which they had been set in ways that would radically define not only how people thought about them but how they behaved. The sixties began an important epoch, but one that built on a view of family life that had been set in place beginning at least a century earlier: families are the result of free choices between a man and a woman in which each party was to have equal rights. The family ended its career as a status and fully accepted its new position as a contract, one that could be modified in many ways, rejected if one found it displeasing, and submitted to court review whenever its terms appear to have been violated.

In the fifteen years that began in 1965, family life and the laws that govern it underwent a remarkable transformation. For a billion or so people in the industrialized nations, divorces and the birth of out-of-wedlock children rose sharply. These changes, as one scholar pointed out, are unique in family history: they were sharp, immediate, and affected virtually every industrialized nation all at once.[87]

Sweeping new divorce laws were passed in England in 1969, Sweden in 1973, France in 1975, West Germany in 1976, and by almost all American states between 1969 and 1985. As Mary Ann Glendon at Harvard has pointed out, not long before these laws were passed, a marriage could only be ended for one of a few serious causes; after they were passed, marriage was more or less terminable at will.[88] The laws of these and other industrialized nations differed in details and implementation, but a fair generalization is that today any married couple that agrees it wishes a divorce can get one. Under no-fault laws, divorce has been essentially deregulated. Even in England, where there has been some effort to maintain a theory of blame, an uncontested divorce is granted, and most divorces are uncontested. It is often not even necessary to confront a judge. In one study, uncontested divorces took an average of less than five minutes.[89] In France there are several constraints, including a waiting period, so that the system, though it makes divorce easily available, does not quite grant it simply on demand. West Germany adopted a more liberal approach so that uncontested divorces are quickly granted. Sweden, needless to say, went the furthest. It replaced its old view that divorce should only be allowed after adultery or desertion with one that eliminates all reference to fault or reasons; divorce is granted on request. In adopting its new procedures, Swedish officials made it clear that in their view all laws bearing on couples should be written so as not to give marriage any advantage over cohabitation. As one said, a legal marriage should simply be "a form of voluntary cohabitation between independent persons."[90] By 1987 eighteen American states had adopted no-fault as the sole basis for divorce; by 1996 almost every other state had added no-fault to existing grievances.[91] Given these changes, it is today the case that for any adult couple, both marriage and divorce are readily available. Easy in, easy out.

Unmarried couples who cohabit have steadily improved their legal claims on society. In Sweden, they are indistinguishable from married ones. In the United States, they have obtained more and more from the courts, though still far less than in Sweden. The greater recognition of cohabitation has built, of course, on an ancient tradition that alternated, as Mary Ann Glendon has put it, between expressions of moral disapproval of cohabitation and covert remedies to help men and women live while cohabiting.[92] Each American state has produced its own view of these alternatives, with a few still recognizing common-law unions. (That recognition created problems for some couples who decided to break up, as with one New York man who discovered that he had to go to court to leave his common-law wife because they had spent a few days in a southern state that recognized common-law unions.[93]) In some states a man and a woman who end their common-law union must divide up their property just as a legally divorced couple must, while in other states a woman who ends a relationship with a man has no claim for what is now called palimony unless while the two were living together there arose an "implied contract"—that is, an informal but clear agreement—that what one partner earned was to be shared with the other.

In Carl Schneider's view, family law in the West has pretty much abandoned the moral basis on which it once rested. That basis was powerfully reinforced in the nineteenth century, when English and American statutes were written that regularized how families were to be formed and on what terms they could be ended. Laws were written governing how marriages were arranged and divorces obtained, what alimony would be owed to whom and for how long, how property was to be divided and who was to have custody of children, the bans on adultery and cohabitation, how adoptions could be arranged, and the circumstances, if any, when contraception and abortions might occur.[94] These laws rested on the moral argument that the family was vital, a decisive determinant of the character and social status of the spouses and their children, and an essential element of any organized society.[95]

Leading figures in England and America at the end of the nineteenth century spoke of marriage as a "state of existence ordained by the Creator," a "consummation of the Divine command to multiply and replenish the earth," "the highest state of existence," and "the only stable substructure of social, civil, and religious institutions." Each marriage, many said, affects not only the spouses, but all other persons. The Supreme Court described marriage as more than a "mere contract"; it was instead "a sacred obligation," "a holy estate," and "the foundation of the family and society, without which there would be neither civilization nor progress."[96]

And in the family the father was the leader. One might quarrel with some of these views, especially the patriarchal one, but what is most important is not whether the views were in each case correct but that they rested on a claim that the family, and marriage in particular, were not simply negotiable contracts but were moral statements about how a good life would be lived.

A century later, virtually every one of these laws has been changed, some for the better, some for the worse, but everywhere in ways that denied that marriage and the family had any moral status. Cohabitation and fornication are no longer crimes, divorce can be arranged without anyone proving that the partner was at fault, child custody shall be decided without regard to "the conduct of a proposed custodian that does not affect his relationship to the child,"[97] contraception and abortion are both legal, and (in many places) an "implied contract" discerned by a court will govern the allocation of property at the end of cohabitation. The Supreme Court put the matter bluntly in a decision upholding the right of people to buy contraceptive devices: "The marital couple is not an independent entity . . . but an association of two individuals each with a separate intellectual and emotional make-up. If the right of privacy means anything, it is the right of the *individual*, married or single, to be free from unwanted government intrusion. . . ."[98]

These changes in family law are fully in accord with the rise of a modern, secular, individualistic state. No one should be surprised that a freely choosing individual should be the centerpiece of family law any more than we would be surprised that such a person is the centerpiece of civil rights or contract law. The rise of the modern marriage market was part of a broad transformation in Western culture from one of ascribed status to one of personal choice. At one time, an individual belonged to a family; today, the family belongs to the individual.[99] At one time, the law was concerned about how families were formed and how long they lasted but little concerned with what happened inside the family. Today the law is much less concerned with how a family is formed or how long it lasts but greatly concerned with what happens inside it. That new concern, expressed by legal inquiries into the possibility of marital rape or the abuse of a spouse or a child, takes with utmost seriousness the experiences of an individual while giving much less attention to the strength of the union.

The change is not simply one in legal arrangements but in how we think. It accords with what Philip Rieff has called the triumph of the therapeutic. "The triumph of the therapeutic cannot be viewed simply as a break with the established order of moral demands, but rather as a profound effort to end the tyranny of primary group moral passion (operating first through the family) as the inner dynamic of social order."[100] What began with the emergence of private property, common law, and the rights of individuals ended, I think inevitably, with a reduction in the role of such institutions as family and church and an elevation of personal choice.

So many benefits have flowed from this change that it may seem petty to quarrel about some of its implications, but the family occupies a special case. Unlike the church, it cannot define a person's relation with God or the hereafter; unlike the government, it cannot resort to orders and physical force. If the family is to have any value, it must be in what people bring to it and which, of course, they can decide to take from it. Marrying is a now a wager that two people enter into because of sexual attraction and personal friendship (sometimes accompanied by the existence of a fetus), a wager that in the future things will work out for the best. But if things don't work out, and often they do not, then the bet has been lost and each party is free to end the attachment. Young people are probably not very good at placing bets of this sort: "I am happy with him or her now, so surely I will be happy with him or her twenty years from now." Nor are they likely to bet much on the practical benefits of marriage that include, as we have seen, good odds on avoiding crime, living longer, and staying healthier. And these bets are even harder to make when personal income now flows to each working person rather than to one united family. Women have always worked in every family going back to the beginning of time, but when they can work independently of the family the family inevitably must lose some of its value.

What is striking is not that there are so many divorces and so many cohabiting couples, but that there are any marriages at all. How can one explain marriage, which taken literally is a solemn and public promise to live together forever, forsaking all others, and to do so in sickness and in health? Simply living together provides the immediate benefits without any legal formalities. Why promise to live together forever instead of promising to live together so long as I find it pleasurable? Why forsake all others instead of forsaking others until someone richer or more beautiful comes along? Why get married if with abortion and the birth-control pill one can avoid having children? Why not just live together for as long as it is enjoyable? Of course cohabitation provides *only* the immediate benefits; it rarely provides what so many men and women in time discover they need— care and companionship over the long term, a term that is getting longer with every improvement in medicine but one that for any cohabiting couple can quickly be interrupted when one partner decides to walk away and find what they imagine is true happiness with someone else.

It is in a way astonishing that people get married at all. How can we explain it? (In Sweden no explanation is necessary, since marriage is rapidly being replaced by cohabitation.) The answer seems to be some combination of love, a desire for children, a hope for long-term companionship, and the expectations of family and friends. But since love is universal, all that can explain differences over time or across cultures is a desire for children, companionship, and cultural expectations. And everywhere cultural expectations are vulnerable to the new individualistic ethos, as we can see with rising levels of cohabitation. Which leaves a desire for children and companionship. And that, I suspect, is where matters now stand. Some people can see far enough into the future to recognize that marriage offers long-term benefits. For them marriage will be preferable. But many people do not see very far into the future, and for them cultural pressures are important. And those pressures are declining.

But marriage lingers on. Some 90 percent of the American people get married by the time they die. Among women who married between 1940 and 1959, nearly two-thirds were still living in that first marriage.[101] Among men and women who are fifty-five years of age or older, fewer than 5 percent have never been married. The majority of children are raised by two parents. Marriage survives despite the absence of many sexual or economic reasons for it. Men and women will make public pledges of loyalty to one another even when both the man and the woman can buy sex on the marketplace and when women can use birth control or abortion to eliminate the chances of unwanted children and take advantage of educational opportunities and an open job market to make their own careers. Despite the apparent advantages of the single life, the desire for children and companionship is not a weak force among humans. This desire is found in most people, perhaps because human experience over the millennia have made such feelings a deep part of human emotions. Evolution has selected for sentiments that encourage marriage but not for those that require it.

Evolution does not make marriage universal. Its existence depends in part on a changing culture. The argument of this chapter implies that the greatest familial problems would exist in countries where the culture has most fully embraced the Enlightenment ideal. The cultural expectation of an enduring marriage would be weakest where the emancipation of the individual has been the strongest. This suggests that high levels of cohabitation, divorce, and children born out of wedlock would be most common in England, the countries founded by England, and much of northwestern Europe, and that, I think, is pretty much what we find. These circumstances exist most dramatically in the United States, the United Kingdom, Canada, Australia, New Zealand, Denmark, and Sweden but are much less true in China, Indonesia, Italy, Japan, Spain, and Taiwan and least of all in countries where clan power remains strong, as in much of the Middle East.[102]

People everywhere enter families, but the strength and endurance of what they have entered depends crucially on culture. In the West, that culture has changed, slowly at some times (as in the eighteenth and nineteenth centuries), rapidly at others (as in the 1920s and the 1960s). Those who are dismayed by what has happened must wonder whether those changes can be altered. We shall see.

Chapter 5
African Americans and Slavery

Everyone knows that African Americans have very high rates of single-parent families, but they disagree as to why this has occurred. And this is where the trouble begins, not simply because the issue is a difficult puzzle but because so much appears to hang on the answer. If you think African Americans have "always" had a lot of out-of-wedlock children, you risk being called a racist, unless you quickly add that families are not important to children, in which case you may be called either a progressive or a fool. If you think slavery caused the problem, you will be reminded that American society after slavery ended put endless roadblocks in the path of black family unity. If you think welfare caused the problem, you must deal with the charge that illegitimate births appear to have risen much faster than welfare payments, and, in any event, you are insensitive to the economic problems African Americans must face. Answering this question is a quick way to earn an ideological label.

But the issue is puzzling, and no easy answer will quite suffice. But let us begin with two important facts. First, there are a lot of people who come to America who are poor, remain poor for a long time, and face great barriers to their acceptance. Latinos now make up about one-eighth of the nation's population, one-third that of California, and nearly half that of Los Angeles. As a boy growing up near Los Angeles, I know how Mexican Americans were once treated. Called *pachucos*, they were denied access to homes in many neighborhoods, made the object of the Zoot Suit Riots of 1943, and thought to be inferior beings. Worse for them, many did not speak much English and a lot were in this country illegally. Even today, when some of the worst forms of discrimination have abated, undocumented Latino men wait on street corners miles from their homes in hopes of being hired, illegally, for a day by someone who is willing to ignore the law. In 1990, Latinos had the highest percentage of families living in poverty of any ethnic group in California and their per-family income was about the same as that of African Americans.

But the proportion of Latino children living in California who are raised by a single mother is only about 20 percent, less than half the rate for African Americans. Controlling for income, the rate at which Latinos take welfare benefits is only about one-fifth the rate at which African Americans do. They are poorer and less educated than blacks, and many are certainly in a risky legal situation, but they are not nearly as likely to have children living without two parents.[1] In 1990 only 16 percent of all households made up of Mexican Americans were headed by a single female (it was much higher for Puerto Rican families).[2] In 1997 for the nation as a whole, the proportion of births to unmarried women was 41 percent for Hispanic women and 69 percent for African American ones.[3] The high rates of out-of-wedlock births for black women cannot be explained by intelligence, for holding IQ constant, black women are three times as likely as Latino and five times as likely as Anglo white women to have out-of-wedlock children.[4] There is, of course, an easy explanation for this difference—culture. Exactly. But what is the cultural difference?

In many nations in the Western Hemisphere—in Barbados, Jamaica, Antigua, Martinique, Surinam, Trinidad, as well as in the United States—black children are likely to grow up in a single-parent family.[5] Most of these places acquired independence from an imperial ruler many decades ago (in Haiti, two centuries ago). In almost every West Indian nation, black leaders responsive to black electorates came to power. Yet the out-of-wedlock birth rate in these places is very high. In Barbados, at the time of its 1990 census, only 30 percent of mothers between the ages of fifteen and forty-nine were married. Of the unmarried mothers, a few—roughly 3 percent—were divorced, but the vast majority had never been married.[6] Much the same story exists in every West Indian nation where the illegitimacy rate ranges from 35 to 72 percent.[7]

There is, of course, a convenient way to minimize this fact. Some people have argued that a child can as easily be raised by an unwed mother or by a man and woman living together in a common-law union as by a married pair. Americans, especially white ones, may think marriage is decisive, but critics argue that in other cultures there is a different view. A common-law marriage provides all of the benefits of a lawful marriage while being as stable as formal ones.[8] But none of those who make this argument show that a common-law union has the same effect as formal marriage and none deals with the fact that many children are raised by mothers who lack not only a husband but any consensual mate. Judith Blake studied Jamaican family life in great detail and noted that one-third of all mothers had no male partner at all, married or unmarried.[9] In a nation as poor as Jamaica, this lack of a father must surely have produced grave child-rearing problems. There would be little money or help.

But the circumstances are worse than what follows from poverty. Even defenders of consensual unions note that priests and middle-class Jamaicans condemn them, unwed mothers must deal with sharp criticism and sometimes beatings from their parents, and unmarried mothers are at a social disadvantage. Married mothers get more respect than unmarried ones. In time most Jamaicans (and most residents of other West Indian nations) do marry, but they marry quite late in life after most of a mother's children have grown up.[10] As William Goode put it, the ancient principle that legitimate births are preferable to illegitimate ones remains true even in societies where the latter are common.[11]

Depending on where she lives, the black West Indian girl is at risk. If she lives in the city or among itinerant cane cutters, her own mother may be unmarried, and so there is no father to protect her, and she may have brothers, but often they will be half brothers with little familial interest in her well-being. The risk arises from her natural desire for sex and acceptance, a desire that many black West Indian boys can grant on their terms because there is no father or brother to challenge them. As Blake suggests, for many Jamaicans there is no such thing as a shotgun marriage: "The sexual exploitation of young girls therefore both results from family disorganization and contributes to it. Men are provided with a far wider range of sexual partners than they would be if girls were protected."[12] If the girl is seduced and has a child, her value to other men is reduced; they often have little interest in raising somebody else's baby (or possibly any baby at all).

Matters may be different in West Indian peasant communities. There, a child may be born out of wedlock but the father is more likely to marry the mother and to play a stable paternal role. And among middle-class West Indians, there is a strong interest in intact, married families. But most West Indians now live in big cities or on plantations, not on individually owned farms, and there men and women spend relatively little time with one another. Their friendships, hobbies, outings, and games are sex segregated. Men meet at bars, in small stores, or on street corners; women meet in churches, homes, and the market.[13] Economic conditions in Jamaica (and probably other West Indian countries as well) contribute to this pattern of casual sexual unions. Much work, such as cutting sugarcane, is seasonal, and some work requires migration to other islands.

But it is not just the economy. As Edith Clarke made clear, "A woman is only considered 'really' a woman after she has borne a child" and "the proof of a man's maleness is the impregnation of a woman."[14]

The woman, having proved by giving birth that she is fertile, needs a husband, but the father, having proved by impregnation that he is a real man, often has little interest in accepting any responsibility for the mother or the child.

When Blake interviewed Jamaican women, she found that they were often deserted by the men who had fathered their children. And once they had a child by one man, their chances of ever marrying another were greatly reduced. The women tried to adjust to this possibility by giving their children away to relatives so that someone else would raise them.[15] So extensive was this farming out of children that by 1986 fewer than half of all Jamaican first-born children were even raised by their mothers.[16] The mother, lacking a husband, had to work. As a result, grandmothers, not mothers, and certainly not fathers, raised many black Jamaican children.[17] Of course, a few common-law unions did lead eventually to marriage, but most did not.[18]

West Indian countries have the same ethnic divide that separates many poor Mexican Americans from many poor African Americans. East Indians, mostly people from the Ganges River basin in India, were brought to the West Indies by planters eager to have enough cheap labor to keep costs down. They often came as indentured servants who confronted, for the few years of their agricultural duties, a great deal of discrimination both from white planters and black workers. But unlike most black West Indians, the East Indians living in the same islands lived in families. They married young, they worked hard to control the behavior of their sons and daughters, and they formed community kinship groups.[19] Most important, they formed families at a much higher rate than did blacks. Blacks and East Indians disliked one another, with much of that dislike expressed by rival attitudes toward personality and family life. Creoles (a common but ambiguous word that often refers to blacks or to persons born on an island who are not East Indian) often think that East Indians are avaricious, stingy, and secretive, while the latter think Creoles are feckless, childish, and promiscuous, shameful in allowing their women so much sexual freedom and in tolerating unwed mothers.[20] Why would African

Americans differ from equally poor Latinos, and West Indians from equally poor East Indians?

Slavery

The black people of the West Indies and of the United States had one thing in common: their ancestors had been slaves. There are deeply poor people living in every part of the world, but among some of the poor—chiefly, forcibly transplanted Africans—the family is weak. Surely slavery must explain a large part of this difference.

For many decades it did. Americans scholars, especially African American ones, assumed that slavery weakened or destroyed families just as it impoverished and oppressed people. William E. B. Du Bois said this in his 1908 book on the black family, and E. Franklin Frazier enlarged upon this in his 1939 book.[21] But when Daniel Patrick Moynihan summarized these arguments in his famous 1965 paper, the political and intellectual roof fell in on him, and a revisionist historical movement began. Du Bois and Frazier would surely have been astonished by the extent to which slavery was being rehabilitated. Well, perhaps not rehabilitated (most of the revisionists had nothing good to say about it), but certainly weakened as a social force. It may have been unpleasant, but it did not destroy the African American family. That family system, the new critics suggested, had been weakened by contemporary forces in American life, chiefly racism and joblessness.

Slavery, in the view of some of these revisionists, scarcely hurt families at all. One writer said in his book on slave communities that "the Southern plantation was unique in the New World because it permitted the development of a monogamous slave family."[22] Another writer remarked on the "impressive norms of family life" for slaves that provided these people with a "remarkably stable base."[23]

A few were prepared to add that, though the evils of modern American society had hurt the black family, its members had found valuable replacements in the form of extended kinship systems or gifted single moms. Given what we now know about the poor prospects of children in single-parent families, it takes one's breath away to read statements such as this, written in 1992: "Black women have a strong tradition of economic independence and collective child-rearing that makes them less dependent on men than are many white women. . . . These are healthy, not pathological, qualities."[24] Another said that the conditions of American slavery helped in the "creation . . . of monogamous families" in which the sex roles were "unusually egalitarian."[25] The author presents no data to support the family-creating aspects of slavery.

The revisionist history of slavery, much of it devoted to proving Moynihan wrong, offered several arguments, each implying that the African American family was not seriously weakened by slavery. Robert William Fogel and Stanley Engerman, in their original and probing analysis of the economics of slavery, said that though marriages were forbidden by the slave code of the South, they nonetheless survived under "plantation codes." Slave owners, they claimed, had a monetary incentive to encourage family life. Families reduced the incentives of individual slaves to flee and encouraged the production of children and hence of more slaves.[26] But the authors supply no evidence for these claims.[27] These material motives were supplemented, Fogel and Engerman argue, by "Victorian attitudes" that emphasized strong, stable families. However, Victorian attitudes, to the extent they arrived in the South at all, did so over two centuries after the slave trade had begun and after at least 80 percent of all American slaves had been imported. If these attitudes affected slavery, they did so long after its main features had been established. The authors were certainly correct to say that the extravagant claims about black family life made by many abolitionists were unsupported by facts, but no new facts were supplied in their place.[28]

Perhaps the best-known study that actually tries to say something about African American families during and after slavery was written by the historian Herbert Gutman. Based in large part on the genealogies he constructed about black children, Gutman argued, contrary to Moynihan, Frazier, and others, that black family life was not chiefly shaped, if shaped at all, by slavery. Upon their emancipation, ex-slave families "had two parents."[29]

But as one generally sympathetic scholar observed, genealogies are not the same as families. The former merely states who were the parents (or grandparents) of a child and what offspring the child would later produce. All this does is describe sexual patterns; everyone, in or out of a family, has a genealogy. But a family means a mother and father living together and caring for their children, whether or not the mother and father are formally married.[30] Gutman had little to say about whether a genealogy amounted to a family, but despite this gap his views exerted a powerful influence on American writers. William Julius Wilson, perhaps this country's most influential student of race, argued in 1987 that Gutman had proved that slavery had not affected black family structure. And to the extent black families were female headed, this was in great part due to the mothers' being widows. To Wilson, the chief problem facing blacks was the lack of jobs in the big cities.[31] As late as 1993, one leading history of fatherhood in America said, on the basis of Gutman's work, that even during slavery "marriages were remarkably stable" and "the great majority of slave families were headed by two parents." Slave fathers "played a vital role in black family life."[32] Moreover, these intact black families persisted through the darkest years of Jim Crow and right on down to the time that they moved to big cities, where unemployment forced fathers "to leave their families to find work."[33]

At this point one is brought up short. Slavery—that vast, cruel system of organized repression that denied to slaves the right to marry, vote, sue, or take an oath; withheld from them the proceeds of their own labor and the opportunity to move about in search of new jobs; allowed their own children to be sold on the slave block; exposed them to their owner's lash and the chance that, if they married, one spouse or another would be sold to a new owner; refused to allow them to buy property—with all of its misery and cruelty, slavery had little or no effect on family life, but moving as free people to a big city did. This is an extraordinary claim about social causes. The greatest social disaster ever to befall a free society did not weaken families, but urban migration did.

Recent research shows this argument to be wrong. Based on a careful analysis of census data, Steven Ruggles concluded that single parenthood was two to three times more common among African Americans than among whites in 1880. The gap widened after 1960, but it was only a widening, not a new event.[34] Now, one can argue that this early difference was the result of greater African American poverty, and no doubt that may have been part of the story. But it was far from the whole story, or even most of it, because in 1880 one measure of social standing, literacy, had the opposite effect. That is, literate black mothers were *less* likely to live with a husband than were illiterate ones. Moreover, single parenthood was *more* common among blacks in counties with a high per capita wealth than it was in places with less wealth.[35] The relationship was reversed for white families; among them, illiteracy and poverty increased the rates of single parenthood.

Urban life probably made a difference, but it was hardly decisive. A group of scholars at the University of Pennsylvania has painstakingly recreated family data from 1910 census manuscripts to discover how the community in which a family lived affected its life. We learn two things. First, African American children living in rural areas were roughly twice as likely as white children in such places to have only a mother present. For them, avoiding a city provided little benefit. Second, when blacks who live in cities are compared to those who live in rural areas, single-parent families are more common in the rural areas in New York and New Jersey and more common in urban areas in most other states.[36] City life may make some difference, but it cannot explain the gap in 1910 between whites and blacks in rural areas or explain all of the differences between urban and rural blacks.

There are several reasons why writers such as Gutman may have gotten this wrong. Many writers relied on some misleading census tabulations. A century or so back, many women reported themselves as widows in order to explain why they had a child but not a husband. In fact, as the University of Pennsylvania group learned, many of these "widows" were in fact never-married mothers.[37] Suppose that in 1910 unmarried mothers were as willing to reveal to the census enumerator that they lacked a husband as unmarried women are today. Some part, perhaps a large part, of the recent increase in single parenthood would disappear as we realized that the proportion of single moms in the past was much higher than we now think. The legendary power of the sixties to create fatherless households would be substantially reduced.

Another difficulty arose when scholars tried to define a family. A man, woman, and child might live together at the moment they are counted, but it is not clear that they are a family in any meaningful social sense. The man may have begat the child, but in what sense was he a father and a husband? He had no claim to the exclusive sexual use of the mother, he could not provide for her materially, and he had no right to prevent a slave sale from ending their union or from wrenching their child from them. Even Gutman's own statistics suggest that many slave children were raised in mother-only families. In 1865–66, he found that between 21 and 28 percent of all the black households containing children were headed by an unmarried mother.[38] After slavery ended, he used 1880 census data to find that in urban areas such as Mobile and Richmond, around one-fourth of all African American families were headed by females.[39] Many of these women described themselves as widows, but as we shall see, many claimed that status only to avoid the criticism that attached to being unmarried.

As Orlando Patterson put it, slavery prevented a black man from being either a father or a husband; he could offer to the mother and the child "no security, no status, no name, no identity." The male slave was placed in an impossible situation, "one bound to reduce him to a state of chronic jealousy and insecurity about women."[40] And even if he managed somehow to overcome these legal barriers, he often had to live apart from the mother of his child. On George Washington's farms, for example, only one-sixth of the slaves lived together as man and wife and two-thirds of those who considered themselves married lived apart from their spouses. Brenda Stevenson has reconstructed these data and used them, and other findings from her research on Virginia, to support the view that there was a great variety of household arrangements, especially ones headed by mothers with no husband and some headed by men who had several wives in various locations.[41]

An additional problem has been the tendency of scholars to rely on available data, and with regard to slave plantations, this information was most often produced only by the largest establishments. Patterson, a distinguished Jamaican scholar who has written about slavery in both his own country and in the United States, has made this point forcefully. Eugene Genovese and Herbert Gutman, by concentrating on large plantations, underestimated the effect of slavery on families. On the big plantations, there was at least a chance that a male and female slave could find one another and act as if they were married. ("As if" because, of course, no formal marriage was possible.) But in the smaller plantations, there were few choices and much less stability.[42] And most slaves lived on small plantations where single-mother families were the most common kind.[43] As Allan Kulikoff was to find, on large plantations about half of the slaves lived in nuclear households whereas on smaller ones, less than one-fifth did.[44]

This is just what other scholars have found to be the case among slaves in Brazil. Nuclear families were the most common form of slave life on the large plantations around Santana de Parnaíba, but the great majority of slaves did not live on these big estates. On these smaller farms "families," if that is what they can be called, were headed by a woman with no husband present. (The polite anthropological term for this arrangement is "matrifocal.") As a result, more than half of the slave children baptized in the Parnaíba parish had unknown fathers.[45] And this low marriage rate existed despite Brazilian slave owners being more tolerant of marriage than their American counterparts.

The problem of African Americans during and after slavery was probably made worse by a low sex ratio. That is, there was a shortage of the most eligible young men. In 1850, the ratio of men to every one thousand freed African American women aged twenty to twenty-nine was 857; in 1870, after slavery had ended (but just as Jim Crow was being imposed), the ratio for all African Americans in this age group was 866.[46] Assuming the census numbers can be taken for granted (a large assumption, given the inaccuracy with which some were tabulated), there were not enough young men around, especially (in 1850) freed men, to marry every woman. And so as we have seen in an earlier chapter, women would have to work harder to find a mate, do without one, or engage in unmarried sex at a man's pleasure.

The shortage of marriageable men in many places was compounded by the fact that a slave woman knew that even if she had a husband he could not protect her. He might be sent to work at a distant location or sold away to a new owner. And a man sent away, married or unmarried, was put in a situation where casual sexuality with any available woman was the only sexual release available. Patterson has written feelingly of what it was like when he grew up in the sugar belt area of Jamaica, where young men worked hard all day and caroused all night with whatever young women were available, departing after the crop had been collected with a legion of broken hearts and pregnant women left behind.[47] This pattern of working away from home made men sexually more predatory and women sexually more casual.

What was left behind in such families as existed was a strong belief that the chief bond of a child was with its mother. Patterson calls this a "uterine society," one that some slave owners reinforced by a policy of separating more sons than daughters from their parents.[48] As a result, slave women turned to their own mothers and women related to their mothers, rather than to their fathers, for help. And should children seek help from the father's side of their family, they were more likely to turn to the father's mother, sister, or aunts.[49] This was true for boys as well as girls. In Jamaica, a boy had little contact and less interest in his father; his chief obligation, he was told, was to his mother, to whom he might contribute money even after he leaves her care.[50] These attitudinal consequences of slavery were probably intensified during the era of Jim Crow because of the continued difficulty men faced in finding worthwhile employment and social standing. Even in the cities, the most common employment for slaves was as domestic help, and women supplied most of this work. And in most cities, the number of black women exceeded the number of black men.[51]

The effect of Jim Crow, and racism generally, on the black family legacy is a difficult matter to unravel. It is not enough to say that blacks were the objects of discrimination and so their families were weakened. In America, the Chinese, the Japanese, the Jews, and many others have experienced racial and ethnic hatred, yet their families stayed together. In India the Untouchables have experienced centuries of discrimination, but family life, though impoverished, was not weakened.

Yet racism cannot be dismissed as an explanation. Orlando Patterson has suggested that in the postslavery period, antiblack racism took an especially sinister form by making black male sexuality an object of hatred. African American men were lynched, often for (allegedly) making sexual advances to white women. Black men were the victims of sexual exaggeration (they were supposedly insatiable) and sexual rejection (for a white woman to have a black lover was much worse than for her to have a Chinese or Japanese one). This unique form of racism may—no one can say for certain—have created a sexual standard for black men that made the display of nonmarital sexual prowess important, provided only that it did not involve a white woman. Though African American men were not told to be fathers, they were expected to be lovers.

Compounding this problem may have been sharecropping. In England and among white Americans, getting married usually meant buying land. But after the end of slavery, there was little land available for black purchase; instead, black men could work land owned by other men and get a share of the crops as their reward. Sharecropping made black men into marginal members of society and ones who were rewarded, not by profits earned from land, but for labor extracted from their families. Sharecropping provided an incentive to have a lot of children (in 1900 the average black rural family had about eight) but no incentive to educate them. And since the land they farmed was not owned by their fathers, the labor never led anywhere. It is possible, as Patterson suggests, that sharecropping meant that many blacks (and not a few whites) were left out of the chance for economic advancement by the customary means—owning land, making progress, and having fewer children. Aggressive sexuality coupled with no capital assets put black men at risk.[52]

The African Legacy

It is possible that some of the patterns of family life that I have ascribed to slavery were in fact rooted in the experience slaves had in

Africa. West Africa, from which most slaves came, had three features that might have made a difference. Slavery* was widespread, children were sent out ("fostered") to be raised by people other than their parents, and agriculture was based on a very different system of land ownership and human labor. It is, of course, impossible to say with any confidence whether these experiences had any present effect even though some anthropologists, such as Melville Herskovits, have tried to make that argument.[53] Consider people who came here freely. A few Americans whose ancestors came from England in the seventeenth and eighteenth centuries may now retain some linguistic habits and possibly sing a few songs or recite some poems that were written in England, but hardly any today would take seriously the idea that they were "formed" by that country in any meaningful sense. It would seem no more likely for people who endured slavery in Africa, a terrifying Middle Passage to America, and the oppression of Southern slavery to retain any links at all to their African past.

But such observations do not settle the matter. More may be retained than people think. Individual property ownership, the Protestant religion, and a belief in personal liberties and the need for a consensual government came to this country with our first English settlers, and they put in place here institutions based on these ancient commitments that have taught countless subsequent generations of their importance. By contrast, slaves came here from a region with much less in the way of individual property ownership, little in the way of a Christian religion, and a tradition of tribal and military rule. Though their chances to create new institutions here were sharply lim-

---

*Slavery in Africa was different from slavery in America. African slavery was (obviously) not based on race and it did not always result from forcible capture (many slaves were abandoned children, some were criminals for whom slavery was their punishment, and some were captured in wars). Some African slaves grew rich and acquired their own slaves, some who were owned could not themselves be sold, and some were related to their owners. These distinctions are important, but they do not alter the fact that forced labor was a feature of African society. On the differences, see Igor Kopytoff and Suzanne Miers, "African 'Slavery' as an Institution of Marginality," in *Slavery in Africa*, ed. by Miers and Kopytoff (Madison: University of Wisconsin Press, 1977), 3–81.

ited, their customs may have lingered on in other ways. And if not, the absence of any rival customs may have lessened their ability to create for themselves a new kind of life after slavery ended. And so the legacy issue must remain open.

The key for us is each group's sense of how a family ought to be organized. The English came here with at least three centuries of familiarity with nuclear families based on individual consent and sustained by agriculture on separately owned plots of land that had to be cultivated intensively. Many slaves came here with no tradition of independent nuclear families but instead with an attachment to broad kinship groups that made marriage possible only after the payment of brideprice and a family life that involved fostering out the children and separating men and women during much of each year. And as anthropologist Meyer Fortes pointed out, the central question in much of West Africa has not so much been "are you married?" but "do you have any children?" It is, he continues, "parenthood not marriage that is the primary value associated with the idea of the family."[54] Given the importance of fertility, many African marriages ended if the wife proved herself barren, not simply because children are a valued asset but also because their presence signifies that parents have added to the kinship line and enhanced the family's patterns of ancestry and descent. Where the culture depended to some degree on valuable cattle, a wife without children would lose the cattle given to her as bridewealth.[55] The power of the African kin network is great; it induces couples to marry and otherwise supplies what resources a child might need. That power is easily exercised among hunter-gatherer cultures where a kin group travels together in search of sustenance. But with the advent of agriculture and the migration of men to work distant fields, the influence of kin groups declines. William Goode put it this way: "A basic origin of high illegitimacy rates [in Africa] lies . . . in the failure of the kin to impose the normal social controls on young people and adults."[56]

No one can say with confidence whether these differences shaped in a lasting way how people lived here. But we cannot rule out the possibility that they made a difference, if only by supplying a familial system that affected how free people adapted to the frontier and how slaves adapted to oppression.

As Sarah Blaffer Hrdy put it, imagine a place where incomes are very low and fertility very high, where women often give birth to children before they are married and fathers are only sporadically in residence with the mothers of their children, and where there are no government programs or charitable organizations that might care for unwed mothers or adopted children. Such a place still exists: it is Africa below the Sahara, especially in those places where people rely on hoe agriculture.[57] This is the family system that many Africans brought with them when they entered slave ships for a trip to America. In Africa, that system may well work, given the agricultural and village realities of life there. But will it work in the United States? Or better put, will it provide much guidance about how to live in a culture where marriage is not allowed, the movement of men away from mothers is made by slave masters, and dissent is punished with the lash?

Recall from the last chapter the essential difference between English (and probably northwestern European) farming and African agriculture. In England expensive and individually owned land was farmed by animal-drawn plows to supply the needs of the family that owned it and to equip them with produce to sell on the market. Wealth grew out of land, and power out of wealth. In much of Africa, by contrast, farming was done by women wielding hand hoes scratching a living out of rather infertile soil while the men went off to hunt or to herd cattle. Since women were important sources of labor, polygyny was common, and so some men had several wives. As land was abundant, land ownership was not a major source of wealth and wealth was not the chief route to political power. Though land was not scarce, access to it was controlled by local chiefs with whom men had to form alliances based on residence or kinship.[58] Because African children had working mothers and (often) absent fathers, the rearing of these children was shared with other women or with older children.

Marriage in Africa was quite different from what it came to be in Europe. It is impossible to generalize about so large and diverse a continent, but a few central facts seem to apply to most of its cultures. The chief one was that marriages were carried out under the influence of kinship considerations because, as Robin Fox has noted, kinship connections in much of the world, and certainly in most of Africa, are more important than marital ones.[59] There people are more concerned about who their clansmen are than who their father is. Because of this, marriage in Africa may follow after some delay the beginning of a residential sexual union. The couple may live together for some time before they are married, an event that may not involve any simple ceremony and may occur only after a child has appeared or the husband has paid bridewealth to his wife's family.[60] Among the Nuer of the Southern Sudan, it may take quite a while for the husband's family to supply enough cattle to meet the bride's price. In the meantime, the man and woman are already sexually quite intimate. Unlike what is true among clan-based marriages in Eastern Europe or the Near East, no one attaches much value to the bride being a virgin. But even after a formal marriage, the Nuer husband often continues to live a bachelor life with his male friends until after the wife gives birth. Then he can move into her house. Of course, the man may marry other women as well, if he can afford to.[61] All of these marriage arrangements are worked out by kin and each person's identity is largely defined by his position in that larger kinship system. "The whole society," Evans-Pritchard has written, "is one great family."[62]

But of course to a European or an American, "one great family" is no family at all. Here we derive our identity from our parents, there they derive it from their kin. In Africa, having a child is important to both mother and father, but this parenthood only defines one partially.[63] Who one is is also determined by one's tribe as well as one's parents. Of course, Americans and Europeans are interested in genealogy, but much of this is a hobby. We do not identify ourselves by talking about the people who lived before us—our ancestral accountants, truck drivers, stock brokers, and horse thieves; we do so by naming our mother and our father and especially the latter, since it is from him that we take our last name.

In many cultures the men left the raising of the children to their mothers. Among the ancient Asante, a slave-owning tribe in Western Africa, the fathers of children had relatively few responsibilities toward them except to ensure, if they could, that their offspring were fed and housed. Often the husband went off to war, an activity that was powerfully rewarded. The mother's brother was often the legal guardian of her children. The husband could and did punish his wife, but she had rights of her own, including a right to initiate divorce.[64] In the Lovedu tribe and elsewhere, polygyny made other wives available to help care for children.[65] In the nineteenth century, upper-status men in Botswana had about three wives each, and even commoners in this period had on the average nearly two wives each.[66]

Children in West Africa are often raised by people who are not their parents. In some communities, more than half of all of the children spend much of their young lives away from their parents, often living with close kin but sometimes with adults who are not related to them at all.[67] This practice is called fostering. In many ways it is similar to English practices that go back to the Middle Ages: send children away as apprentices. So far as we can tell, fostering in West Africa is a centuries-old tradition. It occurs for many reasons, but mostly because one parent is dead or missing. If the husband is dead, the mother may find it difficult to remarry, especially if she tries to bring another man's child into the new household. And if the mother is gone, the child may not be well received by the other wives in a polygynous family. But sometimes fostering occurs when both parents are alive and at home because they think it is in the child's best interests: he or she will learn new skills and find new opportunities.[68] Whatever the motives, many West Africans regard fosterage as a perfectly acceptable means of raising children. Families there approve of delegating parental roles to other people, often beginning at a quite early age, especially if the mother is unmarried or is part of a polygynous family.[69]

But even when they remain at home, children in much of Africa, especially south of the Sahara, grow up pretty much on their own. They learn for themselves the habits of life, taking lessons from the games, songs, and routines of daily existence. Today as in the past, they are overseen by the people who live around them, and these, especially the women, keep an eye on them. Sarah Blaffer Hrdy refers to them as "allomothers," that is, all of a child's caretakers other than the mother.[70] But mothers and allomothers give much less face-to-face instruction or conversation than is true of American mothers, especially those in the middle class. Here mothers talk to their children, teach them lessons, and exchange jokes with them. They play not only a protective but a pedagogical role. But though African adults certainly protect their children, they are much less active as teachers. In many African societies, what is striking is how little parents and children interact.[71] In fact, the main interactions African children have with adults is not with their own mothers or fathers, and especially not with the latter, but with whatever adults in the village happen to be watching them, that is, with their allomothers. The father is usually absent. Among the Gusii people of Kenya, a team of scholars carefully measured how much time other people spent in the presence of an infant or toddler. The mother and a sister gave the child the most attention; the father was scarcely present at all.[72] The absence was partly cultural and partly the result of the father working away from the village. These findings refer to Africans in the modern world; things may well have been different in the eighteenth century, and so we cannot be confident that how children are raised today corresponds precisely to how they were raised more than two centuries ago.

Now imagine how these conditions—assuming, as I do, that conditions like them were in effect centuries ago when the slave trade was under way—might have affected the slaves who came to America and the West Indies. Families were much less important than kinship groups. And as Orlando Patterson has noted, the kin groups were broken up during the Middle Passage and by the sale of slaves in the West. Even worse, when the slaves brought to the West had already been slaves in Africa, their kinship alliances were already in grave disrepair. When they arrived here "they did not belong in their own right to any lineage."[73]

In Africa, women had been economically active as farm workers and produce gatherers. In America and the West Indies, being born to a slave mother made the child a slave and gave to the mother and her child a customary role—working the fields. This fact, combined with the absolute biological and cultural centrality of the mother-child bond, meant that women, despite the horrors of slavery, would find it easier adjusting to it than would the men.

Men had a tougher time. In Africa, fathers did not have a strong role in their youngsters' development; other people, especially nearby women, took over many of these tasks. Not only were they often not available for child-rearing tasks, many had to divide their attention among their several wives. In America and the West Indies, slavery created more barriers—the absence of a marriage bond and any chance at acquiring bridewealth—for any father hoping to play such a parental role. Move them in slave ships to America and it is hard to imagine they would adapt to their new environment by suddenly acquiring what they rarely had, namely, long experience in child rearing and devotion to a single wife, especially since slave work, like African work, took them away from wives for long periods of time.

Life in Africa prepared women to be agricultural workers but it did not prepare men to be attentive fathers. In Africa, kinship was of central importance; in slavery, whether African or American, it was meaningless. As Patterson put it, a slave here or in Africa could have children but no legitimate kin. "They were kinless," and this meant that they were "socially dead."[74] And here, even more than in Africa, the children would chiefly know their mothers. And slave men often resorted to physical violence to control the wives they might have. Whether this reflected past African habits or the mimicking of the brutality of many plantations no one can say, but the relations between husbands and wives were often marred by physical force.[75]

A Legacy of Beliefs

It is hard to believe that two or three centuries of slave life followed by a century or so of Jim Crow left no lasting impression on African Americans, but of course proving such a connection is virtually impossible. But let us for a moment conduct a mental experiment. Given what slaves endured, what would we imagine would be the legacy that their children and grandchildren inherited? We would probably suppose that boys would grow up with little close identification with their fathers and some interest in repeating the youthful sexual exploits that transient work and long absences from home made possible. Few would recall many happy experiences associated with a two-parent family. Girls, on the other hand, would grow up thinking that men were irresponsible and that women would have to make their own careers out of whatever opportunities presented themselves. Children would expect to be raised by their mothers or grandmothers and possibly by other women, perhaps distant ones, and would not be surprised if there were no fathers present. They would expect physical, sometimes harsh, discipline. Of course, these predictions must be stated cautiously, for it is obvious that among millions of African Americans there would be a great variety of adaptations; some would struggle to conform to white American marital patterns, others would try to create a unique marital system of their own, and still others would be unaffected by anything that happened in the past.

But what is striking is that these predictions accord with reality for a large fraction (albeit a minority) of African Americans today. And not only today, but several decades ago when liberal scholars, such as John Dollard, studied a Mississippi town in the 1930s. "African patterns of sexual control," he wrote, "were abandoned probably because of their futility in the new slave milieu."[76] Not abandoned, he added, because blacks were, as some observers thought, childlike, but abandoned because they did not work. Black men had no access to white women and only limited access to black ones, and with the latter the man could offer neither food nor shelter nor protection—the essential requirements of the male social role—to a wife. The man could dominate but not protect the woman, not only during slavery but for at least a century afterward. And since marriage depends on protection more than domination, it got off to a rough start among African Americans.

Orlando Patterson has tried to bring this argument up-to-date. African American men, in his view, sought to embrace the very role that slavery had forced upon them and against which no strong African culture defended them. Sexual predation against black women and violence against black men "would appear to idealize what once dehumanized them," and so "Little Black Sambo became a 'badass' dude."[77] And polls suggest that African American men do not think that marriage will bring them happiness.[78]

Many black women notice how some black men think, and the result is a shortage of marriage. Among people aged twenty-five through thirty-four, more than two-thirds of all white men and women but less than one-third of black men and women are married.[79] What is especially troubling is that educated, affluent African American men are no more likely to marry than their poorer counterparts.[80] And women who get married after they turn thirty-four confront a pool of available males—that is, those who are the same age or a bit older and have promising educational and economic attainments—that has become quite small. This is one of the troubling legacies of the well-known fact that black women greatly outnumber black men in universities. And even were educational attainments the same, the African American sex ratio falls after the age of about forty.

Many African American women get pregnant, often without planning to, and a lot would like to get married, but many fathers are not interested. Both men and women want babies, but the men are much less likely to think that getting married and helping take care of the infants makes much sense. And if they do get married, they are much more likely than their wives to be unfaithful and to be a punitive parent.[81]

The lesson this leaves in the mind of the child is not hard to imagine. The father is absent, and thus fatherhood is unimportant; the father is present, but infidelity and harsh punishments are the result. To children for whom these things are true, the conclusion is clear: do not identify with your fathers. And many do not. One study of African Americans found that men who *rejected* their fathers were more likely to do better in finding jobs than those who identified with them.[82]

One implication of this argument is that single-parent families are likely to be a bit more normal among black than white Americans. By "normal" I do not mean widely accepted or generally endorsed; I mean instead that they will involve people who are less different from their ethnic kin. Given the high rate of single-parent families among African Americans, this must surely be the case; such families are much too common to be limited only to persons with odd dispositions. And scholars have found this to be true. Robert Lerman learned that young African American men who are unwed fathers are much more similar to black men who are married than one finds to be the case between unwed white fathers in comparison to married ones. For example, the reported use of hard drugs and the level of alcohol abuse among young unwed black fathers is roughly the same as it is among young married black men, and much lower than it is among young white unwed fathers. White unwed dads, compared to black unwed dads, are three times more likely to use hard drugs or to be charged with a crime in an adult court and half again as likely to have an alcohol problem.[83] Today, white unwed fathers are clearly deviant, though at the rate at which single-parent homes are growing that may not be true much longer.

All of these facts are about people with acute family problems, but of course most people do not have these problems. About half of all African-American families are part of the middle class, a group for whom the legacy of slavery, at least with respect to income and family structure, has been overcome. In 1995, the income of married black families was 87 percent of that of married white families.[84] It is difficult to write about any social issue without appearing either to overstate the matter, and thus neglect people who have done well, or to recognize these accomplishments, and thus understate the problem. Let me put the matter in language that was endorsed by several African American as well as white students of family life. After a conference at Morehouse College in Atlanta in 1998, the report—*Turning the Corner on Father Absence in Black America*—said that black children born in the early 1980s would spend about eleven years, well over half of their childhood, living in a one-parent home.[85] The signers differed as to what caused this problem. But to the extent slavery contributed to this condition, it is no small matter. Searching for clever language to take into account the remarkable level of African American progress while at the same time recognizing the magnitude of the problem may be a waste of time.

Chapter 6
Mother-Only Families

There have always been children conceived before their parents were married. Though changes in Western culture and the impact of slavery may have increased how often this occurs, our grave social problem is not premarital intercourse or even the birth of a child to unwed parents, but rather the extent to which children are raised in families headed by an unwed mother. Many unmarried mothers (and unmarried fathers) do a splendid job in raising their children, but they are a distinct minority. Single-parent families are the source of the saddest and most destructive part of our society's two nations.

In England, the common law has long held, as Blackstone wrote in the middle of the eighteenth century, that a child born in wedlock is assumed to be legitimate even if the conception occurred before marriage. Peter Laslett estimates that in England around 1550 and again around 1800, about a third of all births were conceived before marriage.[1] The ratio in the United States has been similar. During times of strong social controls, such as the Puritan seventeenth century and the Victorian nineteenth century, premarital pregnancies made up about 10 percent of all births, while in times of personal emancipation, such as the second half of the eighteenth century and in contemporary America, premarital pregnancies have been between 25 and 30 percent of all births.[2]

But traditionally a child *born* before marriage was illegitimate, a word that initially meant that he or she had no right to inherit property. Being a bastard, as such children were then called, put them at considerable risk. They had no legal connection to their parents nor did the parents have an obligation to them. There were two main reasons for creating this empty legal space. In a country, such as England, where livelihood depended on land, everyone had to be confident who would inherit what parcel. (In places, such as much of sub-Saharan Africa, where land was not the basis of wealth and power, bastardy was less important as a legal matter.) And even if inheriting land were not important, avoiding the public expense of rearing a parentless child certainly was.

In much of Europe, a child born to a couple who later married could be made legitimate, and many were. This policy helped the many women who had out-of-wedlock children, a number that increased dramatically around the middle of the eighteenth century. In Paris, Frankfurt, Stuttgart, Rotterdam, and all of Sweden, the illegitimacy rate went up sharply. In Paris between one-fifth and one-quarter of all illegitimate children had their births made legitimate by public authorities. Edward Shorter, who has gathered these facts, argues, I think correctly, that the increase in illegitimacy, and the concomitant increase in premarital intercourse, reflected the spread of the "wish to be free," that massive change toward individual autonomy that grew out of the Enlightenment.[3] Whether making the fatherless children legitimate helped them is not clear, but at least it enabled them to compel parental support and inherit land.

But legitimation was hard to arrange in England. Only an act of Parliament could do that, and this rarely happened. This tough legal barrier, however, was greatly moderated by what one meant by the word *marriage*. As we have seen, a couple living together exclusively might be considered married even if no public ceremony had been performed. The courts could decide they were married even if they had taken no vows, and until 1857 it was the ecclesiastical courts—those speaking on behalf of church tradition—that made the decision. In doing this they tended to follow European practice, not local English law. The common-law courts, by contrast, were bound by secular law and refused to confer legitimacy on out-of-wedlock children. They argued that the purpose of the law was to encourage marriage; the law could do this when it stripped the children of unwed parents of their right to inherit.[4] If a child could not inherit, the parents would be more likely to avoid giving birth until after they were married.

Until the ecclesiastical courts lost their power in 1857, their rulings as to whether a valid marriage existed governed the common-law courts, leaving the latter only with the (often rare) task of deciding simply on matters of inheritance, should any arise.[5] For many people they did not because their parents were often too poor to leave behind much that could be inherited. For many of these youngsters doubts about their parents' marital status may not have had any practical meaning. In addition, England allowed other families to adopt bastards even though this was not legally possible without an act of Parliament. These de facto adoptions often occurred when families took in homeless children, thereby removing them from any risk of legal attack.[6]

What was never tolerated until the recent past were children who lived without parental support and thus who would become a burden on the town. Premarital sex was common, prenuptial pregnancies were routine, common-law marriages were not rare, but giving birth to a child and then expecting the town to support it—this was unforgivable. The community was determined that the father would pay for the support of the child.[7] In England until 1865, if an unmarried mother lived away from her hometown, the overseers in the place where she had landed had the authority to send her back to her original parish.[8] If the girl stayed in her own town, community pressure on her to get married was intense. The Poor Law of 1576 decreed that the parents of an illegitimate child had to pay for its support, and under a law passed in 1733 any man charged by a woman as the father of her illegitimate child had but three choices—marry the woman, contribute toward the child's support, or go to prison.[9] As Lawrence Stone put it, the pressure on a man and woman to marry after the birth of their child was, until this century, quite powerful. If a man deserted a pregnant woman, he was dishonorable; if a woman failed to identify the father of her child, she was unchaste.[10]

These laws and attitudes came to the United States with the immigrants. The Puritans in New England strongly condemned bastardy whereas southerners were more willing to tolerate it, but only on condition that it would create no demand for public support. There, and later in the West, the law recognized common-law marriages. But everywhere people agreed that community support of fatherless children was a bad idea.

The Child-Centered Culture

This hostility to public support soon had to encounter a different, and in time more powerful, political impulse. America gradually became perhaps the most child-centered country in the world.[11] The refugees from England who settled this land increasingly came to think that children ought to be protected even if that meant relaxing old rules about illegitimacy. In 1785, Virginia passed a law that made a child legitimate if, after its birth, the mother and father married.[12] By the 1830s, thirteen states had joined Virginia in allowing illegitimate children to inherit lands.[13]

But protecting the child still left unsettled the problem of support. The courts tried to manage this problem by hearing paternity suits in which a woman might show that a man was the child's father and thus ought to pay for his or her rearing. These suits, of course, occurred long before the invention of DNA testing that could make paternity easily determined. Since courts could not be certain who the father might be, some women had an incentive to bring paternity suits as a way of harassing men. Of course this harassment was one of the few burdens men faced in a world where the father had a dominant legal position. If a married couple separated or were divorced, the father acquired the children whatever the mother might wish. When a New York court tried in 1860 to grant to wives equal custodial rights over their children, the New York Supreme Court objected and the legislature promptly changed its mind.[14] It was not until well into the twentieth century that this aspect of coverture disappeared. Bringing a paternity suit was costly for a woman and the man could easily deny that he was the father. Then as now, collecting money from the real father was no easy task. And even if the money were forthcoming, the help of the father in raising the child was still absent.

By the end of the eighteenth century, the states made greater efforts to attend to the needs of the child if this could be done without impoverishing the town, harming the family, or oppressing the father. This was not easy. As historian Michael Grossberg put it, the essential problem was to decide "whether the individual or the family was the unit to be protected by the law."[15] For a century or more, reformers tried to find ways of helping the child without hurting the family. They thought they succeeded, but all they really did was to decide that it was the individual more than the family that deserved protection. The reformers had three alternatives for helping children: put them in an orphanage, allow those without fathers to be raised by another family, or allow them to be raised by their unmarried mother by paying her some money. For a long time the third choice seemed absurd—paying women to raise their own children was not only a bad use of public money, it might create an incentive for women to weaken their commitment to marriage as the price of sexual access. But what once was thought absurd in time seemed necessary.

Orphanages—or asylums, as they were often called—sprang up in the early nineteenth century to accommodate children who would otherwise be homeless or live with an uncaring parent. In 1800 there were only a half dozen orphanages; by 1910 there were more than a thousand caring for more than one hundred thousand children.[16] One reason for the increase was the Civil War, which left countless children without fathers and many without any parent at all. Many orphanages were organized by churches and other religious organizations, each of which argued that without religious instruction children could not be adequately trained.

But by the end of the nineteenth century, the orphanages were on the defensive. Progressives criticized them for being costly, inhumane, and religious. They were, to be sure, costly; housing, caring for, and educating children is an expensive proposition, as any parent knows. Indeed, many children were in orphanages precisely because their parents—and most had one and some had both—could not pay the bills. As for inhumanity, a few places were inhumane, but these were mostly the large poorhouses into which some children were sent in ways made legendary by Charles Dickens in his portrait of Oliver Twist. But most orphanages were rather small. In 1880 the median institution had only forty-two children; over half catered to fewer than fifty.[17] But even some of the largest ones, such as the New York Catholic Protectory, which might have two thousand children in residence, were not inevitably inhumane. Susan Tiffin, who has reviewed many studies of these institutions, wisely suggests that there were so many differences in size, style, and organization that no simple "aerial view" of orphanages can be given, but then she goes on to argue that they encouraged a "stereotyped and repressive life style."[18] By "repressive" she apparently means that the life of the children was based on a timetable, sometimes relied on military-style coordination, emphasized "unthinking obedience," and failed to encourage a "sense of autonomy."[19]

In this respect she echoes in modern language the criticisms made by Progressives at the end of the nineteenth century. Orphanages isolated children from the real world, they said, and by keeping them in institutions, sapped their independence and energy. When one orphanage supporter noted that children in fact liked doing things in groups—boys liked military games, girls liked tea parties—her views were ignored.

The reformers were also skeptical of the religious basis of the orphanages, with one complaining that the children were "often taught too much about heaven and too little about earth."[20] This view persisted right into the twentieth century, when professional social workers continued to object to church affiliations and worried that the emphasis on religion would prevent the institutions from addressing the needs of the child. Orphanage leaders responded by saying that religion in fact addressed a central need of the child for a secure moral foundation; by teaching morality as well as reading and writing they were helping children prepare for the real world. But this argument was hard to sustain in the Progressive period, and in any event it was often undercut by the deep hostility between Catholic and Protestant institutions. If these two religious groups were always quarreling about religious doctrines, surely, the reformers said, we ought to get rid of those doctrines entirely.

The second method—relying on a different family—seemed to many reformers to be a far better system. It had a long history. For many centuries, unwanted children in England and other parts of Europe had been sent to foundling homes or "baby farms," where other women raised them. The use of these two methods depended on the laws of the country. In England, the fathers of these children were legally obliged to pay for their care, and so baby farms were common and the substitute mothers there were often paid. In France and Russia, by contrast, the fathers were under no such obligation, and so mothers sent unwanted (or at least unsupportable) children to foundling homes.[21]

Moreover, many English parents sent their children to other homes to be servants or work as apprentices. While with these families, the child was expected to conform to commonplace standards of decency—obey their substitute parents, avoid alcohol and fornication, and work hard. The terms of this transaction were often set out in writing, with the child becoming independent after the apprenticeship was over.

In the United States, this idea was adopted by people who created children's aid societies that would place homeless or destitute children in rural homes, many of them in the West, but doing this without any formal contract between birth and substitute families. In 1853, Charles Loring Brace started the New York Children's Aid Society, and other cities soon followed suit. For a while, trainloads of children were sent West so that the youngsters could be deposited in the homes of farmers. The work of Brace and others lent support to the idea of foster care, a view that by 1900 had triumphed over orphanages.

Foster care enjoyed one great benefit. Since people believed that the family was the core of a decent society, putting children in foster families seemed obviously better than putting them in institutions. This may well have been true when the foster family took in the child without any public financing, and many did just that. But increasingly foster families expected to be paid, a change that created the possibility of some foster homes taking children just for the money (or for both the county's money and the income the child could earn when sent out to work). And since there was no good way to check up on foster homes, many children were put in homes where the family care was deplorable. When these conditions were discovered, the children were relocated, sometimes several times, to new homes. Supporters of foster care were aware of this problem and worked hard to create better ways of choosing families, but the problem was hard to solve. The Illinois Children's Home and Aid Society reported in 1900 that 195 of the 494 children it dealt with that year were replacements being sent from one foster home to a new one.[22]

Despite its problems, foster care won the battle over orphanages. The former was cheaper, did not create religious arguments, and involved real families. By 1899 the National Conference on Charities and Correction was able to report that its membership was overwhelmingly in favor of foster homes. Catholic, Protestant, and Jewish leaders began to fall in line. But the transfer to foster care took a long time. In 1923, the Census Bureau found that nearly two-thirds of all dependent and neglected children were in institutions and only one-third in foster homes. It was not until 1962 that these percentages were reversed, with only one-third of the children in institutions and two-thirds in foster homes.[23]

Mothers' Pensions

Paying mothers to raise their own fatherless children was the last idea to gain support. To do so it had to overcome a powerful aversion to making family life dependent on public payment. But two things helped the cause along. The first was that private charities had long been making payments to certain unwed mothers; the call for public help, thus, could be phrased as an effort to backstop private support. This happened with religious charities in Boston, Chicago, New York, and elsewhere. The second was that the women getting this aid were mostly widows who could not possibly be blamed for lacking a husband. Paying pensions to widowed mothers did nothing to challenge the legitimacy and importance of the family, and by the beginning of the twentieth century there was an active movement by Progressives to get states to pass laws making this possible. When people criticized this effort as a way of making women dependent on the government, they were answered bluntly: the pension was payment for services rendered and would no more make a mother a "dependent" than paying a man to hold a job would make him dependent.[24]

Illinois passed the first mothers' pension law in 1911; by 1919 thirty-nine states had followed its example. The pioneering Illinois statute allowed the poor parents of a "dependent or neglected child" who were "otherwise proper guardians" to receive public money as administered by the juvenile court. A judge would decide who was poor and morally fit and then allocate the funds. A citizens' committee was formed to spell out the details. Based on its report, the authorities decided to give aid only to women who were "physically, mentally, and morally fit" and to have court probation officers look in on the applicants to make certain this was the case. No aid would go to women who owned property, had relatives who could help, or had been deserted by their husband for less than two years. Even so, the measure produced controversy. The Russell Sage Foundation issued a report arguing that it would erode family responsibilities and weaken individual initiative (in response, some Progressive leaders called the foundation "reactionary").[25] But social workers employed by private charities agreed with the foundation. It was their task, they felt, to make certain that a woman was deserving and would receive their aid in managing their homes. No state bureaucrat was likely to do this.[26] Moreover, the pensions would encourage fathers to desert their children so that a "new class of dependents would be created."[27] This complaint led the Illinois legislature in 1913 to tighten further the standards by limiting aid to widows or the wives of permanently disabled men. The goal was to ensure that there would be no incentive for errant husbands to abandon their families.[28]

This new policy was easier for the public to accept because no one could argue that an impoverished widow was anything but a member of the deserving poor. Deaths from illness or work in coal mines or on farms created many widows and the First World War added a vast new supply. The war may have helped bring about the 1923 expansion of the law when, for the first time since 1913, deserted women became eligible for county aid, but even this broadening of the law had little practical effect. As late as 1931, 82 percent of all the women getting aid under the Illinois law were widows.[29] Even with an expanded law, mothers who had never married were still excluded because they were "morally unfit," a policy that many states had adopted.[30] When the federal Children's Bureau surveyed mothers' pension laws in 1934, it found that the great majority allowed money to be given to women who had been "abandoned" or "deserted" by their husbands, but only in five states were unmarried mothers allowed to obtain aid.[31]

Many Progressives who fought for the mothers' pension were not about to let the benefits go only to widows or deserted mothers; they wanted them to go to women who had never been married, and they were not enthusiastic about efforts to decide who was morally fit or to limit expenditures. These activists, mostly upper-middle-class women, believed that money given to a mother living alone would reach the home during a crisis and help tide them over "without loss of self-respect."[32] The *Delineator*, a major women's magazine, led the campaign, with stories arguing that mothers are better than orphanages and explaining why widows' pensions are only the first step toward help for all fatherless children. The Scripps and Hearst newspapers endorsed the campaign, and women's clubs worked hard on its behalf. One important leading woman activist said that state governments must help "the deserted wife, and the mother who has never been a wife."[33] Another put the matter more forcefully: "If we cannot have the trinity which God intended—husband, wife, child—we can have the other trinity—mother, child, home—that has a mighty potency in it for good."[34]

But the state laws generally ignored the problem of dealing with children of unwed mothers. A new federal agency soon took the lead in changing this. The Children's Bureau, founded in 1912, estimated that during 1915, 32,400 illegitimate children were born—about 1.8 percent of all live births.[35] Thirty-two thousand children seemed like a big number and helped explain why in cities such as New York there were so many homeless waifs with high death rates. But 1.8 percent was also a very low percentage, and that helped convince reformers that the problem was manageable. By the early 1920s, Julia Lathrop, the head of the Children's Bureau, was able to publish reports about the lot of out-of-wedlock children. Not only could they not inherit property, they were more likely to be ill and to have high death rates. She laid the groundwork for helping provide for unmarried mothers who were not widows.

This was no easy task because people firmly believed that money should not go to an "unsuitable home," and what could be more unsuitable than one in which the mother had never married? An unmarried mom implied immorality, and so most state laws did not allow money to go to such persons. There may also have been a racial motive in this: since unmarried moms were more common among African American than white families, insisting on a suitable home provided a way to restrict aid to blacks. This was nowhere a formal policy, but in some states and counties administrative practice may have produced this result. Gunnar Myrdal, in his famous account of blacks in America, wrote in 1944 that the suitable home rule could encourage some administrators to cut black families off from welfare.[36] But this exclusion of blacks could not have simply reflected racism, since black applicants got old-age assistance at the same rate as whites. What was at stake, in large part, were beliefs about the home.

There were two ideas each leading to a different policy. "Help needy children" meant ignoring how they became needy or whether their mother would produce more needy ones. "Preserve a suitable home" meant judging the parents whatever this might mean for the children. The first lead to helping more recipients, the second to helping fewer. Progressive activists wanted to help more but they knew that this was politically difficult. What they did not see—what in all likelihood hardly anyone then saw—was that some homes would rely on welfare, shun marriage, and produce more out-of-wedlock children. Though almost every historian is critical of the "suitable home" rule, the nations' experience since the mid-1960s suggests that the idea had some merit.

The Rise of Welfare

The Great Depression made state laws part of a new national program. The Social Security Act of 1935 created the Aid to Dependent Children (ADC) program, under which the federal government reimbursed the states for payments they made to low-income mothers of children. The federal law did not include the "suitable home" rule or require that children have "fit parents," leaving it to the states to decide on eligibility. But in its debates, Congress made it clear that the states could impose a "moral character" rule.[37] And most states did.

As time passed, those who managed the program began to change, gradually and subtly, the standards that governed eligibility. The American Public Welfare Association, a group that included the heads of almost every state welfare agency, issued in 1935 a model rule that, if followed, would provide aid to "any dependent child" who is "living in a suitable home" defined as one that met "the standards of care and health" fixed by the laws of the state.[38] A suitable home was one that did not neglect, exploit, or abuse the child. Still, many parents might not be morally fit (the old standard) even though they did not neglect, exploit, or abuse their children (the new standard).

The federal government also began to shift its attitude toward how homes should be evaluated. In 1935 it made it clear in various rulings that ADC was a plan to help needy children, and that this included illegitimate children even if they were delinquent. Doubts were expressed about the constitutionality of taking into account the religious training provided by parents.[39] But the states were slow to take up on these suggestions. The great majority of the mothers getting aid were widows or were separated or divorced from their husbands. As late as 1960, only 4 percent of the children on ADC were living with a mother who had never married.[40] During these early years, the number of mothers receiving ADC went up when the unemployment rate rose and went down when it declined. The increases in how many people got benefits was initially quite modest; in the decade of the 1950s, the number went up by only 7 percent.

Slowly the states began to change under the influence of federal expectations and professional sentiments. By 1931, ten states had changed their mothers' pension laws to permit public money to go to virtually any needy mother; in three of these states, it could even go to mothers who had never married. In only two states was it still limited to widows.[41] Practice did not quickly follow legal opportunity, but in time it did. This slow change has never been adequately analyzed, but in time the result became clear. Under the impact of rising caseloads, bureaucratic obscurity, professional beliefs, and a commitment to racial equality, the rules about moral fitness and suitable homes were dying. What had started as an effort by private charities to uplift mothers had become a government effort to mail out checks. It is not hard to imagine why. Private organizations may have a moral message; government rarely does. Private groups select clients; public agencies serve everyone who meets written criteria. Changing people who are needy is difficult, sending them money is easy. Not only is sending money simple, it also makes it easier to enlarge the definition of the deserving poor from widows to deserted or divorced mothers and then on to unwed ones. If the goal is to help children, then all needy children deserve help equally, whatever the conditions of their parents. Helping deserving families seems worthwhile, but the concern for individual claims will recognize that helping deserving children is important even if they come from undeserving families. Blaming bad or dependent mothers was easy; blaming children for being either bad or dependent seemed nonsensical.

In 1962, the program was renamed Aid to Families of Dependent Children (AFDC) and funds were authorized for intact families that were poor and had an unemployed father. More federal aid was made available for social services aimed at the poor, but now such services no longer implied assessing the moral fitness of the mother. The initial goal was to keep needy children in their homes. For almost thirty years the program did this under conditions that most Americans could accept.

But hidden within this program was an obvious incentive. If you wanted a child but not a husband, the government would help supply the money—but obviously neither the care nor guidance—that the absent father failed to provide. What was remarkable was that for three decades this incentive did not alter very much the behavior of people. One reason may be that though illegitimacy was increasing the results did not greatly affect the welfare rolls. Between 1940 and 1960, the illegitimacy rate among both whites and blacks nearly tripled, but many of these out-of-wedlock children did not go onto welfare because so many families shunned welfare. As late as 1967, less than half the eligible families were on AFDC.[42]

But soon all that changed. Between 1960 and 1980, the number of children receiving AFDC doubled, but the number receiving it because their mothers had never been married increased by a factor of seven. In 1960, 4 percent of the children had never-married mothers; by 1996, 37 percent had them. In 1960, one-quarter of the single mothers were widows; by 1996, when the program ended, only 4 percent were.[43] This meant that welfare payments were now being received, not by women who had once been married, but by those who had never been married. In 1996, more than two-thirds of the AFDC beneficiaries were unmarried when their first child was born, and most were teenagers.[44] Though many mothers stayed on the program for only a few years, one-quarter or more stayed on for at least five years. For them, welfare had become a way of life.

The program was no longer aid for widows and divorcées, but rather in large part for single moms, and very young ones at that. The public was quick to notice this and demanded that something be done to end what it regarded as a system that induced women to have fatherless children and allowed women to get public money without working. In 1996 AFDC was repealed and a new law, popularly called welfare reform, was passed. It limited how much money Washington would send to the states, gave the states freedom to design their own welfare programs, encouraged unmarried mothers to work, imposed a five-year time limit on money paid to them, and told those under the age of eighteen that they would have to live in an adult-supervised setting. The complaints of private social workers in the 1910s that the mothers' pension laws would encourage the emergence of unmarried mothers and the desertion of heedless fathers, complaints that for a time were met by limiting aid to women who were morally fit, suddenly seemed like an accurate forecast of what would happen as the government ran welfare and the need for morality was replaced by the right to a check.

Does Welfare Cause Dependency?

Welfare reform was the object of an intense public debate. The central issue was whether welfare had in fact induced women to bear children without marrying the fathers. Most people believed that it did, and almost any economist would have agreed: if you subsidize something, you get more of it. But there were at least two arguments against this popular conclusion. First, states differed greatly in how much money they gave to an AFDC recipient. In 1997 a three-person AFDC family in Alabama got $164 a month while one in Alaska got $923 and one in Connecticut received $636.[45] But despite these sharp differences in payments there were no corresponding differences across these states in how many women became unmarried mothers. Women in Alaska or Connecticut were no more likely—and certainly not four or five times as likely—to become unwed moms as those in Alabama. In Minnesota, welfare benefits were high but the number of unmarried births quite low; in Mississippi, welfare benefits were small but unmarried births common.[46]

All of this is true, but what it suggests is that there are differences among states created by their cultural, economic, ethnic, and religious features that affect how vulnerable people in these localities are to welfare payments as an alternative to marriage. Minnesota differs from Mississippi in many ways that have nothing to do with welfare, and perhaps these differences affect how willing low-income people are in each state to rely on AFDC payments as a way to sustain single-mother families.

The second argument was that the real (that is, the inflation-adjusted) value of welfare payments went down during the 1970s at the very time when the AFDC caseload was shooting upward. Declining benefit levels surely cannot produce rising welfare rolls.[47] The

AFDC caseload, defenders of welfare said, must be going up for reasons having little to do with how big the AFDC benefits are.[48]

But this criticism leaves out of account the other welfare benefits that low-income people can receive, such as food stamps, Medicaid, and subsidized public housing. AFDC benefits alone rose rapidly in the 1960s and then declined starting in the 1970s. But about the time that decline started, food stamps and Medicaid became available in sufficiently large amounts so that the total package of benefits an unmarried mother would get rose at about the same rate as the national income.[49] By the early 1980s the total benefits going to a poor, unmarried mother living in New Orleans was $654 a month whereas for one living in San Francisco it was $867. And since the cost of living in San Francisco was much higher than it is in New Orleans, the actual benefits were practically identical. As Charles Murray pointed out, the total welfare package amounted to about two-thirds of the median household income in both New Orleans and San Francisco.[50] As a result, that Louisiana and California have similar rates of single-mother families should not be surprising.

The conventional arguments against the idea that welfare can create single-mother families are not, as they are often stated, very convincing. Welfare may well have been a factor, but how large a one? When Robert Moffitt wrote his exhaustive 1992 survey of the evidence, he concluded that welfare did help create more single-mother families, but that its effect was modest.[51] One of the main reasons was that states differed so much and in so many ways that any comparison of welfare benefits and single-mother families across states was likely to be confused by these other, unmeasured features of a state's culture. Moreover, any statistical study had to take into account the real alternatives facing real women. One could not look at any woman (say, one who has been married but is now divorced, or a woman with substantial income) having a child; one had to look at poor women who had never been married who might have a child.

Mark Rosenzweig, an economist at the University of Pennsylvania, did just this by following the women in the National Longitudinal Survey of Youth (NLSY) who have been interviewed every year since 1979. He examined how often young women acquire a child after controlling for their age, parents' income, and personal traits* and looking at the actual AFDC benefits their states offered. He found that the size of AFDC benefits had a small but significant effect on the chances that women would have a child without first getting married but a much larger effect on those chances for young poor women. For this last group, if AFDC benefits increased by only 10 percent, the chances of her having an out-of-wedlock child before she reached the age of twenty-two went up by 12 percent. This held true whether the women were black or white.[52] Welfare benefits made a difference.

Other studies were published that confirmed Rosenzweig's findings. Two economists at the National Bureau of Economic Research found that higher AFDC payments led initially unwed white mothers to postpone getting married and caused unwed African American ones to have their next child sooner.[53] Two other scholars discovered that the level of real welfare benefits were strongly related to the rate at which teenage girls produce out-of-wedlock children.[54] Though teenagers made up only a small part of the AFDC caseload, they stayed on AFDC much longer than others (on average, more than eight years), whereas women over the age of thirty spent much less time on welfare.

The most recent research suggests that welfare unquestionably makes a difference. But how big a difference? On that we are not certain. Robert Moffitt, an economist who wrote a 1992 review of the research, returned to the subject in 1998. He noted that the early studies found that welfare had little effect, but the most recent studies found that it had a significant one. But how big is the effect? On this there is no consensus.[55] This means two things: welfare as it has been administered hurts families, but it is not the only source of that hurt. And those findings imply a policy conclusion: families cannot be fixed just by fixing welfare.

Some of the differences in illegitimacy across states exists not because of what the states spend on welfare but because of the cultural characteristics of those states. David Ellwood and Mary Jo Bane,

---

*The chief personal trait Rosenzweig measured was the woman's intelligence. Less intelligent women, other things being equal, are more likely to have out-of-wedlock children.

who in 1985 were skeptical that AFDC made much of a difference in illegitimacy, nonetheless pointed out that how much money a state spends on welfare may also reflect its social attitudes. Minnesota, for example, has a strong Scandinavian tradition that encourages both strong family ties and generous welfare payments.[56] The number of unwed mothers raising children in Minnesota will thus be the joint result of its shared culture and its welfare payments. Perhaps in Minnesota the culture dominates the payments; perhaps in other states the payments are more important than the culture. How many fewer out-of-wedlock births and single-mother families would we get if the United States had a very different program, or even no welfare at all? Welfare laws are important because if they create out-of-wedlock births and single-mother families, then changing welfare policies can be revised in order to alter these problems. But this is only worth doing if we think a change will make a big difference.

One way to guess at the magnitude of the difference is to remember that for many decades we had welfare laws and no rapid increase in children living with unmarried mothers. Even in the late 1960s, when welfare rolls were rising rapidly, only about 69 percent of the people eligible to be on AFDC were in fact participating. In earlier years the participation rate was even lower.

Jobs and Stigma

There are two possible explanations for this. The first is that at one time the economy supplied sufficient jobs, especially for inner-city neighborhoods, so that men could afford to marry the women with whom they had produced a child. Now those jobs are gone, and so marriageable men—young men with a good job—are in short supply. The second is that the stigma associated with welfare has dissipated, leaving behind women who feel no shame in taking public funds to support themselves and their children.

The jobs argument seems to be more popular among liberals, stigma among conservatives. Of course, both may be true to some degree. Since the sex ratio is an important determinant of illegitimate births, something that reduces the number of available men even further should increase the illegitimacy rate. Sending men to prison in large numbers and making it hard for them to find jobs ought to affect the sex ratio. But there must be limits to this effect because, as we have seen in an earlier chapter, Mexican American immigrants, despite living in the same kinds of inner-city neighborhoods as do African Americans* and despite being even poorer, are much less likely to raise children in single-parent families or to apply for welfare.[57] Hispanics travel by bus to distant places to look for and hold jobs.

Other recent arrivals to our big cities show the same pattern. Since 1980, more than sixteen million immigrants, most of them poor and few knowing English, have entered the United States, many of them moving to inner-city neighborhoods. But the unemployment rate did not suddenly increase nor did their production of fatherless children soar.[58]

These impressions are reinforced by academic research. Christopher Jencks has studied the marriage behavior of mature black men with steady jobs. If jobs make a big difference, then black men who have jobs should not have experienced any large change in the chances of their getting married. But they did. In 1960, 80 percent of these men were married; by 1980, only 66 percent were.[59] Employed black men are marrying less often, not because black women are in short supply (on the contrary!) but because marriage has become a less desirable option for African Americans. Both black men and black women marry less often than they once did.

Everyone knows that mother-only families are more common among black than white Americans (though whites have been working hard to catch up!). The key question is whether for either of these groups the rate at which such families have formed is the result of a lack of jobs. The argument by William Julius Wilson that job shortage was the key factor has not stood up very well to empirical analysis.

---

*South Central Los Angeles was for decades the residential center of African Americans; many people still speak of it as if that remained true. But any visit will quickly reveal that Hispanic immigrants, mostly Mexicans, now live where blacks once lived.

Jencks found that the availability of employed black men old enough to be the husbands of young black women did not change during the 1960s. As a result, we cannot use employment as a way of explaining the sharp rise of black single-parent families in the 1960s. That availability did drop in the 1970s; by 1982, there were sixty-three employed black men aged twenty-five to forty-four for every one hundred black women in that age group (in 1970 there had been seventy men per hundred women). But this decline of 10 percent in employed black men is too small to account for the vastly larger increase in black mother-only families. And as we have already seen, between 1960 and 1980 marriage became less common for fully employed black men just as it did for black men of the same age who were not employed. There was a decline in potential available African American husbands not because their numbers dropped or jobs were harder to find but because fewer such men wanted to get married. Jencks sums up the issue precisely: "Marriage must . . . have been losing its charms for noneconomic reasons."[60]

Other scholars have come to much the same conclusion. Lawrence Mead doubts that the spatial mismatch of blacks and jobs is a main factor affecting employment.[61] Robert I. Lerman notes that the marriage rate of the best-off African American men—those with high earning and a college degree—dropped between 1973 and 1986 by about the same as it did among less educated black men earning less money.[62] William Julius Wilson, in his most recent writings, has acknowledged many of these criticisms of his older theory.[63] Something else is going on; the decline in marriage and the rise of unwed mothers cannot chiefly, if at all, be explained by jobs.

The problem is not a recent one. The low level of black marriage in 1950 was not much different from what it had been in the 1930s. Anyone reading *Black Metropolis*, the magnificent account of African American life in Chicago during the Great Depression, will find a portrayal of family life that reads very much like Elijah Anderson's account of Philadelphia in the 1990s. St. Clair Drake and Horace Cayton wrote of the "social disorganization" of the South Side of Chicago, with high rates of black illegitimacy, divorce, and criminality.[64] Their explanation accords in part with William J. Wilson's, but by taking a longer perspective they make it clearer what may have happened. When they wrote, slavery had only been abolished for eighty years, and so blacks lived in a world where they were the last hired and the first fired. Jobs made a difference when their absence was the still-current legacy of slavery. The combination of that legacy with modern discrimination made the world of black men unstable and thus made them poor risks for women who, working as house maids, often brought home steady incomes. The aversion to marriage may reflect more a culture that was spawned by living an economically ambiguous life than it does a mere shortage of jobs at one historical moment. The history of black single-parent families is so long in this country that it cannot possibly be explained by the current distribution of manufacturing jobs, even though some recent changes may have intensified the problem.

Despite the lack of much empirical support, the job explanation is offered by Elijah Anderson to explain street life among blacks in Philadelphia, but this explanation does little to mar an insightful and revealing portrayal. His years of observing both decent homes and street families left him with this story: To boys on the street, sex is a symbol of social status, and sexual conquests are notches in their belt. Sex is prized, not as a testament of love, but as testimony of the boy's ability to control another person. Boys try to talk girls into sex; their skill at doing this gives them status with their peers. If the girl gets pregnant, the boy is under little pressure to admit it, has little interest in "taking care of somebody else," and values his street reputation as a smooth hustler. The girls may wish a husband, but they are under little pressure to insist upon it unless they live at home with a "decent daddy" who will control their access to boys and insist that the boy do right by them. Without such a father, the girl often lives in an "unprotected nest." For them, welfare offered a means of support.[65]

It is hard to imagine that so self-oriented a pattern of life among this small fraction of one ethnic minority could result entirely or even chiefly from a recent drop in the number of jobs located in the center of a few large cities, especially when the pattern had been found in Chicago in the 1930s and it has of late been duplicated by more and

more white men who never faced a racial barrier to getting a job and
could readily move to wherever jobs may be found.

The non-job explanation is culture. For a variety of reasons, single-
parent families were no longer anathema, and being on welfare no
longer carried a stigma. A lot more people today than previously are
willing to give birth to a child without getting married and raise it
alone at public expense. The stigma attached to dependency for a long
time kept people from "being on the dole." But for a variety of reasons that changed. The National Welfare Rights Organization
(NWRO) was created in part to get people to participate in AFDC
more. Its strategy was to persuade people to abandon any sense of
shame in hopes that by flooding the AFDC offices with so many applicants the program would collapse. Then, somehow, the government
would abandon its alleged belief that poverty was useful to the economy and replace AFDC with a guaranteed minimum income for
everyone.[66] The gamble did not pay off; AFDC grew, but no guaranteed income followed. The NWRO helped bring about the defeat of
its own policy when it fought against President Nixon's 1969–71
effort to create a guaranteed annual income. NWRO said that the
income proposed was too small, but of course it forgot (or pretended
to forget) that every government benefit tends to grow. Daniel Patrick
Moynihan, who talked Nixon into supporting the guaranteed income,
later explained the self-destructive policy of NWRO by pointing out
that its organizational interests—the desire to appear strong by
harassing public officials—was at war with its own policy objec-
tives.[67] The political left wanted a radical change in society; the political right worried about giving money to unwed mothers; the political
center collapsed. Nothing happened.

But whatever the failure of NWRO and the effort to create a guaranteed income, the courts were steadily working to ensure that welfare would become a "right." When Alabama tried to deny AFDC to
a woman who was living with a man who was not her husband, the
Supreme Court overturned the regulation, holding that the woman
must be paid no matter with whom she was living. When Alabama
argued that doing this would encourage immorality, the Court
responded by saying that immorality was an outdated notion; it might

have been relevant to welfare once, but it was not now. The states have no right to limit welfare to a "worthy person" because welfare is designed to help the child, not reform the mother.[68] The old standard of the mothers' pension movement—aid to any morally fit woman without a husband—had been shattered. The morality of the mother no longer counted because welfare was meant to aid children whatever their mother was like. In later decisions the Court also told states they could not employ residency requirements for AFDC and that any person facing the loss of an AFDC benefit was entitled to a full legal hearing.[69]

Welfare activists and a Supreme Court majority completed the revolution in how we think about people. Families do not matter, only individuals count. We may want to limit benefits to women without adequate male help, but we cannot; if a man is there but he is not the child's father, the woman gets the benefit anyway. And when the government gives a benefit, it creates a right to it that will enjoy constitutional protection. In about a half century, most of the assumptions on which mothers' pensions had been founded had flown out the window. We started by asserting that the government ought to help families; we ended by saying that families don't matter.

The result was clear. The proportion of people eligible for welfare who actually took advantage of it increased from 63 percent in 1967 to 91 percent in 1970.[70] This may be the best possible measure of the effect of the sixties: it produced a sharp decline in welfare stigma. And it may also show the limitation of that effect: nearly two-thirds of the eligible people were already on welfare before the sixties had run their course.

The chief transformation that occurred in welfare dependency has been the decline in stigma. Many studies have shown that a lot of people think that being on welfare is shameful,[71] but the number is much smaller today than it once was. Robert Moffitt has even devised and measured a model of stigma to help explain the growth in the use of AFDC.[72] The impact of stigma can be seen by comparing how ready people in different neighborhoods are to leave AFDC. Those in rural communities leave much sooner than do those in urban ones even after controlling for the race of the respondents and the size of their families. For blacks and whites alike, living in a rural community makes you feel the stigma of welfare more keenly and with greater effect than is the case for similar people in cities.[73]

The comments people make in small and large towns reflect this difference. In a rural community everyone knew who was on welfare: the AFDC office was in public view and there were not many other recipients with whom an AFDC mother could associate. One small-town recipient said they called us "welfare cattle"; another remarked that "I always felt like I was bein' watched"; a third said that her neighbors made "nasty comments." But in a big city, everybody a recipient knows is "in the same boat I am" and so they "don't look down on you." Friends even urged women in the big city to get on welfare so they could get some help.[74] And in urban neighborhoods where the majority of the mothers are without husbands, it is hard to imagine how stigma could operate at all.

For African American women, stigma may have been easier to overcome. For centuries they had special problems with African American men: loose sexuality, migrant labor, unrewarding farm tenancy, and familial abuse unchallenged by a white legal system. Once welfare became available without the early restrictions imposed by the mothers' pension movement, black women could take advantage of it as a way out of a historical trap: have children (which almost all wanted) without a husband (which some no longer wanted). To some African American women, welfare offered an escape.

The contemporary willingness to abandon stigma has one obvious reason and perhaps other not-so-obvious ones. The obvious reason is that no one should punish an innocent child for the errors of her mother. The not-so-obvious ones are that it is wrong to criticize the sexual behavior of people, and any kind of family is as good as any other. A good example of this can be found in England, where the National Council for the Unmarried Mother and Her Child (now renamed the National Council for One-Parent Families) has worked since its founding in 1918 to improve the lot of out-of-wedlock children. It has done many commendable things, such as helping create homes for these children and endeavoring to compel absent fathers to pay for their support. But in addition the state has passed new laws that have gone even further. Tax allowances designed for divorced mothers are now available for unwed ones and children's allowances are provided to the first child in any one-parent family just as they long have been for two-parent ones. Fathers are no longer required to be present at the registration of their children's birth. The National Health Service in England made better medical care available for these children, and a series of new laws made it easier to conceal illegitimacy.

The council has worked to eliminate hostility toward unmarried mothers and to get the public to stop using language that is pejorative about illegitimacy. When asked whether doing this would undermine the marriage bond, the council replied that "experience in other countries" shows that this cultural change will produce a "decline in illegitimacy." This was a bad prediction. The number of single-parent families in England rose dramatically. As one author put it, the council's efforts to get rid of "the old forces of shame and disgrace," though they have ensured that that sins of parents would not be visited upon their children, have also made it "easier for parents to commit those sins without much fear of the consequences."[75] One sign that stigma has dropped has been how our language has changed. Proper people, we are told, no longer refer to the child of an unwed mother as illegitimate; we should now refer to them as out-of-wedlock. These changes create a dilemma for society: how can it free children from stigma without freeing prospective parents from it as well? We do not know the answer.

The Shotgun Marriage

When I was growing up in California, many unmarried high school girls became pregnant. But in those days, the girl had only three choices: make the boy marry her, put the child up for adoption, or move to the Midwest and let her aunt or grandmother raise the baby. And the boy had only two choices: marry the girl or hope he could enlist in the navy in order to get out of town before the girl's angry father and brothers caught up with him.

Three economists led by George Akerlof have estimated that if unwed but pregnant girls in the mid-1980s had gotten married at the same rate they did twenty years earlier, then most of the increase in (first-child) illegitimate births would have disappeared. To be exact, the increase in such births among whites would have been only one-quarter as high, and that among African Americans would have been only two-fifths as high as it has in fact been.[76] The decline in shotgun marriages—a decline that reflected the evaporation of the stigma once associated with having a fatherless child—must explain a good part of the current level of mother-only families. Welfare rates may have played a role, the shortage of jobs might have played a small role, but the drop in stigma played the largest one.

Why did stigma decline? Akerlof and his associates suggest that technology made the difference. The advent of legalized abortion and the birth-control pill corresponded to the decline in the shame attached to raising a fatherless child. These devices helped emancipate men from marital obligations because now the woman alone could manage the consequences of her sexuality by either preventing or ending a pregnancy.

No doubt abortions and the pill have made a difference. But there remain some puzzling facts. Adoptions have also decreased so that unmarried women are now keeping children that once would have been sent to a new family. Akerlof and his colleagues estimate that in 1969, before the impact of new technology was felt, unwed mothers kept and raised about one-fourth of their newborn children; many of the rest were put up for adoption. By 1984, however, the fraction of children kept by unwed mothers had doubled, and the number put up for adoption had fallen.[77] Unwed teenage mothers have become *less* interested in abortion. Among teenage women who had an unwanted pregnancy, the proportion that ended in an abortion fell from 53 percent in 1981 to 45 percent in 1994, a drop of about 15 percent.[78]

Technology cannot explain this. Despite the pill, the girl got pregnant; despite abortion, she had the child. But now she was more likely to keep it. Why? One explanation is that abortions eliminated unwanted children so that what remained were children the mother wanted. But the reduction in adoption seems to imply more than this; it suggests that keeping a child without a husband entails no major social costs.

And if the pill and abortions helped men avoid marriage, one still must wonder why it helped white and African American families and not Hispanic or Asian ones. Though they are very poor, inner-city Mexican fathers are more than twice as likely to marry the mother of their child than are black ones. William Julius Wilson, whose own theory on job mismatch has not prevented him from finding and confronting new facts, acknowledges this. Culture matters. Mexican immigrants arrive with a "clear conception of a traditional family unit that features men as breadwinners." If one of these men deserts a pregnant woman, shame descends upon him.[79]

Mexicans are not alone in this regard. When they come to America as first-generation immigrants, people from China, Indonesia, Korea, Laos, Taiwan, and Thailand all have a smaller proportion of their children living in one-parent families than do white, non-Hispanic Americans who have lived here for three generations or more.[80]

When Mexican children arrive in the United States, they are more likely to be in two-parent families than native-born, white non-Hispanics. But slowly that pattern begins to change. Third-generation Mexican-American children (that is, children born in this country to parents who were also born here) begin living with an unmarried parent and take welfare payments even though the proportion of them who are poor has been cut in half and the fraction who are high school graduates has more than doubled. Even though third-generation Mexican-Americans are less likely to be on welfare than are Puerto Ricans and African Americans, being in America has done something to them: living here has changed their culture.[81]

Finally, the technological changes had an odd effect. The people who first took advantage of them were middle- and upper-middle-class women. Even before the Supreme Court decided *Roe* v. *Wade*, abortions were legal in New York and some other states and abroad in countries such as Sweden. Only affluent people could take easy advantage of these opportunities. But the growth in single-parent homes has been most rapid among the poorest women, those who would have been the slowest to buy birth-control pills or search out abortion opportunities. Why did technology work its way up rather than down the income hierarchy?[82]

Though single-mother families are disproportionately headed by relatively poor women, they have become increasingly common among more affluent ones. One was the heroine of a television series, *Murphy Brown*. To the latter, welfare payments are irrelevant. What is not irrelevant is stigma. And that has largely disappeared, as is evident from the wide tolerance young people have for being a single mom. This change raises another problem: if illegitimacy is much more common among poor people than among rich ones, and if stigma declined more among affluent than ordinary people, why did this decline in stigma affect poor people much more than affluent ones? This is a matter about which I shall offer some speculations in chapter 8.

Even though the process by which a loss of stigma affected women is hard to grasp, the reason stigma declined is easily stated. It was the result of the Enlightenment, good health, and modern technology. The Enlightenment made us preoccupied with individual rights and more restless with collective obligations; more interested in contract rather than in status; more ready to search for self-expression than to accept joint endeavors. It only slowly and gradually affected marriage, but once the genie of individual rights was out of the bottle there was no way it could either be put back in or be kept from influencing sex and marriage.

Good health increased the supply of women and decreased the need for many babies. Women gained as modern medicine almost eliminated deaths from childbirth, but what was good for women as individuals may have hurt them as a group. Women survived childbirth and lived longer, but this meant that the number of women grew relative to the number of men. This change in the sex ratio reduced the extent to which scarce women could negotiate with many men the terms of their sexual relationship. As their numbers grew to equal or surpass those of men, they collectively lost some bargaining power; this meant that fewer and fewer could insist on marriage as the price of sex. The health of their children also improved, and so fewer and fewer families felt they had to produce another child every two years.

At one time a woman might have wanted three children but had to give birth to six to allow for the high infant death rate. Now if she wants three, or two, or one, that can be planned in advance using birth-control pills (and in some cases, abortions) with almost no risk of losing any babies to illness. This means that women need be pregnant less often than once was the case, and that fact, coupled with modern technology that makes running a home a part-time job, frees up women to spend more time getting an education and pursuing a career. In a later chapter we shall consider what effect, if any, the rise of female careers has had on the family.

But just how did the reduction in stigma play itself out in our society? Did affluent people, keenly aware of the spread of Enlightenment ideas, abandon the stigma and then somehow teach this lesson to poorer people so that they could incorporate its lessons into their own lives? This is not inconceivable; recall how heroin and cocaine were first taken up by affluent experimenters whose casual habits were then converted into a life-destructive addiction by people too poor to afford any psychiatric or medical help for ending their dependence. Or did the pressures to resist marriage that may have always been felt by poor people—precisely because they were poor and therefore found marriage to be an expensive proposition—erupt into producing babies without marriage as soon as society, without intending to do so, created a payment system that made it possible? I do not know the answers to these questions, but I shall offer some speculations in the final chapter.

Chapter 7
Divorce

Between 1870 and 1950, the rate at which marriages led to divorces increased by a factor of nearly seven.[1] Some of the upsurge around 1950 was the result of the breakup of wartime marriages, many made in haste and a few compromised by the husband's absence during the war, but even so, the increase from 1870 to 1950 was a smooth one, with the rate doubling between 1870 and 1890 and doubling again between 1890 and 1920. But until recent times, divorce was regarded as either a tragedy or a disgrace. A few people spoke out in favor of easy divorces—Katherine Gernould wrote in 1923 that "if you make it possible to marry at sight, you ought to make it possible to divorce on demand,"[2]—but most people were shocked by such sentiments. They were embarrassed by divorce, and politicians worried about revealing their own.

Between 1960 and 1985, the divorce rate doubled again so that roughly half of all marriages would now end in court, but by 1985 it was no longer regarded as a shame. In 1966 as in 1945, most people thought the divorce laws in their states were not strict enough. In 1962, half of the women interviewed by the University of Michigan agreed with the view that when there are children in the family, parents should stay together even if they don't get along. But by 1977, most women disagreed with that statement, and by 1985 the number who disagreed with that view had risen to 82 percent.[3]

Divorce has become more common since the mid-nineteenth century, but the support for divorce has developed, insofar as we can tell, only since the 1970s. And it was during this later period that laws governing divorce became much more permissive. These new laws are associated with—and as I shall argue later in this chapter, in part caused—higher divorce rates. The statutes cemented a radical change in how we conceive of marriage. Today blame has largely disappeared not only from public opinion but from the statute books. If one member of a married couple is adulterous, he or she suffers no penalty. Each is equally entitled to seek a divorce, and, in most states, each is equally entitled to a share in the property, the right to have custody of the children, and the right to alimony. Indeed, "alimony" has in most places been replaced by the phrase "spousal support" and given, not until the recipient marries again, but only for a few years until she has (theoretically) become self-sufficient. Nor must it be a "she" that gets the payment. If the husband is dependent on the wife's earnings, he is entitled to spousal support. The new standard for a no-fault divorce is that an "irreparable breakdown" has occurred. Virtually every state has either a simple no-fault statute or a combination of no-fault together with other, older standards, leaving it up the couple to decide which standard to use.

The new laws replaced older and much tougher standards. In New York, adultery was the only grounds for divorce until the mid-1960s. The law was written by Alexander Hamilton in 1787 in order to provide a way for courts to authorize a divorce; without that law, divorce was only possible by an act of the legislature. For nearly one hundred and eighty years New Yorkers lived under a law that made an honest divorce next to impossible save for a few adulterers. As someone said,

there were two grounds for a New York divorce—adultery and perjury. California had a looser law, one that allowed divorce for cruelty
or desertion as well as adultery. But in both states these laws had one
thing in common: if a couple wanted a divorce but neither party had
been adulterous or cruel, the husband and wife, coached by their
attorneys, had either to lie or go to Nevada and wait out the six-week
residency period.

Since high rates of divorce are in part the result of the passage of
no-fault divorce laws, surely explaining these laws, and thus
explaining the divorce rate, would be simpler than explaining illegitimacy. Moreover divorce affects every part of society whereas out-
of-wedlock births disproportionately (but not exclusively) affect the
poor. And explaining divorce ought to be easy. The first no-fault
divorce law was passed in 1969 in California. It requires no deep or
original insights to imagine the story. The sixties did it, and, naturally,
in California first. The Left Coast, the place where all fads begin,
responded to the demands of feminists, activists of many hues, and an
emancipated public by making it easy for people to get out of a marriage. Soon the rest of the country followed suit, putting in place a
nationwide system of easy divorce to reflect the new, self-indulgent
tint of our sixties culture.

There is only one problem with this theory. It is not true. No-fault
divorce snuck up upon us when, almost literally, no one was watching.
Herbert Jacob, a political scientist who has studied the development of
the new laws with great care, found that this revolution in divorce came
about without a trumpet being sounded, a protest march being organized, or a loud voice heard. At a time when the country was convulsed
with Vietnam, Watergate, abortion, and the Equal Rights Amendment,
nobody paid any attention to the divorce laws. "No party platform or
social protest spurred legislators. . . . Neither national politicians nor
Congress played a part in their adoption. No bureaucracy or interest
group promoted them. Little political conflict accompanied them."[4]
Feminists gave it hardly any notice, and antifeminists gave it less.
There was no organized movement. Whatever the sixties did, it is hard
to find much evidence that they created the divorce revolution.

Feminists did have an indirect effect on divorce. As Jacob notes, their commitment to male and female equality reinforced the drift of public and especially elite sentiment in that direction. Under the rule of sexual equality it seemed only plausible to allow individual men and women to choose to be married or, if married, to separate. Allowing divorce only for cause implied that somebody knew better than the couple whether they should stay together, and in an enlightened society surely no one other than the husband and wife had that knowledge.

The divorce revolution was produced by a quiet group of lawyers, judges, and legislators who calmly worked out, without much controversy, the logical implications of the steadily growing view that men and women were legally and morally equal, that a marriage was not a sacrament but a contract, and that this agreement ought to reflect and reinforce the equality of its members. If this could be done, it would save lawyers and judges a lot of effort. There would no longer be any need to prove that one person wronged another on some narrow ground such as adultery or neglect; the marriage could end whenever its members felt they had irreconcilable differences.

In so doing, the reformers put into law what many judges had created when no one was looking. Mary Ann Glendon notes that by the 1960s, at least 90 percent of all American divorces were uncontested even though they were sought under statutes that required fault to be shown.[5] The reformers saw their job as getting the law to catch up with judicial practice.

Jacob calls what happened an example of routine policy making in which things proceed quietly, no one gets excited, and interest groups are irrelevant. Quiet and unexcited, to be sure, but also a bit misleading. To help prevent people from objecting, many divorce reformers were less than candid about what they were doing. They were inclined to convey their radical proposal in conservative language. In California, a reform commission wrote that the new no-fault law "does not permit divorce by consent, wherein marriage is treated as wholly a private contract terminable at the pleasure of the parties. . . ."[6] Nonsense. That is exactly what the new law did.

In part because an attachment to marriage lingered in their minds, in part because they saw marriage more in psychological than legal terms, and in part because they hoped to disarm potential critics of no-fault divorce, many reformers persuaded states to pass laws that required conciliation before the divorce could take effect. But conciliation never amounted to much; getting out of the marriage turned out to be all that people seemed to want.[7] Perhaps, as Jacob suggests, divorce was part of the therapeutic culture in which family breakdown was no longer seen in moral terms but only in psychological ones. If people who married were immature, had made a bad choice, or suffered from personal maladjustment, what they most needed was an easy out and a chance to start a new life.

Getting the no-fault laws through state legislatures turned out to be remarkably easy. In the lead states, the reformers were aided by an important political fact: the governors of California and New York, Ronald Reagan and Nelson Rockefeller, had both been divorced. They signed the new bills with hardly a quibble. Harder to explain is that the Catholic Church failed to object. To the Church, marriage is a sacrament and divorce is wrong. The Church had modified its view (and sometimes in practice corrupted the administration) of annulment, but it had never approved of divorce. And yet the Church was silent. One explanation is that Catholic bishops, believing that marriage is indissoluble whatever the civil law may say, mistakenly supposed that changes in that law would not affect Catholics' practices. They were wrong. Another explanation is that, as Jacob notes, divorce laws were being debated at the same time as abortion, and the latter issue galvanized the Church.[8] I would add, however, an important qualification to his view. Divorce laws have been passed in Italy, Spain, and Portugal, all Catholic countries and none obsessed with abortion rulings because in none did the courts try to impose them.

A major reason for the failure of no-fault divorces to reduce the divorce rate was that many of the authors of the no-fault divorce laws were conservatives who, aware that a right to divorce had trumped religious constraints on it, believed that modern therapy and marriage counseling could supply what sacraments once provided—a support for troubled marriages. The secular right to divorce had won out by the end of World War I; from then on, the only question was whether couples could be persuaded not to exercise that right.[9]

The pro-marriage reformers gambled that eliminating all fault-based grounds for divorce would lure "divorce-minded couples to submit to a reconciliation-minded social welfare establishment."[10] It was a gamble they lost. They had supposed that divorce seekers were immature, selfish, or sick and could be cured by therapy. Couples could have a no-fault divorce if, in exchange, they underwent pre-divorce counseling. Instead, California (like other states) showed no interest in paying for expensive therapy sessions, the divorce courts had little interest in enforcing a therapy order, psychiatrists said they were not inclined to supply court-ordered therapy, and the divorce-seeking couples had even less interest in enduring such treatment. Seven years after California adopted no-fault divorce, not a single divorce petition had been denied.[11]

What Happens to the Children?

By the time Glendon wrote about divorce in 1989, one spouse could terminate a marriage without the other spouse's fault or consent in forty-one American states.[12] The attorneys who designed these laws attended to the preferences of judges, a desire for legal clarity, and the reduction of perjury, but not, insofar as I can tell, to the needs of children. Child *custody* was, of course, a major concern, but not child *welfare*.

The custody of children had already gone through an extraordinary change. Until the mid-nineteenth century, American law was like English law: the child belonged to the father. He not only owned the family's income and property, he owned its offspring. Then over the course of the next century, with fathers working outside the home and the needs of working women coming to the fore, state after state allowed the mother custody. She was seen as the natural guardian of the child, suitable by temperament and experience to managing children. By the time the modern revolution in divorce law occurred, the courts changed again, now giving chief emphasis to the "best interests of the child," a rule that could allow either the father or the mother to have custody. The principle was that each young child went through "tender years" that must be aided by giving custody to whichever parent was most likely to be helpful. Today a new standard has emerged, joint custody.[13] If you believe that husbands and wives are equal, if you ignore who is to blame for the divorce, if you are prepared to divide marital property more or less equally, then allowing the mother and father to take turns having custody of the child seems to make sense. Under the maternal custody rule, the mother always got the child; under the "best interests of the child," the mother usually got the child. The joint custody rule allowed fathers to lobby for more custody rights and often to get them.

The custody issue divided scholars. Some argued that the child was better off being always with one parent (it could be either, but practice suggested it would usually be the mother). Others rejoined that joint custody created no problems and was fairer to both parents.[14] California passed a joint-custody law in 1979, and several other states followed suit. In practice, however, the best-interests rules still dominate, as mothers usually get custody but with an agreement for paternal visits and limited control.

The test of any rule ought to be what most benefits the child. The child is the one actor in the divorce drama who has neither a vote nor a lawyer, and it is his or her character that is as yet unformed. And there are many such children, perhaps one million a year who are involved in a divorce.

The central question is how great a risk divorce poses for children. You might think that by now scholars would have come to some agreement on a matter of considerable national importance, but in fact there are two schools of thought. The first is that whatever harms befall children, it is not the result of the divorce but of the conflict between the parents before they divorced. The second view is that divorce harms children independently of predivorce conflict and the harm lasts a long time. The implication of the first view is that divorce is not the chief cause of any psychological harm and in fact may constitute a cure for it; the implication of the second is that society ought to do whatever it can to cut back on the rate of divorce. Of course, many scholars think that both forces are at work and they quarrel only over the emphasis that should be given to each. Let me guide you through a few of the leading studies and then suggest that the second view is gaining the upper hand.

The first view initially rested on the confident predictions by counselors and therapists that divorce was a way of solving marital problems and even liberating the child from parental tension. In fact, a divorce may make children more tolerant of others with an accompanying increase in cooperation and respect. And even if the child is hurt by the divorce, the hurt will last only briefly, especially if the financial loss to the mother and child can be set right.[15] This claim about the advantages of divorce meant that its advocates, in Barbara Dafoe Whitehead's words, had "shifted the weight of expert opinion from protecting the interests of children to defending the rights and prerogatives of parents to pursue their own satisfactions."[16]

The most influential writings about divorce asserted that it was marital conflict, not divorce itself, that hurt the child; divorce added little lasting burden to this problem. Frank Furstenberg and Andrew Cherlin, two distinguished students of family life, argued in 1991 that long-term studies of children showed that their problems mostly arose from marital discord. A minority of them might be hurt by divorce, but it was only a minority; children differ greatly, and most adjust reasonably well to parental breakup. And when the mother remarried and the children acquired a stepfather, most seemed to do quite well.[17]

Cherlin repeated this view the following year. Some studies, he said, showed that divorce can be beneficial in the long run for some children because it takes them out of a conflict-ridden family. At the same time, he noted, it can impose serious psychological distress on other children, but fortunately this tended to last only a short time.[18] In part this happens because most divorced parents remarry.

This is a remarkable argument, for it suggests one or both of two implausible views. One is that children can be raised as well by a mother as by a mother and father. Since the great majority of children live with the divorced mother rather than with the father, lacking a father does not make much of a difference. And they indeed lack a father: "The vast majority of children [of divorced parents] will have little or no contact with their fathers."[19] David Popenoe notes that more than half of all adolescent children living with separated or divorced mothers had not seen their fathers in over a year; only one-seventh saw them as often as once a week.[20]

The weight of scientific evidence seems clearly to support the view that fathers matter. We have already seen that children in mother-only families are worse off, even after controlling for income, than are those in two-parent ones. Matters may be better among the most affluent single moms, but most mothers will suffer a significant loss in income after they divorce and at a minimum expose their children to frequent relocations. One study found that the standard of living of a divorced woman fell by 27 percent whereas that of a divorced man increased by 10 percent.[21] Glendon has argued that the United States appears unique among Western countries in failing to assure either public or private responsibility for "the economic casualties of divorce." We have, she suggests, "no-fault, no-responsibility divorce."[22] School-age children who have a father do better than those without one in cognitive development, academic achievement, and impulse control.[23] Of course, an inattentive father at home can produce some of the same effects, but father absence, owing to a divorce, almost guarantees inattention.

Of course, many divorced women remarry, taking their children with them. If that happens, we come to the second argument: stepfathers will do as well as biological ones in raising children. If the first argument is true, then marriage itself is a questionable venture, since fathers are not really necessary beyond providing sperm and money. If the second argument is true, then all of the stories we have heard about wicked stepfathers must be no more than fiction designed to frighten but not teach its readers. Those who deny that divorce is very harmful may be right, but they have a steep hurdle to overcome.

Earlier in this book we noted that the rate at which children are abused or killed is vastly higher when they live with stepfathers rather than their biological ones. (Nine out of ten stepchildren live with a stepfather and their biological mother.) To repeat: preschool children living with a stepfather were forty times more likely than those living with their biological parents to become the victims of child abuse and seventy to one hundred times more likely to be murdered by the step-parent.[24] Though there are many caring and devoted stepfathers, on average they create a much greater risk not only for abuse but for inattention and emotional distance. They do not watch, monitor, and control their children as much as do parents who are genetically connected to their offspring. In their careful study of stepfamilies, Sarah McLanahan and Gary Sandefur show that, even after controlling for family income, children with a stepparent are more likely than those living with both biological parents to drop out of high school; female children are more likely to become teen moms and male children more likely to be idle.[25]

Some scholars had reached a view different from that of Cherlin and Furstenberg. In a long follow-up of divorced children, Judith S. Wallerstein and various coauthors found that divorce is a long-lasting and wrenching experience for many of them. Almost half entered adulthood as "worried, underachieving, self-deprecating, and sometimes angry young men and women."[26] Boys had a tougher time than girls and that adolescence was a worse time for divorce than childhood. But these findings were dismissed by their critics on the grounds that Wallerstein had found the families they studied from among the ranks of people who had sought marriage counseling, suggesting that they represented, not the universe of all divorced families, but those that had particular psychological problems. The authors, by contrast, had claimed that their families were middle-class people who had not sought psychological help (other than marital advice). Though they were initially praised, the Wallerstein books were soon criticized by journalists writing on behalf of a culture that had come to see divorce as a rational way to dissolve the marriage contract. And, in fact, it is hard to know just how representative were the families that Wallerstein studied. We know they were middle-class people from around San Francisco, but the authors seem to have taken volunteers that (except for having weeded out children in psychological distress) may or may not have been typical of families undergoing a divorce.

The disagreement between Cherlin and his colleagues with Wallerstein and hers was overstated by many observers. The former found some children who were hurt by divorce, the latter found some who were helped by divorce. It was a question of numbers. What proportion suffered long-term problems? The former said that "a substantial portion" of boys' problems preceded the divorce and that perhaps only 6 to 9 percent of their postdivorce problems were caused by the divorce itself. The latter said that about 30 percent of both boys and girls had serious postdivorce problems. Though the differences might strike you as modest, they carried a lot of weight. If only 6 to 9 percent of the children had lasting problems, divorce seemed like a good bet for many people, but if 30 percent or more were made worse, the odds had shifted dramatically against you.[27]

The most recent data tend to lean more in the direction of Wallerstein. In 1997, when some scholars compared teenagers living in intact, divorced, and about-to-be-divorced families, they found that divorce was much more important than marital discord in explaining difficulties in adolescent adjustment. Earlier views that children are already unhappy in families that later divorced, the authors wrote, must be modified.[28] Another study published at about the same time came to much the same conclusion. This group discovered that adolescents in divorced families are much more likely to become delinquent, engage in early sex, and suffer from depression than those living in intact families, even after taking into account the quality of the parents' marriage.[29] But the most important study was done by Cherlin himself. In 1998 he and his colleagues published a new study of divorce in Great Britain in which they measured its long-term effects on the mental health of children. Some of the adverse effects were, as they had suggested some years earlier, the result of marital discord or other things not involving divorce. But now they added that divorce itself is harmful. Their earlier views "should be modified," a commendable and wholly scholarly attitude toward how one expresses new and unexpected findings.[30] Not so commendable was much of the national press that gave great publicity to his earlier view that marital conflict was much more important than divorce and next to no coverage to his later view that divorce itself is a large problem.

Cherlin's new findings were reinforced by a study done by Paul R. Amato and Alan Booth. They interviewed more than two thousand married people several times between 1980 and 1992 and their children in 1992 and 1995. They looked at how happy or discordant the marriages were and studied the couples who later got divorced, and they related all of this to how well the children fared. Their findings make it clear that both discord and divorce make a difference. Not only does a lousy marriage produce unhappy children, so does a divorce. Both forces operate: "Low parental marital quality lowers offspring well-being, and parental divorce lowers it even further."[31] But what is most worrisome about these results is that most divorces do not result from conflict-ridden marriages. Only about one-third of all divorced couples reported any prior abuse, frequent arguments, or serious quarrels. But they got divorced anyway. As the authors put it, "People are leaving marriages at lower thresholds of unhappiness now than in the past."[32] For the children of these marriages, the divorce alone was the chief source of harm.[33]

This conclusion ought to be unsettling to those who see divorce in purely legal terms. Max Rheinstein argued that none of the harms to marriage are produced by divorce because an unhappy family will find one way or another, such as separations, formal or informal, to cope with that distress. Divorce, he argued, was merely a legal device, a decree of a court, that gives public recognition to an established social fact.[34] I think he was mistaken. While it is true that a divorce decree is a legal formality, its significance does not end with the document. The decree sets aside a lifetime commitment on the basis of which two people have managed their emotions, attachments, income, property, and children. When people believe that commitment, they behave differently than when they doubt it. As we have seen, married couples share income and wealth more readily than do cohabiting ones because they assume that their relationship is permanent. Suppose divorce is very difficult. That provides a constraint on your freedom of action so that you will take a different view of your spouse's faults than you will if the law makes divorce very easy. That constraint will, at the margin, lead many people to stick it out by coping with their spouses and helping their children. Marriage is a commitment that alters how people evaluate each other.

If you think divorce is difficult and wrong, you stick together for "the sake of the children." If you think divorce is easy and acceptable, you break apart for the sake of yourselves. There is some evidence that supports this view. "There is no such thing as a nice divorce," a character in a Hollywood movie once said, and by and large he is right. The divorce may occur for very good reasons—perhaps infidelity or abuse—but the wrangling over the children is still likely to be intense. When two scholars studied forty-four elementary schoolchildren who had lived with contentious parents, each parent tried to mobilize the child against the former spouse after the divorce. Three children were in their mothers' cars when the raging women rammed their ex-husbands' cars, with an injury to at least one child. One was in her mother's car when the ex-husband threw a piece of furniture that broke the windshield. And even when there was no violence, the children were often mobilized in a tug-of-war between two angry parents, with angry speeches, denials of visiting rights, and hiding (or even kidnapping) a child to keep him or her away from the former spouse.[35]

Obviously, some married couples should get a divorce, even if a child feels hurt. And just as obviously, some children, distressed by long periods of parental conflict, will feel better after the divorce occurs. But just as obviously, many children will be hurt by a divorce, with the hurt lasting for many years. Some intact families hurt children through discord, some divorced families hurt children by separating, and some families do both. The problem is to find, somehow, the optimum number of divorces. It surely will be greater than zero and probably lower than what it is today. The optimum number, one that nobody can calculate, would look like this: It would be high enough to permit the correction of a serious mistake but low enough so as not to encourage couples to think that they have made only a weak commitment. A weak commitment destroys the idea of marriage by leading people to think that tough but manageable problems need not be addressed.

The optimum number is not the one we have now. Suppose that divorce meant only that bad marriages were ended by rational people who realized they had made a mistake. If that were true, then our rising level of divorce would simply mean that a lot of couples once made a mistake. As a result of increasingly easy access to divorce, the surviving marriages would be happier; all the unhappy ones would have ended. But that is not the case. When Norval Glenn looked at poll data that asked how happy people were in their marriages, he found that between 1973 and 1988 they had become less happy. This was true not only of people whose marriages ended in divorce but of those who had never divorced. Marriage has become less of a route to personal happiness; the reason, Glenn suggests, is that there has been a "decline in the ideal of marital permanence." When people vow at their weddings to live together "till death do us part" or "as long as we both shall live," they really only promise to remain a couple "as long as we both shall love" or "as long as no one better comes along."[36]

Other evidence supports this view. When two sociologists looked at more than two thousand married persons over an eight-year period, they found that their attitudes toward divorce affected how happy they were. Those who believed that an unrewarding marriage could readily be jettisoned led many couples to invest less time and effort in their marriages and work less at resolving marital disagreements.[37] As some of these people acquired more favorable attitudes toward divorce, their level of marital happiness declined. The reverse—less marital happiness producing more favorable attitudes toward divorce—was also true, but to a lesser extent. Both processes were at work, but the first—an increased acceptance of the value of divorce causing less marital happiness—was the more powerful one.

The problem of easy marriage is most acute for fathers. In an earlier chapter we saw that human evolution created a relatively weak link between man and woman. Men can sow their seeds widely, but women are bound by pregnancy; fathers can in many places legally acquire other wives, but mothers can never acquire additional husbands; men may value their children, but women usually raise them. When a divorce occurs, the mother usually gets the children and the father often ends contact with them. Marriage is a cultural contrivance designed to prevent weak paternal roles. Looser bonds of marriage weaken those roles because in very few divorces does the father maintain a close contact with his children. "The responsibilities of fathers are carried from one household to the next as they migrate from one marriage to the next."[38] What millennia of human experience taught has now been greatly eroded, a testimony to both the cultural foundations of marriage and the capacity of humans to undo their most important arrangements.

The Effect of Divorce Laws

When easier divorce laws came to the Western world, and especially to the United States, many scholars thought they would make little difference. Max Rheinstein, for years a powerful legal thinker at the University of Chicago Law School, said in 1972 that he could find no connection between the leniency of divorce laws and the practice of divorce.[39] Right after the California no-fault statute was passed, studies appeared suggesting that Rheinstein was right: the law did not produce any increase in marital dissolution.[40] There is one obvious reason why these writers may be right: divorce rates were rising well before the no-fault laws were passed. That they had been going up since the mid-nineteenth century shows the power of a changing culture. Indeed, that the no-fault laws were quickly adopted by legislators who are keenly attuned to popular sentiments suggests that the public, even if it had not made up its mind that it wanted easier laws, was certainly ready to accept them when they were proposed.

But the view that law makes no difference will discourage anyone from thinking that something can be done about high divorce rates and the harm they impose on children. In time, scholars took a fresh look at the evidence and, using more sophisticated statistical methods, found compelling evidence that no-fault makes a difference.

One study looked at divorce rates over a nearly fifty-year period, from 1950 to 1995, examining the effects of no-fault laws while taking into account a host of other factors, such as social and economic conditions in each state, the extent to which Catholics lived in each state, and an estimate of each state's political culture. The results showed that, even after allowing for the rising divorce rates, the passage of a no-fault law made divorce rates rise even faster. There was on average one more divorce for every three thousand people in a state after it had adopted the no-fault rule. (This was no small increase, since the average state in 1995 had about fourteen divorces for every three thousand people.) At the same time; states that had a traditional or moralistic culture, many Catholics, and a low rate of female employment had fewer divorces than states with a politically liberal culture, relatively few Catholics, and many employed women.[41] Law, culture, and demography all make a difference. A similar conclusion was reached by two other scholars who defined a no-fault state as one in which the law both makes divorce easy and allows for the equal division of property no matter whether anyone was at fault. (Some states, such as Virginia, allow a no-fault divorce but take fault into consideration when dividing property and awarding spousal support.)[42]

Divorce hurts many children, though not all, and the harm affects many of them for a long time. When Judith Wallerstein followed the children of divorce for ten years, she found that half saw their father or mother get yet another divorce, half found that their parents stayed angry at one another, and half became "worried, underachieving, self-deprecating, and sometimes angry young men and women"; one-fourth experienced a sharp drop in their standard of living; few were helped with college expenses; and most felt rejected by at least one of the parents.[43] Though some children did well after the divorce, most did not, and this pattern persisted well into adulthood.[44] She also raised serious questions about the tendency of the courts to impose joint custody rules, observing that this policy, never really supported by adequate evidence, was based on a doctrine of parental equality that often had little relevance to the children's best interests.

Easy divorce was greatly encouraged by the no-fault divorce laws that began in the 1960s, but we must not forget that the rate at which marriages ended in divorce had been growing at least since 1870 (we have no Census data that goes back any further). Between 1920 and 1944, the rate of divorces for every one thousand married women increased by 50 percent; between 1944 and 1970 it increased by 24 percent, a fact that suggests that, though no-fault divorce and looser contemporary customs may well have made a difference, the biggest rate of increase preceded the sixties. The new laws were readily accepted by legislators who would have objected had anybody thought to complain. Hardly anyone did.

Chapter 8
Working Mothers

One of the most profound changes in the economic life of America in the last half century has been the dramatic increase in the number of working mothers. In 1940, less than one-tenth of the mothers of children under the age of eighteen worked outside the home; by 1948, with the experience of wartime employment behind them, that fraction had risen to about one-fourth; forty years later, nearly two-thirds of such mothers had outside jobs.[1] (Over 40 percent of women with children under the age of seven work full time.) Accompanying this remarkable change has been an equally great shift in public attitudes. In 1936, 82 percent of all Americans thought a married woman should not work outside the home if her husband was able to support her. By 1996 that viewpoint had fallen to 17 percent.[2] It is hard to find a more striking change in popular beliefs about marriage.

The increase in working mothers might have either of two consequences for marriage. If you are an economist who thinks the marital union is the result of a man and woman coming together in order to improve their economic (as well as social and emotional) benefits, then the income of the woman will make a difference. Having her own resources before marriage and confident that she can retain much of that income after it, she will be more choosy about her partner and even the idea of getting married at all. She will not be as dependent on her husband's earnings as she would if she were a housewife, and so we might expect a decline in marriage and an increase in divorce with rising female wages.

The other view is that a woman with her own income is more, not less, likely to marry. Marriage provides insurance against a loss in income but does not alter the emotional benefits of the union. A working woman can pick sexual partners more carefully without gambling her sexual value on any man who promises her a home. She may, indeed, be more choosy about whom she marries, but by being choosy she will select a man who meets her emotional and intellectual needs and who is likely to remain with her for life. In this view, higher female wages will lead to more marriages and fewer divorces, but also to having fewer children, since child care will reduce the amount of time (and seniority and experience) a woman can acquire in the labor force.

The evidence is complicated. As educated women have earned more money, they are likely to marry men who also have high incomes. But if men do not have rising incomes, marriage becomes less likely. Marriage has also become less common when the wage gap between men and women narrows. High-income women are less likely to marry if their incomes are catching up with men's earnings; lower-income women are less likely to marry if men's incomes are falling. This earnings squeeze helps explain why semiskilled and unskilled men who take jobs for which income levels are not rising rapidly will find it harder to get married, while men who can quickly find profitable opportunities in a technological society will have a better chance of getting married. At the same time, working women, once married, are more likely to go through a divorce than those not working, but it is not clear whether it was the work, the time away from home, the educational level that work required, or the amount of money earned that contributed to divorce.[3]

However, women who work while married may create a problem because they spend a lot of time away from their children. If that problem exists, perhaps we should strengthen marriage by reducing the extent to which women work. When both parents work, the child is at the mercy of day-care providers or the hectic efforts of mom and dad to schedule their lives so that one is around to give a few minutes of "quality time" to the children. In this view, the expansion of female careers has hurt children.[4]

No doubt countless employed mothers worry about the time they do not spend with their children; many feel that they are in an endless struggle to juggle countless balls in the air, each one of which—wife, mother, employee, business leader—appears to be a full-time job. A book has been written arguing that women raised by mothers who spend all of their time at home were better off than those raised by mothers who worked.[5] But the evidence on which this book is based is weak, coming, as it did, from self-selected women who responded to newspaper ads requesting volunteers for the project. We have no way of knowing whether these self-chosen subjects were representative of any population or whether they were just people who have something to complain about.

There have been many efforts to measure the effects of maternal employment on children, and the message so far is not consistent with the criticisms one hears. Of the dozens of studies, some compare the children of employed mothers with those of stay-at-home mothers, and others follow children through time while measuring the effects of maternal occupations. This kind of research is hard to do with great scientific rigor because we cannot randomly assign women to the role of homemaker or careerist. But to make up for that, the best studies have held constant socioeconomic and other demographic differences. Though there are some discrepant findings, overwhelmingly the studies conclude that maternal employment has no harmful effect on the development of children. In fact, some children may do better when their mothers are employed.[6]

But if working does not hurt a mother's children, failing to work may hurt her. Accompanying the increased support for female economic independence has been a growing suspicion of women who are "merely" housewives or who, worst of all, actually enjoy making a home. This view is more common among highly educated people than among all Americans, but among the former its power is keenly felt. When I was teaching at various universities and I introduced my wife to colleagues, many would immediately ask her, "What do you do?" When she said that she kept house, their unspoken reactions ranged from concern to disdain. Somehow, they suggested, she had failed. She didn't think so, but her views were not taken seriously. Recently a woman who is a lawyer and law school professor wrote a book about how to keep house. On the first page she had to explain how difficult this was: homemaking, she said, was her "secret life" that she had struggled for years to conceal from friends. "Being perceived as excessively domestic can get you socially ostracized," she remarked. But she also found a few friends who wanted to learn homemaking after their own mothers, concerned for their daughters' future careers, denied them the knowledge. And so Cheryl Mendelson wrote a book about how to keep a house.[7] And she still works outside it.

Day Care

The story about day care is more complicated. Research about it has become much better, but the controversy over its meaning remains intense. Mothers who use day care think it supports that decision; mothers who stay home with their children think it supports that choice. And the scholars doing the research are just as divided, with a good deal of angry arguments being exchanged.

When day care first came to public attention in the 1930s it was because people were upset by nurseries established to care for the children of poor, working mothers. This concern was strong enough to lead to legislation creating mothers' pensions so that women could remain at home with their children, thereby avoiding any need for day care.

By the 1960s and 1970s, however, day care was back in vogue. Scholarly articles and popular essays were published endorsing it in part because working women needed it and in part because it was thought that children would do well being in the company of other children. The most common method for figuring out the effect of day care on youngsters was to use the Strange Situation test to measure how a setting, such as day care, affects mother-child attachment. Invented by Mary Ainsworth, the test involves assessing how a child who is separated from its mother behaves and then how it reacts to a reunification. It is popular among some scientists but criticized by others.[8]

As a result, different judgments have been reached. Jay Belsky, who has studied day care intensively for many years, concluded early on that it did not harm children. Then, new studies led him to a different view. Full-time day care outside of the home raised concerns that it might harm children during their first year of life.[9] He and others found evidence that for some children day care produced disagreeable and aggressive behavior.[10] Belsky's critics, and there were many, strongly disagreed.[11] Scholars began to attack one another. Day care, it turned out, was not simply an academic curiosity but an issue that cut deeply into how scholars viewed the world.

The most recent wave of research, begun in the early 1990s, was an effort to settle these quarrels. It brought together more than two dozen researchers (including Belsky and some of his critics) who jointly studied for several years a large number of children. This group, called the Early Child Care Research Network and sponsored by the National Institute of Child Health and Human Development, began to study more than one thousand children and their mothers selected randomly from thirty-one hospitals located in or near ten cities. These youngsters were selected before the scholars knew what kind of care they would receive—from a parent, from a relative, or from a day-care program. The children's behavior was measured in various ways—how compliant and self-controlled they were, how much problem behavior they revealed, how well their intellectual and language skills developed, and how strongly the child was attached to its mother. A lot of facts were gathered about each child's intelligence and personality, about each mother's race, ethnicity, education, income, psychological state, and interactions with her child, and about the quality of the parent's home life and of the child care that each child received, whether at home or elsewhere.

Though intellectually sophisticated, the study had some limits. Of all the mothers contacted when their infants were born, a large number did not participate and mothers under the age of eighteen were not included. As a result, the mothers in the study, compared to those first contacted, were better educated and had higher incomes and were less likely to be African American or to be unmarried. Moreover, the scholars decided not to study those living in neighborhoods that the police thought were "too dangerous."

As of mid-2001, we know the results of this study for children who have reached the age of four and one-half years (and in some cases, a bit older). Under certain circumstances, day care produces both risks as well as rewards. If the day care is of high quality, children who spend a lot of time in it show an improvement in their preschool and language skills. But at the same time, children who are in day care a lot—thirty-five hours a week or more—increase the chance that they will have behavior problems whether or not the day care is of high quality. These behavior problems were identified separately by mothers, day-care providers, and kindergarten teachers. On average, and after controlling for many other factors, a lot of day care is correlated with (we cannot yet say causes) being more ready for school and becoming harder to manage.[12] This raises a problem: does intensive day care produce children who are, as one scholar put it, smart and nasty?

When this finding about behavior problems was made public in April 2001, it led to an enormous outburst of publicity accompanied by arguments that the study was either quite correct or entirely wrong. Some of the strident statements were surely mistaken. Moreover, these findings about cognitive and behavioral effects were statements about average behaviors, and these averages of course combine children who benefited with those that were harmed. The latest study suggests that 14 percent of the children in full-time day care are aggressive compared to only 9 percent of those who stay home with mother. It is a difference, but it is not obviously a large one.

We cannot be certain how the family life of these children may have affected their experiences in day care. We know that poor home care hurts the child, and poor home care coupled with poor day care often makes matters worse.[13] These scholars have made great efforts to assess home care, but even the best measures may miss some underlying forces that affect how the children will be affected by day care.

The most general conclusion one can reach from these studies is that, in general, day care "need not have harmful effects on children's development and on their family relationships, although it can do so."[14] By and large, how the children are attached to their parents and how rapidly their language skills develop do not differ very much between those raised at home and those in day care, but some aspects of their behavior may be affected. To the Early Child Research Network the 2001 findings were not unprecedented. They had already learned from studies done earlier in the lives of these children that more time in day care was associated with less harmonious relations between mother and child.

Day care can be done by relatives or by paid professionals, in small groups or large ones, involve just baby-sitting or be linked to education, begin at infancy or later in life, involve preschool care or after-school care, and be carried on in ways that range from neglectful to compassionate. The enormous variation among the kinds of day care means that any simple conclusion about its effects may be misleading or incomplete. And that variation has created changes in how scholars evaluate it. Some have looked at day care in a relative's home, others at such care in a professionally run center that was not part of anyone's home; some have examined a representative group of children, others have looked at the children of professors (in easily accessible university-connected centers), at middle-class children, and at poor children. One study by the Early Child Care Research Network found that children acquired language skills and social competence more readily in day-care centers that met more of the standards set down by the American Academy of Pediatrics, such as having a small ratio of children to staff and teachers with some professional certification.[15]

As for the kinds of children in the programs, one must bear in mind that some studies focus on populations that are not representative of all children. As we have seen, the study does not include mothers under the age of eighteen (hence few teenage moms), many with little education, or those that had a drug-abuse problem.[16] Moreover, there may be a close connection between day care and home care, one that is not yet well-understood. Some day-care programs may help overcome adverse family influences whereas others may make those harmful influences even stronger. Good family care and good day care probably leave the child quite well off, but a lot of day care is not of good quality.

Taken as a whole, it is hard to reach many definitive conclusions about day care because we cannot yet be confident that it causes, rather than is simply correlated with, a child's behavior, nor are we sure that we know how to assess accurately a child's well-being. It is a dispute that may last a long time, since scholars (happily) cannot randomly assign toddlers to homes or day care. Long-term studies of day care in Europe, where there is a much older tradition of such care than in the United States, suggest that good day care either causes no harm or is mildly helpful.[17]

These findings about day care need to be carefully followed up since nearly one-third of all American children under the age of three spend thirty-five hours or more each week in nonparental care. If working moms and day care were a disaster, the country would be in bad shape. There is no evidence of a disaster but some of harm for some children. But these findings may change when more is known. In the 1970s and 1980s, scholars thought that welfare payments had no effect on the formation of single-parent families; a new generation of research has called this view into question. That may happen to day care.

And even if the evidence on maternal employment and day care showed that it harmed children, how could that harm be prevented? Surely few people think that women can be denied the right to work or that a mother who does work must leave her child behind unattended as a latchkey kid. Each family must decide for itself who works outside the home and who works inside it, and today most do just that. When both choose to work, they may wisely choose good day care or foolishly choose bad care, but it is not easy to see how their choices could be improved, at least beyond the obvious legal requirement that external care not subject the child to illegal, brutal, or neglectful supervision.

Gender Equality

If little can or should be done about limiting female employment, an alternate view, one much supported by some enthusiasts of female careers, makes little sense either. That is the belief that the world would be made better by achieving "gender equality," by which is meant an exactly even division of tasks within the family, an exactly even set of opportunities outside of it, and exactly equal levels of compensation for men and women who take similar jobs.[18] Now, if the phrase meant only the end of male dominance over women or equal pay for equal work, hardly anyone in this country would object. But the phrase seems to mean much more to those who use it. It implies that men and women are interchangeable entities, differing only in certain sexual characteristics, and that each has an equal obligation to care for children and to pursue a career.

This view is at odds with how most men and women think and act. Men and women differ in what qualities they bring to one another, how they approach marriage and family life, and how much time they take away from work to be with families. Men can become fathers any time after puberty, for years stretching on to their deaths. Women can become mothers for only a few decades. The latter have biological clocks, the former do not. Becoming a mother is very different from becoming a father. The mother carries the child inside her, feeds it at her breast, and explores its little body wondering whom it most resembles. The father neither carries nor nurses a child and suspects that the infant looks like—well, a baby. Men and women both love their children, but they love them differently. An unmarried father will love his children but spend little time with them; an unmarried mother will love her children and spend much of her life with them.

Men and women think somewhat differently, a matter that probably reflects some complex interaction between nature and nurture.

Women are much more accurate than men in interpreting all of the unspoken messages that make up so much of human communication—the gestures, facial expressions, and tones of voice by which people convey their subtler meanings.[19] Men and women have roughly the same intelligence but not the same talent at finding meaning in a posture, photograph, or glance; in these matters, women are more skillful. The latter have more expressive faces, gaze and smile more, and are less restless. Some of this may result from how their brains are wired, some from coping with being a subordinate person, and some from having babies. Watching an infant means being acutely alert to nonverbal cues. When a husband and wife disagree, the man is more likely to stonewall whereas the woman is more likely to criticize. Men like to avoid arguments (though they are likely to explode after an argument begins), women think arguments will help solve problems (though they will get upset when the man does not respond appropriately).[20] Given these differences, marriages almost always involve disputes, and so if divorces are readily available marriages will end more frequently. Women use more of their brains when they feel sad and are better able than men to detect sadness in others.[21] "Because they're so good at seeing nuances," Raquel Gur has remarked, "women can read what's happening quickly and ask: 'What should I do now?'"[22] Marian Diamond has put these differences into an evolutionary framework: "A male's main function is to find territory, find food, find a female. He has to be able to focus to survive. What the female needs as a mother is to be ready to go in all directions in order to protect her young."[23]

Sweden is probably the nation where women have more freedom than anywhere else. When fathers there take time off from work to stay home with their children, they typically say they want to be the primary caregiver; nevertheless, the women in these families remained in fact the chief caretaker. "Regardless of their family type," the authors of this study wrote, "mothers and fathers behaved in characteristically different ways."[24]

When men go off to work, the child looks forward to his return; when the mother goes off to work, the child may not want her to leave. Children intuitively react differently to mothers and fathers. Fathers are often less alert to the needs of their children—their sicknesses, their schedules, their daily drills—than are their mothers.

Fathers and mothers often earn different amounts of money, but usually it is not because they are of different sexes. From the age of twenty-seven to thirty-three, women earn 98 percent of what men earn, but that changes when they become mothers, for then they take time out (and lose seniority) or accept a less demanding post (and thus step back in the promotion race).[25] There is, of course, still a glass ceiling in some enterprises, but even if it could be wished away in its entirety, most working men and women over their lifetimes would earn quite different amounts of money because of how they choose to spend their time.

In view of these differences, what does it mean to talk of gender equality? Creating equal opportunities is, of course, desirable, but complaining that equal opportunities do not lead to equal results is an argument that can only be based on a view of human nature that is wildly at odds with reality. Though young married men now spend more time on household tasks than did their fathers, I doubt that we shall see them giving the same attention to children as do their wives. Speaking of "equality" in this sphere is speaking nonsense. Ordinary men and women do not think that way. They recognize and, in general, are satisfied with significant differences in male and female roles.[26] There is even better evidence than social science: notice the things about which people complain, sing songs, and write novels. Marriage is mainly about love, companionship, and shared endeavors. When men complain, it is that their wives are moody and too easily upset; when women complain, it is that their husbands are inattentive and insensitive. Men and women are morally equal, but they can be equal without being identical.

Working mothers are hardly a new thing; throughout most of human history, they have always worked outside the home, usually on a farm. Today women want to have a career open to them that is off the farm, and they think they can have a career and be a good mother. Most working mothers agree with this. But at the same time, they have a competing view, saying that "it would be better if she could stay home and just take care of the house and children." Only one-fifth of all women disagree with that view.[27] I am not asserting that they should stay home, or even that they are unhappy with their work (most, I believe, enjoy it quite a bit), only that they think this, and they probably think it for a reason that the argument about gender equality has failed to address.

And gender equality has little meaning at all for a poor fifteen-year-old girl who has a child, no husband, and precious few earning skills. For her, getting the husband to do half the housework is meaningless; she has no husband. Getting equal pay is easy but of little value, since she may have no training that would prepare her for more than flipping hamburgers. Breaking the glass ceiling is irrelevant, since the ceiling is so far above her head. Gender equality is a fancy of the upper middle class, one that has had some effect on how college-educated people live together in a marriage but little effect on how most people behave, or would like to behave.

Helping Working Mothers

Perhaps paying money can help adults, especially women without husbands, raise children. Economists, along with most of us, think that you get more of what you pay for. The United States could in theory have had a different way of supporting single-parent families than the old AFDC system. We might have paid, as most industrial nations do, a child allowance to every family with a baby. In every nation, parents are required to support their children, but we might have adopted the Swedish policy of not only trying to extract payments from absent parents (typically, the father) but also of making tax-supported payments to every parent (typically, the mother) if that paternal support was not forthcoming. Early on, of course, we could not have done those things; in 1935, the Constitution as then interpreted would not have allowed the federal government to do this.

But suppose it had, or suppose we started now. We would then face some practical difficulties. We would not know how to find the absent fathers. In Sweden, the paternity of a child born out of wed-lock is known to the government in the vast majority of cases because most such children are born to a cohabiting couple. The location of any defaulting father can readily be learned from that country's central population registers, which track the movement of everybody throughout the nation.[28] It is inconceivable that any government agency here would be allowed to have that level of information. In the United States, we cannot even take steps to make the Social Security card a reliable source of personal identification. Here children are often born to couples who have not lived together. In Sweden, births to teenagers are only one-third as common as they are in the United States.[29] Even though teenage girls produce only a minority of all births to unmarried women in this country, they are much more common here than abroad and the overwhelming majority of those births are to poor, unwed girls living alone. The absent father, even if he could be found, is often financially unable to make any payments.[30] The Swedish system might have been useful here for women whose husbands had left them, but it would have done little good for girls who never had even a live-in boyfriend, much less a husband. Paying money to help raise children does not solve the fundamental problem here, and perhaps not even in Sweden: the need a child has for the enduring love and undivided attention of two parents.

But perhaps money can be spent in ways that will help reduce the number of single-parent families that raise children. There have been several efforts to do this, most of them without much success. Arkansas and New Jersey said it would deny additional payments to women on welfare who had additional births. These efforts were tried on an experimental basis, but not with much success. There were problems in the experiments, but even allowing for these the family-cap limits seemed to have little effect on additional births. Even when mothers were paid to attend meetings to discuss contraception, as they were in Colorado, not much changed. And when efforts at family planning were combined with a major effort at improving the education of mothers, as was done in Camden, Newark, and Chicago, there was still no change in subsequent birthrates.[31]

One welfare program has produced some modest gains, though not quite the "extremely positive" effect claimed by the *New York Times* when it hailed the new state plan.[32] Minnesota randomly assigned more than fourteen thousand families to either a new state program, one that gives recipients financial incentives to work and pays them child-care subsidies, or to the old AFDC program. The key difference between the two programs involved how much money a recipient could keep if she worked. Under AFDC, the working recipient faced, in effect, a huge tax. If she earned $520 a month from work, she would have to forfeit $407 in welfare and food stamp benefits. Under the Minnesota Family Investment Program (MFIP), by contrast, a mother's welfare payment was increased (to offset work-related expenses) and 38 percent of her earnings were disregarded before calculating her total welfare payment. As a result, the tax on earnings was sharply reduced. Now, if she earned $520 a month, she would get to keep all but $107 of her welfare payment.

The two groups of families were followed for about three years. Not surprisingly, the MFIP recipients earned more money than the AFDC ones, and so the number living in poverty declined. Among the single-parent, long-term welfare recipients, there was also a reduction in the proportion who were ever abused and some improvement in their children's school performance. On the key issue of marriage, there was an improvement, but only a modest one. After three years, the proportion of unmarried moms in MFIP who got married was 11 percent, while among those in the old AFDC program it was 7 percent. This was a gain, but not much. Among welfare recipients who were already married, however, the gain was larger: after three years, two-thirds of MFIP families were still married, while less than one-half of AFDC ones were.[33]

The Minnesota experience suggests, not surprisingly, that money can help make people better off, but that over a three-year period it has only a small effect on the number of single moms who get married. It has a major effect, on the other hand, on the number of already-married couples who stay married. It is an old lesson: getting single moms to marry is harder than keeping married couples together.

Another, very different way of spending money has been suggested by Richard and Grandon Gill. They note that more and more people retire from the workforce at an early age and more and more women work when their children are young. They suggest that this tradeoff between early retirement and early child care, though it may help people, may not help society because it puts children at risk. They are neglected when they are young but enjoyed when they are older. Since society has an obligation to children, perhaps it should alter the incentives so that people begin their careers later.

To do this, they suggest creating a Parental Bill of Rights under which parents who care personally for their children would be financially rewarded by an investment that gives them tax-supported access to educational programs that will enhance their earning power. The arrangement would exactly parallel the GI Bill of Rights, under which an important compensation for people serving in low-paid military jobs when they were young was subsidized access to higher education when they were a bit older. The Parental Bill would make it easier to pursue an early parenting track followed by an enhanced career track. Since there are large economic payoffs to higher education, the parents who took the benefit would be made better off.[34]

As a practical matter, most of the beneficiaries of such a program would be women because when parents choose who will spend the most time with children the mother is the overwhelming (though not unanimous) first choice. One would think that this should create no difficulties, but of course any program that induces women to remain at home with young children would be criticized for "privileging" child care. Such a criticism ought not defeat this program; it would, at most, be an argument to which individual women could respond as their preferences required. But there is a deeper problem. As the Gills point out, it would do little for poor, unmarried mothers, especially teenagers. Of mothers with infants, two-thirds of those with four or more years of college are in the labor force compared to fewer than one-third of those who have less than a high school education.[35] Subsidized higher education might make a large difference for women with career ambitions, but for teenage moms who lack even a high school diploma, paid-for access to college or a technical school would have little effect.

In short, money, though it can help existing families and rebuild a few, is not likely to be a sovereign remedy. Few women become single moms because they are poor; they do it for other, more subtle reasons. Were that not the case, almost every mother would have been unmarried a century or two ago, when poverty was so common as to be the inevitable lot in life for the vast majority of all people. Money is supposed to be able to buy anything, but apparently it does not buy in-wedlock births.

That is not the fault of economists who assign so much importance to money; they assume that preferences remain stable as money arrives or departs. But for marriage, the object is to change preferences. What is at stake is not simply or even mostly money, it is a set of attitudes that lead people to choose commitment before they choose sex, defer children until after marriage, and attach shame to those who violate these rules. The central problem is how we care.

There are ways of helping poor mothers care for their children. These programs do so, not by conveying facts but by changing expectations. One of the most remarkable of these defies the expectations of any serious economist, because behavior is changed without money changing hands. Visiting nurse services, pioneered by Dr. David Olds, sends trained female nurses into the homes of poor, unmarried pregnant women to advise them on prenatal health and child care. It starts before the infant is born and continues for a couple of years after the birth. The nurse—ideally, the same one repeatedly visits each mother—comes once every week or two for an hour or so. The program was started with mostly white women in Elmira, New York, who were followed for fifteen years. Later the plan was copied in several other locations. The mothers-to-be were randomly assigned to either the program or to a control group.

Fifteen years later, the Elmira women visited by the nurses had fewer subsequent births, spent less time on welfare, and were less likely to be arrested. Their children were less likely to run away from home, had fewer arrests, smoked less often, drank less alcohol, and had fewer sex partners. When the program was tried in Memphis with mostly African-American women, many of the same results occurred. They had about one-third fewer subsequent births.[36]

Why do nurse visits produce such dramatic results? Because, I suspect, the nurse is a professional welcomed into a home in order to help prepare a woman to be a mother and whose advice is both valuable and not limited to health and child care. The pregnant women fall under the care of a person whom they see repeatedly. Care—one-on-one devotion to the well-being of another—is the essential element. And since in theory the care is just about health, it is not controversial. In practice, it is surely about many other things as well, because the pregnant women will ask the nurses for advice on how to cope with the difficulties of life. Nurses appear in their uniforms to teach health but in fact teach something about how to live.

How we care for children is the central problem. A mother may work, and if she has a husband to help her and good day care on which to rely, her children may do very well. But if she does not earn much money, has no husband, or cannot find or afford decent day care, her children may do very poorly. We can invent ways to provide a mother with more money. Child care tax credits help families with children in day care, but as the law is written most of the money goes to upper-income families.[37] The benefit to poorer families could be increased if the tax credit were fully refundable so that a person who paid no taxes would get a cash grant. Even better might be a tax credit for stay-at-home as well as day care.

But no matter how we arrange money incentives, we have not induced people to marry. And unless they marry, and stay married, the children will suffer.

Chapter 9
The Cultural Challenge

For two nations to become one again, marriage must become more common. Many Americans wish this, but despite some encouraging trends, history is marching in a different direction. The number of teenage girls giving birth to children has dropped since 1991, but although there are fewer births, the great majority of them remain out of wedlock.[1] The divorce rate has declined a bit from what it was in 1980, but it is still twice as high as it was in 1960,[2] and much of the decline in divorce can be explained by the decline in marriage. It is hard for more people to get divorced if fewer people are getting married. In 1987 the proportion of college freshmen who thought that it is "all right for people to have sex even if they've known each other for a very short time" dropped from 52 percent in 1987 to 42 percent in 1997, but it was only a small decline.[3]

The 1996 welfare reform law offered cash bonuses to those states that reduced illegitimacy the most, but so far state leaders have interpreted the law to mean getting women off welfare and into jobs. Although many states have created programs to reduce illegitimacy, for most bureaucrats who deal with the women who apply for benefits, work trumps legitimacy. It is easy to see why: getting women to work is a readily measured goal, saves the state money, and can readily be discussed. By contrast, getting them to have babies only after they are married produces no immediate gains, may cost more time and effort, and requires bureaucrats to talk about delicate matters. An evaluation of efforts to reduce illegitimacy is under way, and when its results are known, perhaps we shall see some gains.[4]

Meanwhile the elite culture of the United States and much of Europe remains deeply divided about marriage. To some, it is wrong to prefer it to other forms of sexual contact; marriage should not be "privileged" (by which is meant, endorsed). Alternatives to marriage, such as cohabitation and civil-union agreements, are desirable. In Sweden cohabitation is almost as common as marriage. In France, a *pacte civile di solidarité*, or PACS, is now law. Under it, a couple, heterosexual or homosexual, may appear before a court clerk and, in a few moments, have their application approved. It confers on them many, though not all, of the benefits of marriage without any need for divorce should their romance cool; a PACS can be ended almost instantly. The law is silent about children.[5]

When the Institute for American Values convened a conference to discuss the growing effort to get schools to teach courses about marriage, the meeting collapsed into a debate over whether the schools ought to teach about "marriage" as opposed to "relationships." Although Florida requires marriage instruction throughout the state and isolated school districts in other states do the same, many of the curricula for such courses do not have what one investigator called a "marriage focus," which would convey the message that marriage is usually beneficial to its partners.[6] Many teachers said that what teenagers really need is not a message about marriage, but one about improving their relationships with people of the opposite sex (or even the same one). Some teachers went even further. "To get these curricula past school boards, principals, and parents, many of whom are divorced, and to enlist the efforts of teachers who don't want to look judgmental, you must simply soft-pedal marriage."[7] And so the curricula soft-pedaled marriage.

A law school professor has argued that an "obsession with marriage prevents us from looking at our social problems." Marriage, after all, is "nothing more than a piece of paper."[8] In her writings, she argues that "marriage would be abolished as a legal category," replaced by a commitment by "society" to raise children on the basis of subsidies to "caretakers," most of whom will be women. She assigns no value to a child having a father as well as a mother.[9] These advocates of what David Blankenhorn has called the "post-marriage society" agree that adults should take care of children, but they disagree that the adults need to be married to do that. The immense body of research supporting the value of marriage is dismissed as not showing "cause and effect."[10] The goal of the post-marriage critics is Sweden, where unmarried couples care for children and the state pays money to help them do that.

A concern for marriage is being replaced by a concern for relationships. Anthony Giddens, the distinguished English sociologist has described these "pure relationships" as the natural consequence of sexual freedom. Girls no longer "lose" their virginity; in their eyes, they gain sexual experience. Their problem, of course, is to make something meaningful out of this gain, no easy matter when men have decided that there no longer need be any connection between sex and reproduction and thus between sex and marriage.[11] Daniel Cere has written about how many intellectuals now view this new world. Our laws and customs should be changed to support "close personal relationships" in ways that imply little, if anything about marriage. At one time our youthful passions had to adjust to the legal and moral demands of marriage; today, those demands are supposed to change to match our youthful passions.[12]

Nor is this the view simply of the political left. Richard A. Posner, the distinguished appeals court judge appointed by President Ronald Reagan, has argued that companionate marriage (that he wrongly dates from the English Reformation) "fosters puritanical attitudes" by making offensive a "husband's adultery." Far better, he suggests, is the modern Swedish arrangement, one that probably reflects the relative unimportance of religion in that country, in which marriage conveys so few benefits that cohabitation is preferable. There, intensive sex education, widespread female employment, publicly financed day care, and long and well-paid maternity leaves emancipate women from men, meaning that child care is now a matter that is individually arranged in ways that (Posner supposes) help children. These aspects of the Swedish program, he thinks, "may be the essential elements of a realistic (and inexpensive) program for dealing with our [America's] national blights of teenage pregnancy, teenage parenthood . . ."[13]

Of course, these policies will only work if they promote the existence of a two-parent family, and Posner correctly notes that when he wrote there was very little research on that matter in Sweden. That has begun to change. In 1995, two Swedish scholars found that boys living in a single-parent family (or who had otherwise experienced some familial disruption) were much more likely to become delinquent than those raised in an intact family.[14] And Posner wrongly supposes that American research shows that it is the tensions preceding divorce and not divorce itself that harms children, and that it is poverty rather than absent fathers that hurt children in single-parent families.[15] But the evidence in this book, some of which was not available when he wrote, proves that divorce and not just predivorce tension, and being fatherless and not just being poor, hurts children. Even in Sweden, where research on these matters is scarce, one of the few studies suggests that in all but one income group boys raised in one-parent homes had appreciably higher rates of serious psychiatric disturbance than did those from two-parent families. The same was true of boys in families broken by separation or divorce.[16] Another study of several thousand Swedish teenagers found those who grew up in a family where one biological parent was absent achieved lower educational levels than those who grew up with both such parents. The first group may have suffered in part from lower incomes, but after controlling for income the gap between single-parent and two-parent youngsters was significant. "Living in a stable two-parent family," the author wrote, "is conducive to the educational career of an adolescent."[17]

The postmarriage society that is advocated by some American thinkers rests on two beliefs: that the state can ensure the supply of whatever the child may need and that Sweden has shown us how to do it. Against this view we have the belief of virtually every society and certainly every religion since the beginning of recorded time that the family is the central feature of human society. I think that the latter view is correct. Human history, not social science, has privileged marriage. But that history is not an ineluctable force. The ideal of marital child care can be changed and in fact has been changed over the last century or so. The views of some sociologists and law-school professors that now appear to represent only a tiny avant-garde movement could well become far more powerful and widely shared.

How Culture Was Once Changed

The Victorian era was the last great Anglo-American effort to combat social disorder and strengthen families by a massive investment of private effort. Its general features were described in chapter 4, but a closer look at what was done will give us an idea of what a cultural change requires. Queen Victoria came to the throne at a time when both countries were experiencing a profound social erosion. Disraeli's novel *Sybil*, in which he described how England had become two nations, was written in the early 1840s, a time when there was a sharp increase in crime and illegitimacy.[18] In America, Andrew Jackson was president, and crime rates were rising and social turmoil intensifying. At that time we had no national crime data, but the painstaking work of Roger Lane in Philadelphia, Paul E. Johnson in Rochester, and James Richardson in New York City tells us that orderly communities were under attack.[19] Ted Robert Gurr has found evidence of this change in London and Stockholm.[20]

To speak of the Victorian era today is to invite, at best, bemused smiles and at worst hostile glances. But whatever we may think of what was done, the cultural change worked. Despite rapid industrialization, massive urbanization, the emergence of a factory-based working class, and (in America) high rates of immigration into the country, both America and England became safer. Boston in the late nineteenth century was less violent than Boston in 1840, and the homicide rates in Philadelphia declined as that century wore on.[21] Eric Monkkonen surveyed all of the studies of crime in the nineteenth century and found that, with perhaps two exceptions, each reported falling or stable crime rates in industrializing America.[22] The same decline occurred in London and Stockholm.[23] Drunkenness and disorderly conduct also declined in American cities during the second half of the nineteenth century.[24] In England, the illegitimacy ratio fell sharply between 1860 and 1900.[25]

One obvious explanation for this change was that the population was getting older. The birth rate fell and the average age of the population increased. The fewer the young men, the fewer the crimes and out-of-wedlock births. Aging made a difference, but not the whole difference. The murder rate fell by 55 percent in Boston and by 36 percent in Philadelphia, but the proportion of the population in the age group twenty to twenty-nine fell by only 15 percent. The scholars who have looked at this matter closely agree that though aging made a difference it does not explain all or even most of the decline in crime.[26]

Another explanation is policing. American cities created police departments toward the end of the century; London created its police force even earlier. No doubt professional policing helped curtail crime, but we would have to make some heroic assumptions about its effectiveness to imagine that the Boston police force could have cut that city's murder rate by more than one-half between the middle and the end of that century.[27]

Still another possibility is the Industrial Revolution itself, a force that, far from weakening social ties, in fact enhanced them by replacing the old discipline of small towns and strong families with the new discipline of organized factories and public schools. Economic efficiency required punctuality, industriousness, and cooperation, all taught by both factories and schools and all enforced by the prospect of poverty or the poorhouse for those who did not grasp the lessons.[28] This argument may be true to some extent, though it is not clear how factory life reduced crime or illegitimacy; after all, the factories were closed at night and on Sundays, when a growing and largely male working class was looking for something fun to do.

What inhibited those young workers at night and on Sunday and what helped the police reduce crime rates was to some significant degree the inculcation of a stronger set of moral habits. That inculcation is what we mean by Victorianism. Proving how this cultural order influenced behavior is difficult if not impossible, but many leading scholars have come to believe it, and for good reason. How else can we explain that industrialization and urbanization (and in America, immigration) did not unleash social discord? The answer, it seems, is that bourgeois morality gained an extraordinary ascendancy owing mostly to private efforts.[29]

The Young Men's Christian Association, Sunday schools, religious revivals, church membership, and temperance movements became the order of the day. Their goal was character and their reach was extraordinary. The people leading these movements meant different things by character. For some, it meant a religious reawakening; for others, moderation in drink and circumspection in sex; for still others, orderly habits and a suitable occupation diligently pursued. Joseph F. Kett, in his study of how adolescents were treated during the nineteenth century, explains how the growth of a big-city workforce composed of unattached young men was met by a religious and secular effort to intensify the commitment to character, by which was meant not some set of rules, but "an internal gyroscope, a self-activating, self-regulating, all-purpose inner control."[30] By this effort, its sponsors hoped to emphasize self-restraint as a force that would strike a balance between youthful ambition and urban opportunity.

In large measure these efforts had a religious foundation that was sparked by the Second Great Awakening that began toward the end of the eighteenth century and led to the creation of many American colleges, the formation of the antislavery movement, and the spread of church-based activities in the cities. In 1820, fewer than 5 percent of the adult males in New York City were on the lay boards of that city's many Protestant organizations, but by 1860, after an intense mobilization effort, the proportion had more than quadrupled. About 20 percent of all adult males served on such boards and more than half of all adult Protestant men were members of at least one church-related voluntary association.[31]

One of the most important of these associations was the Sunday school. These were, of course, church-based activities built on religious goals, but they soon acquired secular goals as well. Sunday school was not merely a brief lesson from the Bible but a day-long exercise in "decorum and restraint" that used the minute application of rules and procedures to teach the students their civic duties and civil obligations.[32] Enrollment in these schools, both here and in England, was very large. In 1825 the American Sunday School Union claimed to enroll one-third of all the children in Philadelphia between the ages of six and fifteen. In New York City in 1829, more than 40 percent of all children ages four to fourteen were said to be in Sunday school.[33] In England, Sunday school enrollment tripled between 1821 and 1851 and accounted for more than half of all children between the ages of five and fifteen (and three-fourths of all working-class children).[34] These schools are sometimes criticized today as efforts by the middle class to impose its will on the poor, but research suggests it was quite the opposite. Sunday schools were largely financed and staffed by working-class persons who sought by means of drill, regulation, and punctuality to establish what one author has called "moral hegemony." In this way, he added, "the bourgeois world view triumphed largely through consent, not through force."[35]

On leaving Sunday school and joining the labor force, young men found the YMCA, an institution designed to serve as a functional alternative to the family. Brought to the United States from England in 1851, within a decade there were more than two hundred YMCAs here with more than twenty-five thousand members.[36] The original YMCA was not, however, merely a place for rest and relaxation. Its members were expected to participate actively in some organized effort at urban moral betterment.[37]

Throughout most of the nineteenth century, temperance was a powerful movement, so powerful, indeed, that the passage of a prohibition law in Maine helped prompt John Stuart Mill to write *On Lib-*

erty, in which he said prohibition was objectionable as an infringe-
ment on the rights of those who wished to buy alcohol.[38] He may have
been right, but it was worth recalling that whatever the practical problems of legal prohibition, the temperance movement was mostly a vol-
unteer effort that had a profound effect on popular habits. In 1829 the
average American drank ten gallons of alcohol per year; by 1850, that
amount had fallen to about two gallons per year.[39] The Civil War, the
perfection of large-scale beer production techniques, and European
immigration all caused an increase in alcohol consumption, but it
never rose again to the level it had achieved in 1829.

Perhaps the most intensive form of child care outside the family is
the orphanage. The first American orphanage was established in Baltimore in 1856 by Roman Catholic nuns, and soon more such institutions were created by Christian and Jewish groups and by private
philanthropies.

When Nurith Zmora examined three orphanages in Baltimore out
of the twenty-eight that operated there in 1910, she found that all were
decent places run by caring professionals who maintained close ties to
the community. The buildings were adequate, the food good, and the
schooling better than what was available outside the institution. Many
of the children in these institutions were not literally orphans, but the
sons and daughters of impoverished or single-parent families. When
she traced their graduates, she found that most had done well.[40] There
are many different kinds of residential institutions that care for children, of course, and so it is hard to make any simple generalization. But
other studies in addition to Zmora's have come to reasonably positive
conclusions.[41] Even a survey of orphanage studies written by a person
who wrongly believes that poverty alone is the cause of weak American
families concludes that "asylums provided a reasonably stable, if not
necessarily loving, environment" because they focused on children as
"innocents needing help."[42] Moreover, the quality of life of children in
asylums improved dramatically between the 1830s and the 1930s.[43]

Richard McKenzie, himself a graduate of an orphanage, sent a ques-
tionnaire to four thousand or so alumni of nine orphanages. About half
returned them. More than three-fourths said they found their time at

the orphanage (which averaged nine years) to be "very favorable"; only
2 percent gave it an unfavorable rating. One-third or so missed having
a family, but very few complained of work, punishment, or lack of freedom, and scarcely any wished to enter the foster-care system. The
alumni had, for their age groups, incomes and educational levels equal
to or higher than that of the white population generally.[44]

These findings cast some doubt on the view, widely shared among
many social workers, that separating children from their families will
greatly harm them and that living in a group home is worse than living in a family setting. But whatever the doubt, orphanages were
doomed. In 1910 two-thirds of all children living away from their
families were in orphanages and one-third were in foster care; a half
century later, the proportions were reversed. Today only a few group
homes for children remain. Orphanages declined because they had too
many critics: social workers opposed them because they weakened the
family, liberal reformers because they involved "social control," and
fiscal conservatives because they were too expensive. Public policy
strongly favors family preservation (even if the family to be preserved
is weak, abusive, or neglectful) and foster care (even if the foster family is uncaring). Federal law requires that the states make "reasonable
efforts" to leave children with their biological parents, but as McKenzie observed, a "reasonable effort" has been interpreted to mean
"every possible effort."[45]

The nineteenth century was not of one mind about the virtues of
family life. The Children's Aid Society disliked orphanages because
they were asylums that might quench the energy and skill of young
boys and even worried a bit about familial conformity. Charles Loring
Brace used the society to sweep up tens of thousands of street urchins
and ship them to small Midwestern and western towns where they
could develop their own individuality and resourcefulness away from
urban problems.

All of these efforts—revivals, YMCAs, temperance, orphanages,
Sunday schools, and the Children's Aid Society—were attempts to
give to people a bourgeois interior whatever their economic exterior.[46]
To the extent circumstances permitted, the fallen were uplifted, the
abandoned were sheltered, the young were taught, and the drunks

were urged to remain sober. We have no data that will enable us to trace their effect on the conditions of family life, but what we can study—crime rates, alcohol consumption, religious involvement, abandoned children—suggests that the Victorian era was not, as we sometimes think today, merely a stuffy and hypocritical effort to adopt the facade of a dubious middle-class life, but in fact a massive private effort to inculcate self-control in people who were confronting the vast temptations of big-city life. The Victorians thought that people had a fallible human nature that would often lead them to choose self-indulgence over self-restraint. The task of society was to emphasize the latter in order to minimize the former.

By the end of the nineteenth century, matters had sufficiently improved so that many writers were ready to argue against Victorian constraints and in favor of individual emancipation. Crime rates were down, mass disorder was rare, and out-of-wedlock births had declined. In this new atmosphere of social peace, more and more thinkers began to see people not as moral agents but as victims of social circumstances.[47] The appeal of evangelical religion had begun to evaporate and its secular companion, utilitarianism—that is, doing whatever will make most people better off—had lost its radical edge. These philosophical impulses were now thought to be too earnest, too self-righteous; they took the fun out of life. By the first part of the twentieth century, the First World War ended any talk of Victorian morality; after all, civic duty had sent millions of people to their deaths in trenches.

The nineteenth century witnessed a profound transformation in elite views. At the beginning, the emphasis was on moral exhortation, social control, voluntary prohibition, personal accountability, religious endeavor, and the denunciation of illegitimacy; by the end of the century, it had shifted to environmental improvement, personal empowerment, secular leadership, and mothers' pensions.[48]

Can Culture Be Changed Again?

I doubt that most people would want to return to all the things that reinforced the familial culture during the nineteenth century, when rapid social change was placing it under so strong an attack. Most people want to enhance popular support for marriage. But consider what would be required if you tried that on the scale attempted in past centuries. Would you insist that farms be clan controlled, with no right of individual inheritance? Would you ignore the Enlightenment, with all that it has meant in terms of economic growth, political freedom, scientific invention, and artistic imagination? Would you tell women that they could not own property, initiate divorce proceedings, or retain custody of their children? Would you insist that all dependent children either starve or live in foundling homes? Would you require everyone to live on a farm or in a small town, without moving to a big city despite the opportunities that urban life confers? Would you say that no fatherless family should get any public aid? Would you insist that a divorce be based on a fictional account of adultery? Would you support a wide array of moral reform organizations based on an openly religious impulse? I think many people would resist most if not all of these efforts to challenge history.

And even if you wished to mobilize people on behalf of marriage without altering what the past has bequeathed them, by what means would you reach them? Americans generally remain religious, but many of their leaders do not. We will look in vain for contemporary church leaders like Lyman Beecher, Charles G. Finney, or Dwight L. Moody or for wealthy businessmen who supported them, such as William E. Dodge and John Wanamaker. If you prefer a secular approach to helping families, you would not find today anything like the Charity Organization Society that in a hundred or more cities sent some four thousand female volunteers into the homes of poor families to make friendships with disadvantaged women and tell them that in order to improve their lot they had to improve their character. Today this effort would be scorned as the worst form of middle-class preachiness. Its less moralistic rival, the neighborhood settlement houses and such leaders as Jane Addams, are thought well of today, but in part because they took the lead in saying that the moral defects of some poor people were not the cause but the consequence of their poverty. That is true to some extent, but so also is the opposite view.[49]

The religious backbone of the cultural change movement has

largely disappeared among elites even though it remains alive and well among the rank and file. Today a revivalist is a figure to be caricatured, just as Sinclair Lewis ridiculed Elmer Gantry. Religious activity that touches on the political world is generally denounced even though church ministers are often sought out as political allies. An openly religious movement to alter human character is called by the media "right-wing Christian fundamentalism." But research has suggested that religious orientation is in fact a powerful force for helping people despite adverse economic circumstances. When more than two thousand young black males living in poverty-stricken areas of three cities (Boston, Chicago, and Philadelphia) were studied around 1980, those who attended church frequently were much less likely to commit crimes or sell drugs even after controlling for their age, income, education, and housing quality.[50] Church attendance was a protective factor in disorderly neighborhoods; it created a moral community that helped people resist the disorder.[51]

The effect of religion on behavior may be great, but encouraging church attendance is no longer important to cultural and political elites in America or in most Western nations. Except in recent political campaigns, religion is either ignored or denounced; even the leaders who think it may be desirable are, at best, arguing for a commitment that they themselves are unwilling to make. Many of us who believe religion is helpful think it is useful only for "other people." That utilitarian (and probably self-defeating) detachment did not exist during the nineteenth century.

At the end of that century, there were some voices calling for a weakening of the commitment to marriage, but they were so few they could be safely ignored. But by the end of the twentieth century, those views have become far more common and are embraced in college textbooks, celebrated in motion pictures, and given a vulgar rhythm in that part of popular music about sex without love, passion without commitment, and violence without shame. Today the world is more vulnerable to new cultural pressures. Virtually everyone has immediate access to radio, television, and the Internet. Magazines have increasingly focused on revealing snapshots of celebrity lives and the enjoyment of one's own life. Someone once summarized the evolution of American magazines in the twentieth century this way: We began with *Life*, then went to *People*, then to *Us*, and finally to *Self*.

At the beginning of the twentieth century, only a little more than 6 percent of all seventeen-year-olds had graduated from high school and only about 2 percent of the young people between the ages of eighteen and twenty-four went to college. Now more than 80 percent of all Americans have graduated from high school and more than one-quarter have completed four years of college.[52] If students wish to study marriage in college they will confront textbooks that rarely provide a sound treatment of how marriage benefits its members, the extent to which commitment and not just pleasure is essential to a marriage, and the difficulties facing children who are raised outside of marriage (or, indeed, the effect of marriage for better or worse on children at all). After he studied the twenty leading textbooks, Norval Glenn found that only one book, that by Andrew Cherlin, relied on sound scholarship and gave a balanced treatment to controversial subjects.[53] As an old college professor I am not certain how depressed I should be about these texts, because I learned long ago not to suppose that students will be much affected by what they read. But many will read these and some will believe them. What is more unsettling is that a small army of college professors write and assign such books.

Ideas affect people more profoundly today than they once did because the idea industry is larger, richer, and more extensive. This may help explain why so many people attribute everything they like or dislike to the sixties. That decade was, to be sure, one of rapid cultural change, but it was also one in which the idea industry took hold, expanding its impact with new technology, drawing into its ranks people who had their own thinking shaped by the adversary culture, and competing vigorously for ways to increase the size of its audience by shock, revelations, and excitement.

It is important to remember how much progress we have made in making life bearable for people, especially for those whose ancestors were hurt by slavery. Millions of African Americans have overcome that legacy. Even in the slums of Philadelphia, ones that have been studied for many years by Frank Furstenberg and his battalion of colleagues and assistants, many African American families are raising their children reasonably well, quite a few by getting their children involved in religious activities.[54] But many other blacks have not done well even though slavery ended a century and a half ago. Perhaps in another century all will have escaped that legacy, but one cannot yet be optimistic because the rate at which black families bear illegitimate children has grown sharply in the last half century. And the problem is no longer chiefly that of blacks, as young white girls have increasingly taken the same path.

In some ways, continued economic growth will make a difference. In the United States, better-off people are more likely to marry and less likely to head single-parent households than are poorer ones.[55] Make more people better off and perhaps marriage rates will go up and single-parent families will decline. The poor suffer the most from the decline in marriage, just as they suffer the most from drug abuse and street crime. And they suffer not because they hate families, like drugs, or value crime, but because something in their environment or their culture makes it hard to form families, shun drugs, and avoid crime.

It is hard to be clear about what the problem is; certainly it is not any of the grand simplicities—racism, neglect—with which our society is often described. Rather, I suspect, it lies in the model our culture sets for people, especially poor ones. I have used before a metaphor to describe what I think has happened; I repeat it here. Imagine a game of crack the whip in which a line of children, holding hands, starts running in a circle as the first child rotates so as to require the others to follow. The first child, or the first few, move slowly, but at the end of the line the last few must run so fast that many fall down. In part, crack the whip has become institutionalized.

Cocaine and heroin were first used by the affluent; by the time many of them stopped and sought out help, drug use had spread to the poor at the end of the line. They found it hard to stop and impossible to find help. The consumer benefits of an affluent society were first bought by the rich, but demand for them quickly spread down the line to people who found it harder to afford them; at the end of the line, some of them decided to steal what others were buying. The pleasures of loose sexuality were celebrated by the affluent who wrote articles about sexual freedom or made motion pictures glamorizing the lives of unmarried mothers; the people at the end of the line thought sexuality without marriage was desirable, but there was no place for their children to turn for help. It is hard to keep up at the end of the line, and if we add to those in that tail-end position some ancient burdens, such as the legacy of slavery that left men detached from families, their problems are compounded. Myron Magnet has made this argument with some effect in *The Dream and the Nightmare,* and it may well help us understand why a changed culture—the decline of stigma, the embrace of cohabitation, and the acceptance of divorce—may influence most powerfully the people who did the least to create it.[56]

And increased affluence brings with it its own cost. Divorce is common among better-off people. It is not hard to see why. In the first place, they are more likely to be married and hence to have divorce as an option. Even more important, they can more easily afford divorce. Though women tend to be made worse off by these splits, their own earning power makes it easier for them to get by than is the case for their poorer, unskilled sisters.

Suppose you wish to reduce the rate at which divorces occur. The first thing you will discover is that the spread of individual rights makes it hard to improve divorce laws. You may wish to make divorce more difficult, but you cannot easily go back to the New York statute when an abused wife had to pretend she or her husband had been adulterous in order to get out of a marriage. But perhaps some other statute, one that allows divorce on grounds of cruelty? That helps the abused wife but does nothing for a woman whose husband is drunk, improvident, and neglectful. Well, let us add alcoholism, improvidence, and neglect. But how can we stop there? There are almost as many causes for divorce as there are married couples; on what philosophical or legal basis can we say that some causes are more important than others? It may be possible to craft a defensible list of grounds, but to do so we must claim that we, the authors of the statute, know better than married men and women what ought to count, and only a few men and women, married or not, will concede that right to the legislature.

We may, of course, slow divorce by making it more costly whatever the grounds. We can impose a mandatory waiting period from the time the petition is filed to when it may be granted, and another waiting period before either spouse can marry again. (This will prevent a future Eddie Fisher from marrying Elizabeth Taylor three hours after he had divorced Debbie Reynolds.) But when cohabitation has become acceptable, a deferred marriage is scarcely any burden at all; the new couple will live together until the waiting period is over. There are other costs, however, that might be more powerful. The distribution of property can be based on an assessment of fault even though the marriage itself is granted by consent, but who will determine fault? A judge, of course, but on what grounds? Answering that question puts us back at square one—what is fault? Perhaps the easiest way to make divorces costly is to require that the husband have custody of the children, as once was the universal Anglo-American practice. Imagine a successful business tycoon getting a divorce so as to marry a trophy wife when accompanying the trophy will be three young children from his former wife. Not likely.

Perhaps we can require lengthy predivorce conciliation or allow, as some states now do, "covenant marriages" that create greater obstacles to divorce, obstacles the couple have accepted, in writing and in advance, as the condition of their marriage. Since 1997 Louisiana has offered covenant marriages to couples. If they agree to be married under this law, they must be counseled by a religious leader or secular therapist as to the importance of marriage and agree that they can only be divorced on proof of adultery, a capital felony, physical or sexual abuse, or malicious desertion. Separation is also allowed in grounds of habitual intemperance or cruelty. Should the couple be unwilling to make these commitments, they can then be married under the ordinary statute that gives them the right to a no-fault divorce. (Predictably, the covenant statute has been attacked because it allegedly restricts sexual freedom and smuggles Biblical teachings into marital law.[57]) Such a law is an attractive alternative to an easy-in, easy-out marriage statute, but of course everything depends on couples agreeing to this procedure, and many will not.

There is, of course, a quite different view of the world we have made. It can be found among those who have written that marriage is outmoded or is at best one ("middle-class") way of arranging a sexual union. One can live alone and be happy, cohabit with a partner and be fulfilled, or raise a child by oneself and be rewarded. Marriage should not be "privileged."

Some popular writers have suggested that we replace a marital contract with a parenting contract. Barbara Ehrenreich has argued that in the future, couples should make a contract, not with each other ("because I think these relationships don't last forever"), but in a way that requires "co-parenting." The man and the woman would agree ("perhaps with some beautiful ceremonies") to help raise the child.[58] One wonders what might be in such a contract. Obviously, some financial commitments would appear, but what of the more important commitments—love, companionship, a walk in the park, a day at the ball game, help with a music lesson? And one wonders how such parenting contracts might be enforced. Should each child be given the right to an attorney, at somebody else's cost? And imagine the judge when such cases come before him or her. What body of law and precedent should guide the court's decision as to who should supply the love and companionship, who should take the child on a walk or to the ball game, who should help with the music lesson?

Is Anything Possible?

Public policy strongly favors family preservation (even if the family to be preserved is weak, abusive, or neglectful) and foster care (even if the foster family is uncaring). Federal law requires that the states make "reasonable efforts" to leave children with their biological parents, but as McKenzie observed, a "reasonable effort" has been interpreted to mean "every possible effort."[59]

Certainly preserving good families is desirable and drawing on the help of competent foster parents is helpful, but as practiced the family preservation movement has often protected incompetent families and the foster-care movement has sometimes catered to bad foster parents.[60] Residential care centers—what once were called orphanages—still exist, though in much reduced numbers and have, I suspect, an important role to play once one scrapes off the overheated political rhetoric that surrounds them. New residential schools for poor children have opened, and more are planned even though running them is costly. But there is also emerging a new strategy to care for unwed mothers and their children.

This alternative is called a second-chance home. Though many such homes have existed for decades, a new impulse for their expansion grew out of the 1996 federal welfare reform act. That law requires that unwed teenage mothers receive public assistance only if they live with their parents or legal guardians or, if such care is unavailable or inappropriate, live in an "adult-supervised supportive living arrangement," or second-chance homes. These facilities were pioneered in Massachusetts and have now spread to several other states. If unmarried teenage mothers lacked adequate parents, they are required to live in a publicly funded home under the supervision of experienced mothers. No alcohol or drugs are allowed. Boyfriends could visit only during approved hours. Every mother would attend school. Learning effective child care would be the central goal; staying off the street would be the central constraint. They aim at teaching not self-esteem but self-respect.

In Massachusetts second-chance homes are called the Teen Living Program. All are run by private groups such as the Salvation Army, the YWCA, and the Crittenton Services. A girl can enter in the third trimester of her pregnancy. The average entering girl is fifteen years old; the average age of a child is two. The girls can leave when they are eighteen and claim regular welfare benefits, but if they leave before they are eighteen, no such benefits are available. While in the program, the young mothers pay into the homes a portion of their welfare benefits and all of their food stamps.

The young mothers are selected because their own mothers cannot provide suitable shelters owing to child abuse, drug problems, or the like. Most of the men who impregnated the girls are older, and they rarely visit. Some of the girls don't like the rules and leave these homes, but others stay to the limit and come back as alumnae. The homes work hard at teaching girls how to be mothers, how to deal effectively with other people, why it is important to get an education, and how to cope with the temptation of drugs.[61]

In 1999 the Massachusetts program costs $38,000 per mother, and because the program is new, we do not yet know whether it makes a difference. These two facts—high costs and unknown results—might doom this program for policy wonks. But it has one great attraction: it directs our energies at infants in the critical years of their lives, when a chance—perhaps the best chance, possibly the only chance—exists for saving them from reproducing the life of abuse and dependency that they might otherwise inherit.

A less expensive version of the same approach was suggested by Elizabeth Gill. An experienced guardian of abused and neglected children, she has proposed that each state create Parent-Child Centers for unwed teenage mothers. Each small center would be headed by an experienced mother or two who would supervise a day-care program in which the teen moms would care for their own children and be enrolled in educational programs run at the center. The centers would not be residential; at night the moms would live in their own homes or with their parents. The cost of the centers would thus be less than that of second-chance homes but the goals would be the same: caring for both the children and their young mothers so that the former get a decent start in life and the latter learn how to manage a family.[62]

Caring for unwed mothers costs a lot, but the damage it might prevent can be equally large. Having allowed a second nation of single-parent families to emerge in ways that supply new recruits for gangs, new girls to be exploited, and new recipients for welfare, we should not be astonished to learn that fixing the problem will be expensive. Not only expensive, but with benefits that may be limited to only a few mothers and their children.

But reviving old institutions, such as orphanages, or installing new ones, such as second-chance homes, will not make a large difference unless there is a powerful cultural reassertion of the value of marriage. Although most people want that to happen, the leadership that might make it occur is conspicuous by its absence.

The central problem is how a society manages stigma. Many people confuse stigma and prejudice, but the two are very different. Prejudice means wrongly imputing to people the traits of a group of which they are a member. We are prejudiced when we think that some man thinks likes other men, some woman behaves like other women, or some African American reacts like other African Americans. Stigma, by contrast, means blaming a single person for his or her immoral, dishonorable, or improper conduct. We rely on stigma to reproach individuals for lying, cheating, stealing, or extramarital sex. Prejudice is an erroneous imputation of group traits on individuals; stigma is the attribution of blame to a single individual. Prejudice leads to discrimination, stigma to shame.

Shame is the inner sense that one has violated an important social or moral rule. Shame once inhibited women from having children without marrying and men from abandoning wives for trophy alternatives. Today it does much less of either. We wrongly suppose, I think, that shame is the enemy of personal emancipation when in fact an emancipated man or woman is one for whom inner control is sufficiently powerful to produce inner limits on actions that once were controlled by external forces. A truly free man or woman is a person whose actions are controlled by gyroscopes rather than opportunities.

But our society has managed to stigmatize stigma so much so that we are reluctant to blame people for any act that does not appear to inflict an immediate and palpable harm on someone else. In Muncie, Indiana, a middle-American town whose people have been repeatedly studied for more than three-fourths of a century, we learn that in 1924, when parents were asked what were the most important values that their children should learn, they said obedience and religion. Today, they say independence and good manners.[63] This change reveals both what we value and what we deplore. Children ought to be independent, and apparently they are, but they also ought to restrain that independence with an equivalent concern for decency and moral conduct. Outside of Muncie, the decline of stigma has gone much further, as is evident to any school principal who must contend with parents who oppose instructional discipline, any police officer who must confront a gang member, any welfare worker who must deal with an unwed mother, or any citizen who might wish to reproach an unruly boy.

The lasting power of our civil emancipation can be seen in the First Nation as well as in the Second. Many affluent parents appear to be indifferent to their own children's misconduct. For example, there was a massive outbreak of syphilis among more than two hundred chil-

dren in a nice Atlanta suburb. The parents of these youngsters were
often unengaged. One scholar put it bluntly: "We see parents who are
either clueless or blatantly unconcerned about their children." They
have replaced "caring and personal involvement with the purchase of
material goods."[64]

Shame has not been entirely discarded by elite opinion. Of late
there has been a revived interest in shame as a way of controlling juvenile delinquents. As described by John Braithwaite, an Australian
criminologist who is its chief proponent, neighborhood groups should
be empowered to rely on certain forms of shame as a way of disciplin-
ing young people convicted of less serious offenses.[65] Efforts to use
reintegrative shaming for this purpose are under way in many cities; if
they succeed, they will give shame a good name again. But even if successful, creating an *organization* to deliver stigma is a bit different
from encouraging a society to do it.

Cultures are like lunches: none is free. Both offer benefits, but always
at a price.

Why Do People Marry?

Despite all of these problems, what is astonishing is that Americans
think marriage is a good idea and that a married couple does a better
job of raising children than do unmarried persons. They are critical of
parents who emphasize their personal happiness over the well-being
of their children.[66] Why should they believe this when for a century or
more almost every reason to be married has been under assault? The
family no longer has a large economic role or any political role at all.
Sex is available outside it as well as inside it, and with modern contraception and abortion technologies the risk of any unhappy consequences can be dramatically reduced. The rise of individualism has
made many of us believe that personal rights are more important than
collective goods. But still people want to get married. Why do people
believe that making a commitment to live together forever is better
than just living together so long as it is convenient? It seems so easy to
suppose that one can arrange one's own life with a partner without

any contractual obligations. Why do couples with no religious beliefs often get married in churches or synagogues? The lesson that Western culture has tried to teach us has been that, though religion may play some role in one's private life, it has no larger meaning.

Marriage is a cultural response to a deep-seated desire for companionship, affection, and child rearing, desires so deep seated that surely they are largely the product of our evolutionary history. Ask anyone why he or she married, and you will get no clear answer. "We love each other." "We want to have children." "We thought it was the right thing to do." All true, but the love and the children can come without marriage, yet the third answer—it was the right thing to do—dominates the decision. "Why did I marry?" one historian asked at the end of his book on husbands and wives in America. "Hell, I married. Reasons fail. I am happy I did, but why I did will always remain just beyond my horizon of self-knowledge. I thought I was acting as a free agent, but I was also working off scripts and patterns that I barely recognized."[67]

Marriage is a commitment that profoundly alters how a man and woman deal with one another. The collective good—that is, the obligation to share resources, live together, raise children in concert, and avoid sexual temptations—seems to improve individual lives. But to understand the benefits of that commitment one has to be—well, grown up. One way to act grown up is to accept the importance of a formal, and often a religious, ceremony. By doing so one is boldly saying that marital commitments are so important you wish to make yours publicly, in front of friends and relatives, and with the endorsement of a religious leader who confers on the commitment a blessing that you may or may not accept but that emphasizes, whatever your beliefs, how serious that commitment is.

But not everyone is grown up. Some are too young to understand commitment; their goal instead is romance, sexual access, having a child, or remaining free. Some remain young a long time because their own parents have set no model for them, and their friends celebrate a teenager's child because it is "cute" and not because it is important. Some are old enough to understand a commitment but still do not grasp its meaning. They would just as soon live together until they get bored with that, and if they marry they do so quickly and privately in front of a judge, not a minister, and with few, if any, witnesses. For them, Sweden is the answer. And perhaps Sweden is the answer—for Swedes.

For Americans, however, Japan may be a better model than Sweden, because the former has succeeded in taking advantage of the Enlightenment without bearing some of its costs. In Japan, science is encouraged, democracy is practiced, industry flourishes, arts are cultivated, citizens are free, and the government is accountable, but shame remains a powerful force for controlling behavior. Crime, drug abuse, and out-of-wedlock births are all remarkably rare, and that rarity has been achieved without much in the way of a coercive government program. Divorce rates are about one-third of what they are here. However, the one thing Japan cannot export is its culture.* That America cannot adopt it is a fact of history. What is not a fact of history is why American elites prefer Sweden to Japan.

This country does not quite face a disaster because most people believe in marriage even though some activists are trying to talk us out of it. Between 1995 and 2000, the percentage of children living with married parents increased slightly among blacks and Hispanics. But if there is no marital disaster, neither is there marital success. The root of our present cultural problems flows from the failure of marriage to hold its ground among many poor people. The recent increase among children living with married black parents was only from thirty-five to thirty-nine percent. The tolerance and individualism of the affluent have exacted a heavy price from the poor. From the 1600s until near the end of the nineteenth century, we told black slaves they could not marry. After slavery ended, African Americans were allowed to marry but white law was indulgent toward—better, neglectful of—the problems of some of these marriages. From 1935 to 1996 we told the poor that somebody else would take care of their familial problems, but of course no one else did, and when we ended that message in 1996 we

*But perhaps Japan can import Western culture. Recent news accounts have announced the stirrings there of greater individualism and what the Japanese call the "era of personal responsibility." (Yumiko Ono and Bill Spindle, "Japan's Long Decline Makes One Thing Rise: Individualism," *Wall Street Journal* [December 29, 2000]: A1.) But Japan still has a long way to go before personal responsibility becomes doing your own thing.

did so with an equally odd message: unwed mothers will be better off if they work more. The correct message should be that out-of-wedlock children will be better off if parents care for them. One provision of the 1996 law, the one that encourages second-chance homes, is a step in that direction, but it is one that most states have only gingerly embraced.

Our object should be to restore for everyone the authority of marriage. The history of mankind has taught us this lesson and we ignore it at our peril. But restoring that value is not something that can be done by a public policy. As Daniel Patrick Moynihan once remarked, "if you expect a government program to change families, you know more about government than I do." Culture is the legacy of human reflection about ordinary experiences, a legacy that is reinforced by religion. Religion greatly increases the likelihood that young people will marry rather than cohabit.[68] The problem for Anglo-American society is to find a way whereby marriage is restored. That effort must be done retail, not wholesale, by families and churches and neighborhoods and the media, not by tax breaks or government subsidies.

Will it happen? We do not know. But the effort to do so can draw upon one great strength: the persistence of marriage among people for whom it could so easily be dismissed. Most of us wish to be part of our own family. We find something deeply satisfying in an intimate arrangement that, though weakened, persists. Our task is to teach our children to seek out the same satisfactions by insisting on a simple rule: Do not have children before you are married.

Historian Steven Ozment has written that the family, though "the smallest and seemingly most fragile of institutions," is "proving itself to be humankind's bedrock as well as its fault line." This book has been about the fault lines; I end it with an acknowledgment of the bedrock strength of marriage. That strength "lies in the cohesion and loyalty of the parent-child unit around which the larger worlds of household and kin, community and nation . . . necessarily revolve."[69] The parent-child bond is the source of much of our moral nature and the foundation of social organization.[70] Most people know this, and act upon it. But the commitment that will nurture and sustain that bond is under attack, not by the enemies of children, but by our own desire for extinguishing shame and achieving an illusory emancipation.

Notes

Chapter 1

1. Benjamin Disraeli, *Sybil* (London: Oxford University Press, 1926), 67.

2. Elijah Anderson, *Streetwise* (Chicago: University of Chicago Press, 1990).

3. For an account of his report and the ensuing anger, see Lee Rainwater and W. L. Yancey, *The Moynihan Report and the Politics of Controversy* (Cambridge: MIT Press, 1967).

4. Committee on Ways and Means, *1998 Green Book* (Washington, D.C.: House of Representatives, 19 May 1998), 1252–53.

5. Annie E. Casey Foundation, *When Teens Have Sex* (Baltimore: Casey Foundation, 1998), 32.

6. David R. Hall and John Z. Zhao, "Cohabitation and Divorce in Canada," *Journal of Marriage and the Family* 57 (1995): 421–27; Larry L. Bumpass et al., "The Changing Character of Stepfamilies," *Demography* 32 (1995): 425–37; James H. Bray, "Children's Development in Early Remarriage," in *Impact of Divorce, Single Parenting, and Stepparenting on Children,* ed. E. M. Hetherington and J. D. Arasteh (Hillsdale, N.J.: Lawrence Erlbaum, 1988), 279–98; and Wade F. Horn, *Father Facts, 3d ed.* (Gaithersburg, Md.: National Fatherhood Initiative, 1998).

7. Martin Daly and Margo Wilson, *Homicide* (New York: Aldine de Gruyter, 1988), 89.

8. Survey Research Center, "Monitoring the Future Survey," University of Michigan, 1995. Cited in David Popenoe and Barbara Dafoe Whitehead, *Should We Live Together?* report of the National Marriage Project (New Brunswick, N.J.: Rutgers University, 1999), 4.

9. Deanna L. Pagnini and Ronald R. Rindfuss, "The Divorce of Marriage and Childbearing: Changing Attitudes in the United States," *Population and Development Review* 19 (1993): 336.

10. Larry L. Bumpass and James A. Sweet, "National Estimates of Cohabitation," *Demography* 26 (1989): 620–21.

11. Ibid., 621.

12. Neil G. Bennett, Ann Kilmas Blanc, and David E. Bloom, "Commitment and the Modern Union: Assessing the Link Between Premarital Cohabitation and Subsequent Marital Stability," *American Sociological Review* 53 (1988): 127–38.

13. T. R. Balakrishnan et al., "A Hazard Model Analysis of the Covariates of Marriage Dissolution in Canada," *Demography* 24 (1987): 395–406; F. Althaus, "Young Dutch Women Are Less Likely than Before to Marry, Have Children," *Family Planning Perspectives* 23 (1991): 190–91.

14. Larry L. Bumpass, "What's Happening to the Family?" *Demography* 27 (1990): 483–98.

15. William G. Axin and Arland Thornton, "The Relationship Between Cohabitation and Divorce: Selectively or Causal Influence?" *Demography* 29 (1992): 372.

16. David Popenoe, letter to author, 26 February 1999.

17. Eric Nagourney, "Study Finds Families Bypassing Marriage," *New York Times*, 15 February 2000.

18. Susan L. Brown and Alan Booth, "Cohabitation Versus Marriage: A Comparison of Relationship Quality," *Journal of Marriage and the Family* 58 (1996): 668–78.

19. David Popenoe, *Life Without Father* (New York: Free Press, 1996), 34; Larry L. Bumpass and James A. Sweet, "Children's Experience in Single-Parent Families," *Family Planning Perspectives* 6 (1989): 256–60; and Bumpass and Sweet, "National Estimates of Cohabitation," *Demography* 26 (1989): 615–25.

20. Wendy D. Manning and Daniel T. Lichter, "Parental Cohabitation and Children's Economic Well-Being," *Journal of Marriage and the Family* 58 (1996): 998–1010.

21. Larry Bumpass and Hsien-Hen Lu, "Trends in Cohabitation and Implications for Children's Family Contexts in the United States," *Population Studies* 54 (2000): 29–41.

22. Pamela J. Smock, "Cohabitation in the United States," *Annual Review of Sociology* 26 (2000): 1–20; Arland Thornton, "Influence of the Marital History of Parents on the Marital and Cohabitational Experiences of Children," *American Journal of Sociology* 96 (1991): 868–94.

23. Robert Whelan, *Broken Homes and Battered Children* (London: Family Education Trust, 1993). See Table 12.

24. Teresa Castro-Martin and Larry L. Bumpass, "Recent Trends in Marital Disruption," *Demography* 26 (1989): 37–51; Fjalar Finnas, "Entry Into Consensual Unions and Marriages Among Finnish Women Born Between 1938 and 1967," *Population Studies* 49 (1995): 57–70.

25. Sara McLanahan and Gary Sandefur, *Growing Up With a Single Parent: What Hurts, What Helps* (Cambridge: Harvard University Press, 1994), 39–63.

26. Deborah A. Dawson, "Family Structure and Children's Health: United States, 1988," *Vital and Health Statistics*, 10th ser., no. 178 (1991).

27. Horn summarizes these studies, and supplies the references, at pages 54–73.

28. McLanahan and Sandefur, 95. There appears to be only one recent study that contradicts these findings, and it was limited to the school readiness of six- and seven-year-old children: Henry N. Ricciuti, "Single Parenthood and School Readiness in White, Black, and Hispanic 6- and 7-Year Olds," *Journal of Family Psychology* 13 (1999): 450–65.

29. Cynthia C. Harper and Sara S. McLanahan, "Father Absence and Youth Incarceration," paper presented to the American Sociological Association (August 1998). See also Amy Conseur, et al., "Maternal and Perinatal Risk Factors for Later Delinquency," *Pediatrics* 99 (1997): 785–90.

30. Nicholas Eberstadt, *Prosperous Paupers & Other Population Problems* (New Brunswick, N.J.: Transaction, 2000), 33–50.

31. McLanahan and Sandefur, 95–115.

32. Robert J. Sampson, "Neighborhood and Crime: The Structural Determinants of Personal Victimization," *Journal of Research in Crime and Delinquency* 22 (1985): 7–40; Sampson, "Neighborhood Family Structure and the Risk of Criminal Victimization," in *The Social Ecology of Crime*, ed. J. Byrne and Robert Sampson (New York: Springer-Verlag, 1986), 25–46; D. R. Smith and G. R. Jarjoura, "Social Structure and Criminal Victimization," *Journal of Research in Crime and Delinquency* 25 (1988): 27–52.

33. William Galston's statement is based on facts drawn from Charles Murray, "According to Age: Longitudinal Profiles of AFDC Recipients and the Poor by Age Group," Working Seminar on the Family and American Welfare Policy, Washington, D.C., 1986, 89–90.

34. Tom Wolfe, *Hooking Up* (New York: Farrar Straus Giroux, 2000). See also the detailed study by Norval Glenn and Elizabeth Marquardt, *Hooking Up, Hanging Out, and Hoping for Mr. Right.* (New York: Institute for American Values, 2001).

35. Quoted in Barbara Dafoe Whitehead, "The Plight of the High-Status Woman," *Atlantic Monthly* (December 1999), 122.

36. Ibid.

37. "Flying Solo," *Time* (August 28, 2000), 47–55. [no author]

38. Ibid., 49.

39. Quoted in Ferdinand Mount, *The Subversive Family* (New York: Free Press, 1992), 4, 156.

40. Stephanie Coontz, *The Way We Never Were: American Families and the Nostalgia Trap* (New York: Basic Books, 1992), 111.

41. Quoted in James Q. Wilson, "The Family-Values Debate," *Commentary* (April 1993): 24.

42. Jesse Bernard, *The Future of Marriage* (New Haven, Conn.: Yale University Press, 1982), 245–7, 271.

43. Christopher Lasch, *Haven in a Heartless World: The Family Besieged* (New York: Norton, 1995), 6.

44. "Flying Solo," 48.

45. Linda J. Waite and Maggie Gallagher, *The Case for Marriage* (New York: Doubleday, 2000).

46. Steven Stack and J. Ross Eshelman, "Marital Status and Happiness: A 17-Nation Study," *Journal of Marriage and the Family* 60 (1998): 527–536.

47. Waite and Gallagher, 47–64.

48. Robert H. Coombs, "Marital Status and Personal Well-Being: A Literature Review," *Family Relations* 40 (1991): 97–102; Catherine E. Ross, John Mirowsky, and Karen Goldsteen, "The Impact of the Family on Health: The Decade in Review," *Journal of Marriage and the Family* 52 (1990): 1059–1078.

49. Waite and Gallagher, 55.

50. Ibid., 59–61.

51. Catherine E. Ross, John Mirowsky, and Karen Goldstein, "The Impact of the Family on Health: A Decade in Review," *Journal of Marriage and the Family* 52 (1990): 1059–78; Richard G. Rogers, "Marriage, Sex, and Mortality," *Journal of Marriage and the Family* 57 (1995): 515–26; I. M. A. Joung, et al., "The Contributions of Intermediary Factors to Marital Status Differences in Self-Reported Health," *Journal of Marriage and the Family* 59 (1997): 476–90; Lee A. Lillard and Linda J. Waite, " 'Til Death Do Us Part: Marital Disruption and Mortality," *American Journal of Sociology* 100 (1995): 1131–56; Frank Trovato and Gloria Lauris, "Marital Status and Mortality in Canada," *Journal of Marriage and the Family* 51 (1989): 907–22.

52. Nadine F. Marks and James D. Lambert, "Marital Status Continuity and Change Among Young and Midlife Adults: Longitudinal Effects on Psychological Well-Being," *Journal of Family Issues* 19 (1998): 652–86; Waite and Gallagher, 65–77.

53. Sanders Korenman and David Neumark, "Does Marriage Really Make Men More Productive?" *Journal of Human Resources* 26 (1991): 282–307 and Waite and Gallagher, 97–109.

54. In five developed countries, women devote at least twice as many hours to child care as do men. Judith Bruce et al., *Families in Focus* (New York: Population Council, 1995), 52.

55. Richard T. Gill, *Posterity Lost: Progress, Ideology, and the Decline of the American Family* (New York: Rowman & Littlefield, 1997), 61.

56. United Nations, *Demographic Yearbook, 1986* (New York: United Nations, 1988), table 32.

57. Michael Barone, *The New Americans* (Washington, D.C.: Regnery, 2001), 38–40, 133–5, 166–7, 223–5, 268–9.

58. National Center for Health Statistics, *Report to Congress on Out-of-Wedlock Childbearing* (Washington, D.C.: Department of Health and Human Services, 1995).

Chapter 2

1. Kathleen Gough, "The Origin of the Family," *Journal of Marriage and the Family* 33 (1971): 760–71.

2. Dain Borges, *The Family in Bahia, Brazil, 1870–1945* (Stanford, Calif.: Stanford University Press, 1992), 46.

3. Donald Symons, "Darwinism and Contemporary Marriage," in *Contemporary Marriage*, ed. Kingsley Davis (New York: Russell Sage Foundation, 1985), 133–55.

4. John Tooby and Leda Cosmides, "The Psychological Foundations of Culture," in *The Adapted Mind: Evolutionary Psychology and the Generation of Culture*, ed. Jerome H. Barkow, Leda Cosmides, and John Tooby (New York: Oxford University Press, 1992), 117. This lengthy essay is a most useful introduction to the problems in explaining human behavior by "culture."

5. Ibid., 763.

6. Lionel Tiger and Robin Fox, *The Imperial Animal* (New York: Holt, Rinehart & Winston, 1971), 71.

7. Ibid., 70.

8. Cf. Robin Fox, *Kinship and Marriage* (Cambridge: Cambridge University Press, 1967), 41–50.

9. For a brief overview in Africa, see Thomas S. Weisner, "Support for Children and the African Family Crisis," in *African Families and the Crisis of Social Change*, (Westport, Conn.: Bergin and Garvey, 1997), 20–44.

10. Fox, 31.

11. This view is even offered by a person who seems to favor marriage as simply a contract. See Marjorie Schultz, "Contractual Ordering of Marriage: A New Model for State Policy," *California Law Review* 70 (1982): 204.

12. A good review of these reactions is in Edward Westermarck, *The History of Human Marriage* (New York: Allerton, 1922), 86–94.

13. Martin Daly and Margot Wilson, *Sex, Evolution, and Behavior*, 2d ed. (Belmont, Calif.: Wadsworth Publishing Co., 1983), 286.

14. Robert O. Hawkins, "The Relationship Between Culture, Personality, and Sexual Jealousy in Men in Heterosexual and Homosexual Relationships," *Journal of Homosexuality* 19 (1990): 67–84. See also Robert G.

Bringle, "Psychosocial Aspects of Jealousy," in *The Psychology of Jealousy and Envy*, ed. Peter Salovey (New York: Guilford Press, 1991).

15. Gregory L. White and Paul E. Mullen, *Jealousy* (New York: Guilford Press, 1989), 122. Jealousy is also a problem in group-marriage communes.

16. Nena O'Neill and George O'Neill, *Open Marriage* (New York: Evans & Co., 1972), 256–57.

17. Ibid., 239–40.

18. David M. Buss, *The Evolution of Desire* (New York: Basic Books, 1994), 139.

19. Bram P. Buunk, "Jealousy in Close Relationships: An Exchange-Theoretical Perspective," in *The Psychology of Jealousy and Envy*, ed. Peter Salovey (New York: Guilford Press, 1991).

20. Buss, 129–31.

21. Peter N. Stearns, *Jealousy: The Evolution of an Emotion in American History* (New York: New York University Press, 1989), 121. The quotations from Mead, Davis, and Ellis are taken from Stearns at 115–17.

22. Ibid., 127–29, and David C. Geary, *Male, Female* (Washington, D.C.: American Psychological Association,1998). 131, 148. See also Mark W. Teismann and Donald L. Mosher, "Jealous Conflict in Dating Couples," *Psychological Reports* 42 (1978): 1211–16, Joyce Shettel-Neuber, Jeff B. Bryson, and Leanne E. Young, "Physical Attractiveness of the 'Other Person' and Jealousy," *Personality and Social Psychology Bulletin* 4 (1978): 612–15; David M. Buss et al., "Sex Differences in Jealousy," *Psychological Science* 3 (1992): 251–55; Buss, et al., "Jealousy and the Nature of Beliefs About Infidelity: Tests of Competing Hypotheses About Sex Differences in the United States, Korea, and Japan," *Personal Relationships* 6 (1999): 125–50; Buss, *The Dangerous Passion* (New York: Free Press, 2000), 49–72.

23. For a glimpse of the scholarly debate over the extent to which jealousy reflects innate differences between men and women that have been shaped by evolution or reflects instead some process of social learning, see *Psychological Science* 7 (1996): 359–79. In my view jealousy does indeed reveal some important biological predispositions between men and women that culture can modify up to a point. Scholars who argue that jealousy is wholly learned have no good explanation for why men and women always differ in what they have supposedly learned. But I also feel that a narrow evolutionary view does not explain jealousy for reasons stated in the next few paragraphs.

24. James Q. Wilson, *The Moral Sense* (New York: Free Press, 1993), 40–4, 127, 227–28.

25. Lawrence Stone, "Passionate Attachments in the West in Historical Perspective," in *Passionate Attachments*, ed. Willard Gaylin and Ethel Person (New York: Free Press, 1988), 16.

26. William R. Jankowiak and Edward F. Fischer, "A Cross-Cultural Perspective on Romantic Love," *Ethnology* 1 (1992): 149–55.

27. Thomas Gregor, "Sexuality and the Experience of Love," in *Sexual*

Nature, Sexual Culture, ed. Paul R. Abramson and Steven D. Pinkerton (Chicago: University of Chicago Press, 1995), 330–50.

28. Helen Harris, "Human Nature and the Nature of Romantic Love" (Ph.D. diss., University of California at Santa Barbara, 1995), 68–71. See also William Goode, "The Theoretical Importance of Love," *American Sociological Review* 24 (1959): 38–47.

29. On male jealousy, see Martin Daly, Margo Wilson, and Suzanne J. Weghorst, "Male Sexual Jealousy," *Ethnology and Sociobiology* 3 (1982): 11–27.

30. Jennifer Roback Morse, *Love & Economics* (Dallas: Spence Publishing, 2001), 63, 175, 197.

31. On marriage viewed as an investment, see Elizabeth S. Scott and Robert E. Scott, "A Contract Theory of Marriage," in *The Fall and Rise of Freedom of Contract*, ed. F. H. Buckley (Durham, N.C.: Duke University Press, 1999), 201–44, especially 212–18.

32. Linda J. Waite and Maggie Gallagher, *The Case for Marriage* (New York: Doubleday, 2000), 47.

33. Ibid., 31.

34. Ibid., 43, 53–4.

35. Ibid., 31.

36. David F. Lancy, *Playing on the Mother-Ground* (New York: Guilford Press, 1996), 31–71.

Chapter 3

1. General Register Office, *Census 1961* (London: HMSO, 1966). The decline in the total number of men relative to women was only 2 percent, but the decline for young men was much larger.

2. Pamela Sharpe, "Literally Spinsters: A New Interpretation of Local Economy and Demography in Coylton in the Seventeenth and Eighteenth Centuries," *Economic History Review* 44 (1991): 46–65.

3. Edward Westermarck, *The History of Human Marriage*, 5th ed. (New York: Allerton, 1922), III, 52–63.

4. On China, see China Financial and Economic Publishing House, *New China's Population* (New York: Macmillan, 1988), 114; and Guo Zhigang and Deng Guosheng, "A Theoretical Study on the Marriage Market: Perspectives on the Marriage Market in the Process of Fertility Decline in China," *Chinese Journal of Population Science* 8 (1996): 13–22; and R. Jeffrey, P. Jeffrey, and A. S. Lyon, "Female Infanticide and Amniocentesis," *Social Science and Medicine* 9 (1984): 1207–12.

5. *Too Many Women? The Sex Ratio Question* (Newbury Park, Calif.: Sage Publications, 1983).

6. Guttentag and Secord, 175.

7. Noreen Goldman et al., "Demography in the Marriage Market in the United States," *Population Index* 50 (1984): 5–25.

8. Norval Glenn and Elizabeth Marquardt, *Hooking Up, Hanging Out, and Hoping for Mr. Right* (New York: Institute for American Values, 2001), 10–1; Goldman, 18.

9. Brad Edmonston and Blayne Cutler, "Where the Boys Are," *Atlantic* 263 (1989): 67.

10. Guttentag and Secord, 201.

11. Ibid., 214.

12. For blacks aged twenty to twenty-four, the undercount for males is estimated to be 5.7 percent and for females 2.5 percent, a difference of about 3 percent. By ages thirty to thirty-four the undercount difference is about 10 percent. Howard Hogan and Gregg Robinson, "What the Census Bureau's Coverage Evaluation Programs Tell Us About Differential Undercount," in *Research Conference on Undercounted Ethnic Populations: Proceedings* (Washington, D.C.: U.S. Department of Commerce, 1993), 9–28. I am grateful to Peter Skerry for helping me on this matter.

13. Mark A. Fossett and K. Jill Kiecolt, "A Methodological Review of the Sex Ratio: Alternatives for Comparative Research," *Journal of Marriage and the Family* 53 (1991): 941–57.

14. Guttentag and Secord, 207–11.

15. Bureau of the Census, *Negroes in the United States, 1920 to 1932* (Washington, D.C.: U.S. Government Printing Office, 1935), table 2.

16. Daniel Lichter et al., "Race and the Retreat from Marriage: A Shortage of Marriageable Men?" *American Sociological Review* 57 (1992): 781–99.

17. Guttentag and Secord, 219.

18. Ibid., 221.

19. The connection was estimated by a regression equation. For the illegitimacy rate: There were 3.7 fewer illegitimate births per thousand black women and 4.3 fewer illegitimate ones per thousand white women for every additional male in each race's sex ratio. For the illegitimacy ratio: There were 2.3 percent fewer illegitimate births out of all black births and just under 1 percent fewer illegitimate births out of all white births for each percentage increase in the number of males.

20. Mark A. Fossett and K. Jill Kiecolt, "Mate Availability, Family Formation, and Family Structure Among Black Americans in Nonmetropolitan Louisiana, 1970–1980," *Rural Sociology* 55 (1990): 305–27.

21. Mark A. Fossett and K. Jill Kiecolt, "Mate Availability and Family Structure Among African Americans in U.S. Metropolitan Areas," *Journal of Marriage and the Family* 55 (1993): 288–302. Much the same conclusion was reached in Scott South and Kim Lloyd, "Marriage Markets and Nonmarital Fertility in the United States," *Demography* 29 (1992): 247–64.

22. Scott J. South and Kim M. Lloyd, "Marriage Markets and Nonmarital Fertility in the United States," *Demography* 29 (1992): 247–64.

23. Scott J. South and Kim M. Lloyd, "Spousal Alternatives and Marital Dissolution," *American Sociological Review* 60 (1995): 21–35.

24. K. Jill Kiecolt and Mark A. Fossett, "Mate Availability and Marriage Among African Americans: Aggregate- and Individual-Level Analyses," in *The Decline in Marriage Among African Americans*, ed. M. Belinda Tucker and Claudia Mitchell-Kernan (New York: Russell Sage Foundation, 1995), 121–35.

25. William Julius Wilson, *The Truly Disadvantaged* (Chicago: University of Chicago Press, 1987), 83–86.

26. David Hayes-Bautista, *No Longer a Minority: Latinos and Social Policy in California* (Los Angeles: UCLA Chicano Studies Research Center, 1992), 12–19. For an elaboration of this point, see my chapter 5.

27. Daniel T. Lichter, Felicia B. LeClere, and Diane K. Laughlin, "Local Marriage Markets and the Marital Behavior of Black and White Women," *American Journal of Sociology* 96 (1991): 843–67; and Lichter et al., "Race and the Retreat from Marriage," op. cit. See also Daniel T. Lichter, Robert N. Anderson, and Mark D. Hayward, "Marriage Markets and Marital Choice," *Journal of Family Issues* 16 (1995): 412–31.

28. Jane Waldfogel, "Working Mothers Then and Now: Effects of Maternity Leave on Women's Pay," in *Gender and Family Issues in the Workplace*, ed. Francine D. Blau and Ronald G. Ehrenberg (New York: Russell Sage Foundation, 1997), 92–126.

29. Scott J. South, "Sex Roles, Economic Power, and Women's Roles: A Theoretical Extension and Empirical Test," *Journal of Marriage and the Family* 50 (1988): 19–31. Of course the strength of this study is weakened by the fact that sex ratios often vary greatly across communities within any given nation.

30. David T. Courtwright, *Violent Land: Single Men and Social Disorder from the Frontier to the Inner City* (Cambridge: Harvard University Press, 1996), 133.

31. Ibid., 79.

32. Alan P. Grimes, *The Puritan Ethic and Woman Suffrage* (New York: Oxford University Press, 1967), 14. In at least one state, Utah, the sex ratio was evenly balanced, and female suffrage arrived for religious reasons. But in other states women were generally outnumbered.

33. Ibid., 76.

34. Stanford W. Lyman, *Chinese Americans* (New York: Random House, 1974), 86–88.

35. Ibid., chap. 5.

36. Ibid., 159.

37. Guttentag and Secord, 131–32; Courtwright, 23, 152–69; Lyman, op. cit.

38. David C. Geary, *Male, Female: The Evolution of Human Sex Differences* (Washington, D.C.: American Psychological Association, 1998), 101.

39. Ibid., 317–20. See also Eleanor E. Maccoby and C. N. Jacklin, *The Psychology of Sex Differences* (Stanford, Calif.: Stanford University Press,

1974); and Maccoby, *The Two Sexes* (Cambridge: Harvard University Press, 1998), 89–117.

40. Lawrence H. Keeley, *War Before Civilization* (New York: Oxford University Press, 1996), 86–88.

41. Ibid., 143–47.

42. Ibid., 31–32.

43. David M. Buss, *The Evolution of Desire: Strategies of Human Mating* (New York: Basic Books, 1994), 55–57. See also Geary, 149–51, and the many studies cited therein.

44. Nancy Etcoff, *Survival of the Prettiest: The Science of Beauty* (New York: Doubleday, 1999), 192, and studies cited therein.

45. Jean E. Veevers, "The 'Real' Marriage Squeeze," *Sociological Quarterly* 31 (1988): 180.

46. Buss, 23–24.

47. Ibid., 82.

48. James Boswell, *The Life of Samuel Johnson* (New York: Oxford University Press, 1936), ii, 444.

49. Geary, 102.

Chapter 4

1. R. H. Helmholz, *Marriage Litigation in Medieval England* (Cambridge: Cambridge University Press, 1974), 27–31.

2. Edward Westermarck, *Marriage* (New York: Jonathan Cape, 1929), 48–54.

3. Giri Raj Gupta, "Love, Arranged Marriage and the Indian Social Structure," in *Cross-Cultural Perspectives of Mate-Selection and Marriage*, ed. George Kurian (Westport, Conn.: Greenwood Press, 1979).

4. Boserup published first: see her book *Women's Role in Economic Development* (London: Allen & Unwin, 1970). Goody developed this argument in a 1976 book, cited below.

5. Jack Goody, *Production and Reproduction* (Cambridge: Cambridge University Press, 1976), 109. See the entire book for a full elaboration of the argument I have summarized in the text.

6. Adam Kuper, *Wives for Cattle: Bridewealth and Marriage in Southern Africa* (London: Routledge & Kegan Paul, 1982), 166.

7. Alan Macfarlane, *The Origins of English Individualism* (New York: Cambridge University Press, 1978); and Macfarlane, *Marriage and Love in England* (London: Basil Blackwell, 1986).

8. William I. Thomas and Florian Znaniecki, *The Polish Peasant in Europe and America* (New York: Alfred Knopf, 1927).

9. Ibid., 158.

10. Ibid., 92.

11. Teodor Shanin, "A Peasant Household: Russia at the Turn of the Century," in *Peasants and Peasant Societies*, ed. Teodor Shanin (London: Basil Blackwell, 1987), 21–26; and Shanin, *The Awkward Class* (Oxford: Clarendon Press, 1972), 30–31.

12. Richard Pipes, *Property and Freedom* (New York: Alfred Knopf, 1999), 159–208. See also Peter Czap, Jr., "Marriage and the Peasant Family in the Era of Serfdom," in *The Family in Imperial Russia*, ed. David L. Ransel (Urbana: University of Illinois Press, 1978), 103–23.

13. Thomas and Znaniecki, 113.

14. Macfarlane, 74.

15. Peter Laslett, "Mean Household Size in England Since the Sixteenth Century," in *Household and Family in Past Time*, ed. Peter Laslett (Cambridge: Cambridge University Press, 1972).

16. John R. Gillis, *For Better, For Worse: British Marriages, 1600 to the present* (New York: Oxford University Press, 1985), 15.

17. R. M. Smith, "Some Reflections on the Evidence for the Origins of the 'European Marriage Pattern' in England," in *The Sociology of the Family*, ed. Chris Harris (Staffordshire: University of Keele, 1979), 78–79.

18. Macfarlane, 81, provides a brief summary of the complex relationship between sex and landownership in England. Though the legal superiority of men was undeniable, women could more easily acquire land in England than in countries where there was clan control of property.

19. Brian Tierney, *The Idea of Natural Rights* (Atlanta: Scholars Press, 1997), 344. Tierney offers an excellent account of how natural rights arose in medieval and early modern thought.

20. John Witte, Jr., *From Sacrament to Contract: Marriage, Religion, and Law in the Western Tradition* (Louisville, Ky.: Westminster John Knox Press, 1997). In the pages that follow, I rely heavily on Professor Witte's findings.

21. Alan Macfarlane, *Marriage and Love in England: Modes of Reproduction, 1300–1840* (London: Basil Blackwell, 1986), 125.

22. Jack Goody, *The Development of the Family and Marriage in Europe* (Cambridge: Cambridge University Press, 1983), 68–73, 93–96, 101–2, 123–25, 221.

23. James A. Brundage, *Law, Sex, and Christian Society in Medieval Europe* (Chicago: University of Chicago Press, 1987), 586–87.

24. Frances Geis and Joseph Geis, *Marriage and the Family in the Middle Ages* (New York: Harper & Row, 1989), 83–98; Charles Donahue, "The Policy of Alexander the Third's Consent Theory of Marriage," in Stephen Kuttner, ed., *Proceedings of the Fourth International Congress of Medieval Canon Law*, vol. 5 in *Monumenta Iuris Canonica*. (Vatican City: Biblioteca Apostolica Vaticana, 1976).

25. Witte, 26, 28, 32.

26. Ibid., 33.

27. Ibid., 38–39.

28. Ibid., chap. 2.

29. Steven Ozment, *When Fathers Ruled: Family Life in Reformation Europe* (Cambridge: Harvard University Press, 1983), 28.

30. Witte, 161–63.

31. John R. Gillis, *For Better, For Worse: British Marriages, 1600 to the Present* (New York: Oxford University Press, 1985), 141.

32. Witte, 173.

33. Alan Macfarlane, *The Culture of Capitalism* (London: Basil Blackwell, 1987), 129–35. See also Martin Ingram, *Church Courts, Sex and Marriage in England, 1570–1640* (Cambridge: Cambridge University Press, 1990), 142–45. These findings rebut Lawrence Stone's argument that marriages until at least the sixteenth century, and perhaps for long after that, were arranged by parents with little regard for the emotional ties between husband and wife. Stone's views were unduly influenced by upper-class experience (rich people did have to worry about dynastic ties and property management). See Lawrence Stone, *The Family, Sex and Marriage in England 1500–1800*, abridged ed. (New York: Harper & Row, 1979), 81–82, 414.

34. Gillis, 17.

35. John R. Gillis, "From Ritual to Romance: Toward an Alternative History of Love," in *Emotion and Social Change*, ed. Carol Z. Stearns and Peter N. Stearns (New York: Holmes & Meier, 1988), 100–103.

36. Gillis, *For Better, For Worse*, 127.

37. Don S. Browning et al., *From Culture Wards to Common Ground: Religion and the American Family Debate* (Louisville, Ky.: Westminister John Knox Press, 1997), 75.

38. Michael Grossberg, *Governing the Hearth* (Chapel Hill: University of North Carolina Press, 1985), 19, 103.

39. John Demos, *A Little Commonwealth: Family Life in Plymouth Colony* (Oxford: Oxford University Press, 1970), 85–91.

40. Linda Kerber, *Women of the Republic: Intellect and Ideology in Revolutionary America* (New York: W. W. Norton, 198), 229–31.

41. Philip J. Greven, Jr., *Four Generations: Population, Land, and Family in Colonial Andover, Massachusetts* (Ithaca, N.Y.: Cornell University Press, 1970), 272–73, 281.

42. Alexis de Tocqueville, *Democracy in America*, trans. Harvey C. Mansfield and Delba Winthrop (Chicago: University of Chicago Press, 2000), 558.

43. Ibid., 563.

44. Ibid., 567.

45. Ibid., 566.

46. Quoted in Grossberg, 70–77.

47. Ibid., 69–75.

48. Milton wrote extensively on marriage; his arguments are summarized in Witte, 179–86.

49. David Hume, *A Treatise of Human Nature*, ed. P. H. Nidditch (Oxford: Clarendon Press, 1978), 486.

50. Adam Smith, *Lectures on Jurisprudence*, ed. R. L. Meek, D. D. Raphael, and P. G. Stein (Oxford: Clarendon Press, 1978), 142.

51. David Hume, *Essays*, ed. Eugene F. Miller (Indianapolis, Ind.: Liberty Classics, 1985), 181–90.

52. Adam Smith, *The Theory of Moral Sentiments*, 6: ii, 1.10.

53. Ibid., 6: ii, 1.5.

54. Roy Porter, *The Creation of the Modern World: The Untold Story of the British Enlightenment* (New York: W. W. Norton, 2000), 320, 326.

55. Joyce Ellis, as quoted by Porter, 326.

56. Mary Wollstonecraft, *A Vindication of the Rights of Women*, ed. Sylvana Tomaselli (Cambridge: Cambridge University Press, 1995). Though she did not write them down, Wollstonecraft had new ideas about sex. She suggested to a married woman that the two of them form a ménage à trois with the latter's husband. She later had a child with a man she refused to marry.

57. Edmund Burke, "Three Letters Addressed to a Member of the Present Parliament," in *The Works of Edmund Burke*, vol. 5 (London: G. Bells & Sons, 1910), 208–13.

58. Witte, 208.

59. Gertrude Himmelfarb, *Marriage, Morals, and the Victorians* (New York: Vintage Books/Random House, 1987), 21.

60. Joan Perkin, *Women and Marriage in Nineteenth-Century England* (Chicago: Lyceum Books, 1989), 10–19.

61. Ibid., 15–19.

62. Ibid., 107.

63. Ibid., 18.

64. Marylynn Salmon, *Women and the Law of Property in Early America* (Chapel Hill: University of North Carolina Press, 1986), 44–53.

65. Ibid., 60–61, 187.

66. Browning et al., 95.

67. Ibid., 85.

68. Grossberg, 87–88.

69. Perkin, 123–24.

70. Stone, 416–22.

71. Grossberg, 5.

72. George M. Young, *Victorian England: Portrait of an Age* (Oxford: Oxford University Press, 1936), 5.

73. John Stuart Mill, "On the Subjection of Women." in *J. S. Mill: On Liberty and Other Writings*, ed. Stefan Collini (Cambridge: Cambridge University Press, 1989), 117. Mill first published this essay in 1869 to the dismay of many of his friends, some of whom thought that the liberal enterprise ended with male rights.

74. On this, see the excellent essay by Gertrude Himmelfarb, *On Liberty and Liberalism: The Case of John Stuart Mill* (New York: Knopf, 1974), 169–86.

75. Perkin, 216.

76. Ibid., 224.

77. Bertrand Russell, *Marriage and Morals* (New York: Liveright, 1929), 166, 307–8, 316.

78. Mary Lyndon Shanley, *Feminism, Marriage, and the Law in Victorian England* (Princeton, N.J.: Princeton University Press, 1989), 65.

79. Ibid., 66, 189–95.

80. For a modern criticism in this vein, see Susan Moller Okin, *Justice, Gender, and the Family* (New York: Basic Books, 1989).

81. On this, see Milton C. Regan, Jr., *Family Law and the Pursuit of Intimacy* (New York: New York University Press, 1993), especially 35–42.

82. Paula S. Fass, *The Damned and the Beautiful: American Youth in the 1920s* (New York: Oxford University Press, 1977), 89–93, 97, 146, 151, 263, 266.

83. B. R. Mitchell, *International Historical Statistics, Europe 1750–1993* (London: Macmillan, 1998), 19–42.

84. Quoted in Modris Eckstein, *Rights of Spring* (Boston: Houghton Mifflin, 1989), 256.

85. Glen H. Elder, *Children of the Great Depression* (Chicago: University of Chicago Press, 1974), 275, 279, 287.

86. See the data summarized in James Q. Wilson, *Thinking About Crime*, rev. ed. (New York: Random House/Vintage Books, 1985), 237.

87. Louis Roussel, quoted in Mary Ann Glendon, *The Transformation of Family Law* (Chicago: University of Chicago Press, 1989), 144.

88. Glendon, 149.

89. Ibid., 156.

90. Ibid., 274.

91. Linda D. Elrod and Robert G. Spector, "A Review of the Year in Family Law," *Family Law Quarterly* 29 (1996): 773.

92. Glendon, 255.

93. Ibid., 278.

94. Carl E. Schneider, "Moral Discourse and the Transformation of American Family Law," *Michigan Law Review* 83 (1985): 1805, 1820.

95. Glendon, 291–92.

96. These phrases are quoted in Witte, 194.

97. Schneider, 1811, quoting the Uniform Marriage and Divorce Act.

98. *Eisenstadt* v. *Baird* 405 U.S. 438 (1972). The point is developed in Reagan.

99. Glendon, 292, quoting Alain Benabent.

100. Philip Rieff, *The Triumph of the Therapeutic* (New York: Harper & Row, 1966), 143.

101. Bureau of the Census, *Current Population Survey of Fertility and Marital History Supplement, 1995*. The data were compiled for me from this source by Melissa Knauer.

102. On divorce, see the tables in William J. Goode, *World Changes in Divorce Patterns* (New Haven: Yale University Press, 1993).

Chapter 5

1. David Hayes-Bautista et al., *No Longer a Minority: Latinos and Social Policy in California* (Los Angeles: UCLA Chicano Studies Research Center, 1992), 12–19.

2. M. Belinda Tucker and Claudia Mitchell-Kernan, "Marital Behavior and Expectations: Ethnic Comparisons at Attitudinal and Structural Correlates," in *The Decline in Marriage*, 147.

3. *National Vital Statistic Reports*, vol. 47 (October 25, 1999), table 6.

4. Richard J. Herrnstein and Charles Murray, *The Bell Curve* (New York: Free Press, 1994), 330–31.

5. See David Lowenthal, *West Indian Societies* (London: Oxford University Press, 1972), 105; and William Goode, "Illegitimacy in the Caribbean Social Structure," *American Sociological Review* 25 (1960): 21–30; Edith Clarke, *My Mother Who Fathered Me*, 2d ed. (London: George Allen and Unwin, 1966).

6. *1990 Population and Housing Census*, Barbados Statistical Service, vol. 1, tables 6.02, 6.04.

7. Goode, 23.

8. One of the many exponents of this view is Fernando Henriques, *Family and Colour in Jamaica* (London: Eyre and Spottiswoode, 1953), 87, 90. The same view is defended by Melville J. Herskovits and Francis S. Herskovits, *Trinidad Village* (New York: Knopf, 1947), 17.

9. Judith Blake, *Family Structure in Jamaica* (Glencoe, Ill.: Free Press, 1960), 16.

10. Goode, 26–30; Blake, 18–20.

11. Goode, 21–30.

12. Blake, 90.

13. Lowenthal, 106.

14. Clarke, 96.

15. Blake, 92–93, 83–85, 100–105.

16. Elsa Leo-Rhynie, *The Jamaican Family: Continuity and Change* (Kingston, Jamaica: Grace Kennedy Foundation, 1993), 14.

17. George W. Roberts and Sonja A. Sinclair, *Women in Jamaica* (Millwood, N.Y.: KTO Press, 1978), 161–68.

18. Ibid., 174.

19. Ibid., 157–58.

20. Ibid., 161.

21. W. E. B. Du Bois, *The Negro American Family* (Cambridge: MIT Press, 1970 [first published in 1908]); E. Franklin Frazier, *The Negro Family in the United States* (Chicago: University of Chicago Press, 1939).

22. John W. Blassingame, *The Slave Community: Plantation Life in the Antebellum South* (New York: Oxford University Press, 1972), 77. His view on this matter was restated in the 1979 revised edition of the book (see page 149).

23. Eugene Genovese, *Roll, Jordan, Roll: The World the Slaves Made*

(New York: Vintage, 1974), 451–58, 492. He supported his view with data obtained from Herbert Gutman (see page 747, note 39), which Gutman published two years after the Genovese book.

24. Stephanie Coontz, *The Way We Never Were: American Families and the Nostalgia Trap* (New York: Basic Books, 1992), 252.

25. Deborah White, *Ar'n't I a Woman? Female Slaves in the Plantation South* (New York: Norton, 1985), 68, 158.

26. Robert William Fogel and Stanley L. Engerman, *Time on the Cross: The Economics of American Negro Slavery* (Boston: Little, Brown, 1974), 126–144. The reference to Victorian attitudes is at page 129.

27. Robert William Fogel and Stanley L. Engerman, *Time on the Cross: Evidence and Methods* (Boston: Little, Brown, 1974), 114, n. 4.8. They say that evidence on the effects of slavery on family formation "is still at a preliminary stage" and refer the reader to an unpublished paper that may contain some facts.

28. For a critique of the Fogel and Engerman book, see Paul A. David et al., *Reckoning with Slavery* (New York: Oxford University Press, 1976). The critique of the Fogel-Engerman view of slave families was written by Herbert Gutman, whose own work, published the same year as this volume, seemed to say that the black family had scarcely been affected by slavery. A puzzle.

29. Herbert G. Gutman, *The Black Family in Slavery and Freedom, 1750–1925* (New York: Pantheon, 1976), 9.

30. Stephen Gudeman, "Herbert Gutman's 'The Black Family in Slavery and Freedom, 1750–1920,' " *Social Science History* 3 (1979): 56–65, especially 63.

31. William Julius Wilson, *The Truly Disadvantaged* (Chicago: University of Chicago Press, 1987), 64, 143.

32. Robert L. Griswold, *Fatherhood in America: A History* (New York: Basic Books, 1993), 20.

33. Ibid., 22.

34. Steven Ruggles, "The Origins of African-American Family Structure," *American Sociological Review* 59 (1994): 136–51.

35. Ibid., 148.

36. S. Philip Morgan et al., "Racial Differences in Household and Family Structure at the Turn of the Century," *American Journal of Sociology* 98 (1993): 799–828.

37. Samuel H. Preston, Suet Lim, and S. Philip Morgan, "African-American Marriage in 1910: Beneath the Surface of Census Data," *Demography* 29 (1992): 1–15.

38. Gutman, 11 (table 1).

39. Ibid, 489 (table A-12).

40. Orlando Patterson, *Rituals of Blood: Consequences of Slavery in Two American Centuries* (Washington, D.C.: Civitas/Counterpoint, 1998), 32–35. A similar point is made by Elizabeth Fox-Genovese, *Within the Plantation Household* (Chapel Hill: University of North Carolina Press, 1988), 297.

41. Brenda A. Stevenson, "Black Family Structure in Colonial and Ante-

bellum Virginia: Amending the Revisionist Perspective," in *The Decline of Marriage Among African Americans*, ed. M. Belinda Tucker and Claudia Mitchell-Kernan (New York: Russell Sage Foundation, 1995), 27–56.

42. Patterson, 31.

43. Brenda A. Stevenson, "Gender Convention, Ideals, and Identity Among Antebellum Virginia Slave Women," in *More than Chattel: Black Women and Slavery in the Americas*, ed. David Barry Gaspar and Darlene Clark Hine (Bloomington: Indiana University Press, 1996), 177.

44. Allan Kulikoff, *Tobacco and Slaves* (Chapel Hill: University of North Carolina Press, 1986), 369–72.

45. Alida C. Metcalf, *Family and Frontier in Colonial Brazil* (Berkeley: University of California Press, 1992), 170–73.

46. Bureau of the Census, *Historical Statistics of the United States* (Washington, D.C.: U.S. Government Printing Office, 1975), I, 17.

47. Patterson, 36.

48. Ibid., 34.

49. Ibid., 35.

50. Clarke, 162–63.

51. Claudia Dale Godin, *Urban Slavery in the American South, 1820–1860* (Chicago: University of Chicago Press, 1976), 43, 64.

52. Patterson, 45–49.

53. Melville J. Herskovits, *The Myth of the Negro Past* (Boston: Beacon Press, 1958). This view is disputed by Frazier, chap. 1.

54. Meyer Fortes, "Family, Marriage, and Fertility in West Africa," in *Marriage, Fertility, and Parenthood in West Africa*, ed. C. Oppong et al. (Canberra: Australian National University, 1978), 17.

55. Adam Kuper, *Wives for Cattle: Bridewealth and Marriage in Southern Africa* (London: Routledge & Kegan Paul, 1982), 26, 169–70.

56. William J. Goode, *World Revolution and Family Patterns* (Glencoe, Ill.: Free Press, 1963), 185.

57. Sarah Blaffer Hrdy, *Mother Nature: A History of Mothers, Infants, and Natural Selection* (New York: Pantheon, 1999), 372.

58. Adam Kuper, "African Marriage in an Impinging World: The Case of Southern Africa," in *Contemporary Marriage*, ed. Kingsley Davis (New York: Russell Sage Foundation, 1985), 256.

59. Robin Fox, *Kinship and Marriage* (Cambridge: Cambridge University Press, 1967), 14.

60. Eileen Jensen Krige, "Summary and Conclusions," in Eileen Jensen Krige and John L. Comaroff, *Essays on African Marriage in Southern Africa* (Capetown, South Africa: Juta and Co., 1981), 187–88.

61. E. E. Evans-Pritchard, *Kinship and Marriage Among the Nuer* (Oxford: Clarendon Press, 1951), chap. 3, especially 70, 72.

62. Ibid., 178.

63. On this, see Alan Macfarlane, *Marriage and Love in England: Modes of Reproduction 1300–1840* (London: Basil Blackwell, 1986), 40.

64. Robert B. Edgerton, *The Fall of the Asante Empire* (New York: Free Press, 1995), 40, 259.

65. Krige, "Love, Marriage and Social Change," in Krige and Comaroff, 152.

66. Kuper, 258.

67. Esther N. Goody, *Parenthood and Social Reproduction: Fostering and Occupational Roles in West Africa* (Cambridge: Cambridge University Press, 1982).

68. Joan B. Silk, "Adoption and Fosterage in Human Societies: Adaptations or Enigmas?" *Cultural Anthropology* 2 (1987): 39–49.

69. Uche C. Isiugo-Abanihe, "Child Fosterage in West Africa," *Population and Development Review* 11 (1985): 53–73. See also Renee Pennington, "Child Fostering as a Reproductive Strategy Among Southern African Pastoralists," *Ethology and Sociobiology* 12 (1991): 83–104.

70. Hrdy, 91.

71. David F. Lancy, *Playing on the Mother Ground* (New York: Guilford Press, 1996), 22. Lancy describes this research and says it is consistent with his observations of the village of Kpelle in Liberia.

72. Robert A. LeVine et al., *Child Care and Culture: Lessons from Africa* (Cambridge: Cambridge University Press, 1994), 158.

73. Patterson, 25–27.

74. Ibid., 28.

75. Ibid., 38–41.

76. John Dollard, *Caste and Class in a Southern Town* (Madison: University of Wisconsin Press, 1988), 420. First published by the Yale University Press in 1937.

77. Patterson, 50, 51.

78. Scott J. South, "For Love or Money? Sociodemographic Determinants of the Expected Benefits from Marriage," in *The Changing American Family*, ed. Scott J. South and Stewart E. Tolnay (Boulder, Colo.: Westview Press, 1992), 171–94.

79. Ibid., 58.

80. Ibid., 63, 146.

81. Ibid., 130, 135–36.

82. Ibid., 149. Patterson refers to the study by John Scanzoni, *The Black Family in Modern Society* (Boston: Allyn and Bacon, 1971), 176–90.

83. Robert I. Lerman, "A National Profile of Young Unwed Fathers," in *Young Unwed Fathers*, ed. Robert I. Lerman and Theodora J. Ooms (Philadelphia: Temple University Press, 1993), 39.

84. Stephan and Abigail Thernstrom, *America in Black and White* (New York: Simon & Schuster, 1997), 196–7.

85. *Turning the Corner on Father Absence in Black America*, a report from the Morehouse Conference on African American Fathers (1999). The statement was signed by fifty eminent scholars and activists, both black and white.

Chapter 6

1. Peter Laslett, *The World We Have Lost* (London: Routledge, 2000), 161.

2. Daniel Scott Smith and Michael S. Hindus, "Premarital Pregnancy in America 1640–1971," *Journal of Interdisciplinary History* 4 (1975): 537–70.

3. Edward Shorter, "Illegitimacy, Sexual Revolution, and Social Change in Modern Europe," *Journal of Interdisciplinary History* 2 (1971): 237–72.

4. Blackstone took this view. His remarks are quoted in Michael Grossberg, *Governing the Hearth* (Chapel Hill: University of North Carolina Press, 1985), 198.

5. T. E. James, "The Illegitimate and Deprived Child: Legitimation and Adoption," in *A Century of Family Law, 1857–1957*, ed. R. H. Graveson and F. R. Crane (London: Sweet & Maxwell, 1957), 42.

6. Ibid., 39–40.

7. Lawrence Stone, *The Family, Sex and Marriage in England 1500–1800*, abridged ed. (New York: Harper & Row, 1979), 398.

8. Joan Perkin, *Women and Marriage in Nineteenth-Century England* (Chicago: Lyceum Books, 1989), 182.

9. Ibid.

10. Stone, 398.

11. Viviana A. Zelizer has written a book about the "transformation in the economic and social value of children" between 1870 and 1930 from "economically useful" in the early period to "economically useless but emotionally priceless" in the later one. *Pricing the Priceless Child* (New York: Basic Books, 1985), 3, 209.

12. Grossberg, 204.

13. Ibid., 212.

14. Hendrik Hartog, *Man and Wife in America* (Cambridge: Harvard University Press, 2000), 15, 214.

15. Grossberg, 228.

16. Susan Tiffin, *In Whose Best Interest? Child Welfare in the Progressive Era* (Westport, Conn.: Greenwood Press, 1982), 64.

17. Ibid., 66.

18. Ibid., 67.

19. Ibid., 69–70.

20. Quoted in ibid., 75. A good recent history of orphanages that rightly emphasizes the religious conflicts that surrounded them is Matthew A. Crenson, *Building the Invisible Orphanage* (Cambridge: Harvard University Press, 1998).

21. Rachel G. Fuchs, "Legislation, Poverty, and Child-Abandonment in Nineteenth-Century Paris," *Journal of Interdisciplinary History* 18 (1987), 55–80.

22. Tiffin, 101.

23. Ibid., 105.

24. Mark H. Leff, "Consensus for Reform: The Mothers'-Pension Movement in the Progressive Era," *Social Service Review* 47 (1973): 411.

25. Ibid.

26. Roy Lubove, *The Struggle for Social Security, 1900–1935* (Cambridge: Harvard University Press, 1968), 95.

27. Leff, 404.

28. Joanne L. Goodwin, *Gender and the Politics of Welfare Reform: Mothers' Pensions in Chicago, 1911–1929* (Chicago: University of Chicago Press, 1997), 122–29.

29. Tiffin, 130.

30. Goodwin, 161.

31. Children's Bureau, *A Tabular Summary of State Laws Relating to Public Aid to Children in Their Own Homes* (Washington, D.C.: U.S. Government Printing Office, 1934).

32. Clara Cahill Park, as quoted in Theda Skocpol, *Protecting Soldiers and Mothers* (Cambridge: Harvard University Press, 1992), 427.

33. Quoted in Skocpol, 451.

34. Quoted in Grossberg, 230.

35. Ibid., 229.

36. Gunnar Myrdal, *An American Dilemma* (New York: Harper, 1944), 359–60.

37. Winifred Bell, *Aid to Dependent Children* (New York: Columbia University Press, 1965), 29.

38. Quoted in ibid., 29–30.

39. Ibid., 33.

40. Committee on Ways and Means, U.S. House of Representatives, *1998 Green Book* (May 19, 1998): 1251.

41. Crenson, 280–81.

42. Steven M. Teles, *Whose Welfare?: AFDC and Elite Politics* (Lawrence: University of Kansas Press, 1996), 20.

43. Loc. cit.

44. Ibid., 540.

45. Ibid., 429.

46. Daniel P. Moynihan, *Family and Nation* (New York: Harcourt, Brace, Jovanovich, 1986), 136.

47. David Ellwood and Mary Jo Bane, "The Impact of AFDC on Family Structure," in *Research in Labor Economics*, vol. 7, ed. Ronald Ehrenbert (Greenwich, Conn.: JAI Press, 1985).

48. David T. Ellwood and Lawrence H. Summers, "Is Welfare Really the Problem?" *The Public Interest* 83 (1986): 57–78.

49. See the studies summarized in Robert Moffitt, "Incentive Effects of the U.S. Welfare System: A Review," *Journal of Economic Literature* 30 (1992): 7.

50. Charles Murray, "Have the Poor Been Losing Ground?" *Political Science Quarterly* 100 (1985): 427–45; and Murray, "No, Welfare Isn't Really the Problem," *The Public Interest* 84 (1986): 3–11.

51. Moffitt, 31, 56.

52. Mark R. Rosenzweig, "Welfare, Marital Prospects, and Nonmarital Childbearing," *Journal of Political Economy* 107 (1999): S3–S32. A comparable study done using data from the Panel Survey of Income Dynamics comes to the same conclusion, as noted in Rosenzweig, S23. Studies with comparable findings include C. R. Winegarden and Paula Bracy, "Welfare Benefits and Illegitimacy in the U.S.: Reconciling Contradictory Trends," *Southern Economic Journal* 64 (1997): 167–79; Robert D. Plotnick, "Welfare and Out-of-Wedlock Childbearing," *Journal of Marriage and the Family* 52 (1990): 735–46; and Charles Murray, "Welfare and the Family: The U.S. Experience," *Journal of Labor Economics* 11 (1993): S224–S262.

53. Jeff Grogger and Stephen G. Bronars, "The Effect of Welfare Payments on the Marriage and Fertility Behavior of Unwed Mothers: Results from a Twins Experiment," working paper 6047 of the National Bureau of Economic Research (May 1997).

54. George R. G. Clarke and Robert P. Strauss, "Children as Income-Producing Assets: The Case of Teen Illegitimacy and Government Transfers," *Southern Economic Journal* 64 (1998): 827–56.

55. Robert A. Moffitt, "The Effect of Welfare on Marriage and Fertility," in *Welfare, the Family, and Reproductive Behavior,* ed. Robert A. Moffitt (Washington, D.C.: National Academy Press, 1998), 50–97. A similar view can be found in Daniel T. Lichter, Diane K. McLaughlin, and David C. Ribar, "Welfare and the Rise of Female-Headed Families," *American Journal of Sociology* 103 (1997): 112–43.

56. David T. Ellwood and Mary Jo Bane, "The Impact of AFDC on Family Structure and Living Arrangements," *Research in Labor Economics* 7 (1985): 137–207.

57. Robert I. Lerman, "A National Profile of Young Unwed Fathers," in *Young Unwed Fathers,* ed. Robert I. Lerman and Theodora J. Ooms (Philadelphia: Temple University Press, 1993), 15, 34–36.

58. AFDC beneficiaries were above 20 percent of the immigrant group among people from Vietnam, Jamaica, and the Dominican Republic and below 10 percent for immigrants from China, El Salvador, Mexico, and Korea. David E. Hayes-Bautista and Gregory Rodriguez, *Immigrant Use of Public Programs in the United States 1996,* (Los Angeles: Center for the Study of Latino Health, UCLA School of Medicine, 1997), figure 6.

59. Christopher Jencks, "Is the American Underclass Growing?" in The *Urban Underclass,* ed. Paul E. Peterson and Christopher Jencks (Washington, D.C.: Brookings Institution, 1991), 89.

60. Christopher Jencks, *Rethinking Social Policy* (Cambridge: Harvard University Press, 1992), 133.

61. Lawrence M. Mead, *The New Politics of Poverty* (New York: Basic Books, 1992), 85–109.

62. Robert. I. Lerman, "Employment Opportunities of Young Men and Family Formation," *American Economic Review* 79 (1989): 62–66. Similar

criticisms have been brought by Robert G. Wood, "Marriage Rates and Marriageable Men: A Test of the Wilson Hypothesis," *Journal of Human Resources* 30 (1995): 163–93. See also David T. Ellwood and Jonathan Crane, "Family Change Among Black Americans: What Do We Know?" *Journal of Economic Perspectives* 4 (199): 65–84, especially at 77.

63. William Julius Wilson, *When Work Disappears* (New York: Vintage, 1997), 95 and chap. 4 generally. But he does not back down from his view that somehow the problems are caused by a shortage of jobs (cf. p. 109). This may be because he has studied, not poor blacks generally, but those living in one city, Chicago.

64. St. Clair Drake and Horace R. Cayton, *Black Metropolis* (New York: Harcourt, Brace, 1945), 582. Their view is supported by E. Franklin Frazier, *The Negro Family in the United States* (Chicago: University of Chicago Press, 1934).

65. Elijah Anderson, *Street Wise* (Chicago: University of Chicago Press, 1990), 112-37; and Anderson, *Code of the Street* (New York: Norton, 1999), 142–78.

66. See the brief account in Teles, 85–89. The NWRO was created by Richard Cloward and Francis Fox Piven, two Columbia University professors, and is explained in their book, *The Politics of Turmoil* (New York: Pantheon, 1972). The legal argument that welfare benefits are no longer merely claims that can be evaluated but rights that must be enforced was set forth in Charles Reich, "The New Property," *Yale Law Journal* 73 (1964): 739–43.

67. Daniel Patrick Moynihan, *The Politics of a Guaranteed Income: The Nixon Administration and the Family Assistance Plan* (New York: Random House, 1973), 327–37.

68. *King v. Smith*, 392 US 309 (1968), (1969) esp. 9, 14.

69. *Shapiro v. Thompson*, 394 US 618 (1969); *Goldberg v. Kelly*, 397 US 254 (1970). These cases are carefully examined in Teles, 107–16.

70. Lawrence M. Mead, *Beyond Entitlement: The Social Obligations of Citizenship* (New York: Free Press, 1986), 62.

71. Patrick Horan and Patricia Austin, "The Social Bases of Welfare Stigma," *Social Problems* 21 (1974): 648–57; Harold R. Kerbo, "The Stigma of Welfare and a Passive Poor," *Sociology and Social Research* 60 (1976): 173–87; Chaim I. Waxman, *The Stigma of Poverty* (New York: Pergamon Press, 1977).

72. Robert Moffitt, "An Economic Model of Welfare Stigma," *American Economic Review* 73 (1983): 1023–35.

73. Mark R. Rank and Thomas A. Hirschl, "A Rural-Urban Comparison of Welfare Exits," *Rural Sociology* 53 (1988): 190–206.

74. Loc. cit.

75. Peter Hitchens, *The Abolition of Britain* (San Francisco: Encounter Books, 2000), 169.

76. George A. Akerlof, Janet L. Yellen, and Michael L. Katz, "An Analysis of Out-of-Wedlock Childbearing in the United States," *Quarterly Journal of Economics* 111 (1996): 277–317.

77. Ibid., 289–90.

78. Stanley K. Henshaw, "Unintended Pregnancy in the United States," *Family Planning Perspectives* 30 (1998): 24–29.

79. Wilson, *When Work Disappears*, chap. 4. The quotation is from page 98.

80. Donald J. Hernandez and Evan Charney, eds., *From Generation to Generation: The Health and Well-Being of Children in Immigrant Families* (Washington, D.C.: National Academy Press, 1998), table B-2A, pp. 237–41.

81. Sandra L. Hofferth, "Receipt of Public Assistance by Mexican American and Cuban American Children in Native and Immigrant Families," in Donald J. Hernandez, ed. *Children of Immigrants* (Washington, D.C.: National Academy Press, 1999), 546–583.

82. David D. Friedman, *Law's Order* (Princeton, N.J.: Princeton University Press, 2000), 177.

Chapter 7

1. Paul H. Jacobson, *American Marriage and Divorce* (New York: Rinehart, 1959), 21, 90.

2. Quoted in Nelson Manfred Blake, *The Road to Reno: A History of Divorce in the United States* (New York: Macmillan, 1962), 232.

3. Andrew J. Cherlin, *Marriage, Divorce, Remarriage*, rev. ed. (Cambridge: Harvard University Press, 1992), 45–48; and Arland Thornton, "Changing Attitudes Toward Family Issues in the United States," *Journal of Marriage and the Family* 51 (1989): 873–93.

4. Herbert Jacob, *The Silent Revolution* (Chicago: University of Chicago Press, 1988), 3.

5. Mary Ann Glendon, *The Transformation of American Family* (Chicago: University of Chicago Press, 1989), 188.

6. Quoted in Jacob, 55.

7. Glendon, 190.

8. Jacob, 56–57, 72, 86–87.

9. J. Herbie DiFonzo, *Beneath the Fault Line: The Popular and Legal Culture of Divorce in Twentieth-Century America* (Charlottesville, Va.: University Press of Virginia, 1997), 10. See also William L. O'Neill, *Divorce in the Progressive Era* (New Haven: Yale University Press, 1967).

10. DiFonzo, 12.

11. Ibid., 171.

12. Glendon, 189.

13. Jacob, 127.

14. The one-parent rule was defended by Joseph Goldstein, Anna Freud, and Albert J. Somit, *Beyond the Best Interests of the Child* (New York: Free Press, 1973); the joint custody rule was defended by Carol Stack, "Who

Owns the Child? *Social Problems* 23 (1976): 505–15; and by Mel Roman and William Haddad, *The Disposable Parent: The Case for Joint Custody* (New York: Holt, Rinehart, and Winston, 1978).

15. For a useful, and critical, summary of these views, see Barbara Dafoe Whitehead, *The Divorce Culture* (New York: Alfred A. Knopf, 1997), 45–65, 85–90.

16. Ibid., 89.

17. Frank F. Furstenberg, Jr., and Andrew J. Cherlin, *Divided Families: What Happens to Children When Parents Part* (Cambridge: Harvard University Press, 1991), 62–76, 82.

18. Cherlin, 72. Among the empirical studies that support this view are Andrew J. Cherlin et al., "Longitudinal Studies of Effects of Divorce on Children in Great Britain and the United States," *Science* 252 (1991): 1386–89; P. Lindsay Chase-Lansdale, Andrew J. Cherlin, and Kathleen E. Kiernan, "The Long-Term Effects of Parental Divorce on the Mental Health of Young Adults," *Child Development* 66 (1995): 1614–34; and Jeanne H. Block, Jack Block, and Per F. Gjerde, "The Personality of Children Prior to Divorce: A Prospective Study," *Child Development* 57 (1986): 827–40.

19. Furstenberg and Cherlin, 36.

20. David Popenoe, *Life Without Father* (New York: Free Press, 1996), 31.

21. Richard R. Peterson, "A Re-evaluation of the Economic Consequences of Divorce," *American Sociological Review* 61 (1996), 528–38; and Peterson, "Statistical Errors, Faulty Conclusions, Misguided Policy: Reply to Weitzman," *American Sociological Review* 61 (1996): 539–42. In the same vein, see Karla B. Hackstaff, *Marriage in the Culture of Divorce* (Philadelphia: Temple University Press, 1999), 205–09.

22. Mary Ann Glendon, *Abortion and Divorce in Western Law* (Cambridge: Harvard University Press, 1987), 105.

23. Henry B. Biller and Jon Lopez Kimpton, "The Father and the School-Aged Child," in *The Role of the Father in Child Development*, 3d ed., ed. Michael E. Lamb (New York: John Wiley & Sons, 1997), 143–61.

24. Martin Daly and Margot Wilson, *Homicide* (New York: Aldine de Gruyter, 1988), 87–88; Wilson and Daly, "Risk of Maltreatment of Children Living With Stepparents," in *Child Abuse and Neglect*, ed. Richard Gelles and Joan Lancaster (New York: Aldine de Gruyter, 1987), 215–32.

25. Sara McLanahan and Gary Sandefur, *Growing Up with a Single Parent* (Cambridge: Harvard University Press, 1994), 89. The differences are not huge but they are significant. See also E. Mavis Hetherington and Sandra H. Henderson, "Fathers in Stepfamilies," in Lamb, *The Role of the Father*, 212–44.

26. Judith S. Wallerstein and Sandra Blakeslee, *Second Chances: Men, Women, and Children a Decade After Divorce* (New York: Ticknor & Fields, 1989), 299. See also the other books she wrote: Wallerstein and Joan Berlin Kelly, *Surviving the Breakup: How Children and Parents Cope with Divorce* (New York: Basic Books, 1980); and Wallerstein, Julia M. Lewis, and Sandra Blakeslee, *The Unexpected Legacy of Divorce* (New York: Hyperion, 2000).

27. See the argument between Cherlin and Richard Gill, an economist who has studied the same subject, in Cherlin, "Nostalgia as Family Policy," *The Public Interest* (winter 1993), 1–8; Gill, "For the Sake of the Children," *The Public Interest* (summer 1992), 81–96; and Gill, "Family Breakdown as Family Policy," *The Public Interest* (winter 1993), 8–15.

28. Rex Forehand, Lisa Armistead, and Corinne David, "Is Adolescent Adjustment Following Parental Divorce a Function of Predivorce Adjustment?" *Journal of Abnormal Child Psychology* 25 (1997): 157–64.

29. Ronald L. Simons et al., *Understanding the Differences Between Divorced and Intact Families* (Thousand Oaks, Calif.: Sage, 1996), especially 204–05.

30. Andrew J. Cherlin, P. Lindsay Chase-Lansdale, and Christine McRae, "Effects of Parental Divorce on Mental Health Throughout the Life Course," *American Sociological Review* 63 (1998): 239–49.

31. Paul R. Amato and Alan Booth, *A Generation at Risk: Growing Up in an Era of Family Upheaval* (Cambridge: Harvard University Press, 1997), 219.

32. Ibid., 220.

33. These findings do not rule out the possibility that the children themselves contribute to the likelihood of divorce. Our genetic makeup helps shape our personality, such as whether we are extroverted or neurotic. And these traits may affect how easy it will be for us to get along with others. Two scholars have compared identical twins with fraternal twins and ordinary siblings, and they found that when one member of an identical twin pair got divorced, the odds that the other member would get divorced were three times higher than was true of two members of a pair of fraternal twins. Though there is obviously no such thing as a "divorce gene," our personalities do make a difference. This intriguing suggestion that genes affect divorce cannot, of course, be the whole story, for the American gene pool did not change enough to explain why divorces became seven times more common between 1870 and 1950. Matt McGue and David T. Lykken, "Genetic Influence on Risk of Divorce," *Psychological Science* 6 (1992): 368–72.

34. Max Rheinstein, *Marriage Stability, Divorce, and the Law* (Chicago: University of Chicago Press, 1972), 266.

35. Janet R. Johnson and Linda E. G. Campbell, *Impasses of Divorce* (New York: Free Press, 1988), 151–52.

36. Norval Glenn, "The Recent Trend in Marital Success in the United States," *Journal of Marriage and the Family* 53 (1991): 261–70; quotations at 268.

37. Paul R. Amato and Stacy J. Rogers, "Do Attitudes Toward Divorce Affect Marital Quality?" *Journal of Family Issues* 20 (1999): 69–86.

38. Frank Furstenberg and Kathleen Mullan Harris, "The Disappearing American Father?" (paper presented at the Albany Conference on Demographic Perspectives on the American Family, April 1990).

39. Rheinstein, 406.

40. Robert Schoen, Henry N. Greenblatt, and Robert B. Mielke, "Cali-

fornia's Experience with Non-Adversary Divorce," *Demography* 12 (1975): 223–43; Elizabeth Peters, "Marriage and Divorce: Informational Constraints and Private Contracting," *American Economic Review* 76 (1986): 437; Gerald C. Wright, Jr., and Dorothy M. Stetson, "The Impact of No-Fault Divorce Law Reform on Divorce in American States," *Journal of Marriage and the Family* 40 (1978): 575–80; Harvey J. Sepler, "Measuring the Effects of No-Fault Divorce Laws Across Fifty States," *Family Law Quarterly* 15 (1981): 65–102; Alan H. Frank, John J. Berman, and Stanley F. Mazer-Hart, "No-Fault Divorce and the Divorce Rate," *Nebraska Law Review* 58 (1978): 1–99.

41. James C. Garand, Pamela A. Monroe, and Denese Vlosky, "Do No-Fault Divorce Laws Increase Divorce in the American States?" (paper presented at the 1980 annual meeting of the American Political Science Association). This issue is still in dispute. Norval Glenn, for example, argues that no-fault divorce has little effect on divorce rates: Glenn, "A Reconsideration of the Effect of No-Fault Divorce on Divorce Rates," *Journal of Marriage and the Family* 59 (1997): 1023–25, and Glenn, "Further Discussion of the Effects of No-Fault Divorce on Divorce Rates," *Journal of Marriage and the Family* 61 (1999): 800–2. J. L. Rogers and his colleagues take issue with this view. Rogers, et al., "The Effect of No-Fault Divorce Legislation on Divorce Rates," *Journal of Marriage and the Family* 59 (1997): 1026–30, and Rogers, et al., "Did No-Fault Divorce Legislation Matter? Definitely Yes and Sometimes No," *Journal of Marriage and the Family* 61 (1999): 803–9. I agree with the Rogers, et al., view. In their last article, consider the dramatic results shown in their state-by-state tables of divorce rates before and after adopting a no-fault law.

42. Margaret F. Brinig and F. H. Buckley, "No-Fault Laws and At-Fault People," *International Review of Law and Economics* 18 (1998): 325–40.

43. Wallerstein and Blakeslee, 298–99.

44. Wallerstein, Lewis, and Blakeslee, 329–36.

Chapter 8

1. *Statistical Abstract of the United States, 1998* (Washington, D.C.: U.S. Government Printing Office, 1998), tables 654, 655, 656.

2. Theodore Caplow, Louis Hicks, and Ben J. Wattenberg, *The First Measured Century* (Washington, D.C.: AEI Press, 2001), 40–41.

3. Andrew Cherlin, *Marriage, Divorce, Remarriage* (Cambridge: Harvard University Press) 52–53; Robert A. Moffitt, "Female Wages, Male Wages, and the Economic Model of Marriage," in *The Ties That Bind*, ed. Linda J. Waite (New York: Aldine de Gruyter, 2000), 302–42; Valerie Kincade Oppenheimer, "The Continuing Importance of Men's Economic Position in Marriage Formation," in Waite, op. cit., 283–301.

4. An example of this argument is Brian C. Robertson, *There's No Place Like Work: How Business, Government, and Our Obsession with Work Have Driven Parents from the Home* (Dallas: Spence, 2000).

5. Martha Hahn Sugar, *When Mothers Work, Who Pays?* (Westport, Conn.: Bergin and Garvey, 1994).

6. For a useful summary, see Adele Eskeles Gottfried et al., "Maternal and Dual-Earner Employment," in *Parenting and Child Development in "Nontraditional" Families,* ed. Michael E. Lamb (Mahwah, N.J.: Lawrence Erlbaum Associates, 1999), 15–37. Some of these studies are summarized in Adele Eskeles Gottfried and Allen W. Gottfried, eds., *Maternal Employment and Children's Development: Longitudinal Research* (New York: Plenum, 1988). See also Paul R. Amato and Alan Booth, *A Generation at Risk* (Cambridge: Harvard University Press, 1997), 145.

7. Cheryl Mendelson, *Home Comforts: The Art & Science of Keeping House* (New York: Scribner's, 1999). The quotations are from page 3.

8. A defense of the Strange Situation Test can be found in Mary D. S. Ainsworth et al., *Patterns of Attachment* (Hillsdale, N.J.: Lawrence Erlbaum, 1978); a critique is Jerome Kagan, *The Nature of the Child* (New York: Basic Books, 1984), 57–64.

9. Jay Belsky and M. J. Rovine, "Nonmaternal Care in the First Year of Life and the Security of Infant-Parent Attachment," *Child Development* 59 (1988): 157–67; Belsky, "A Reassessment of Infant Day Care," in *The Parental Leave Crisis,* ed. Edward F. Zigler and Meryl Frank (New Haven: Yale University Press, 1988), 100–119.

10. Jay Belsky, "The 'Effects' of Infant Day Care Reconsidered," *Early Childhood Research Quarterly* 3 (1988): 235–72; K. R. Thornburg et al., "Development of Kindergarten Children Based on Child Care Arrangements," *Early Childhood Research Quarterly* 5 (1990): 27–42; Deborah Lowell Vandell and Mary Anne Crosatini, "Variations in Early Child Care: Do They Predict Subsequent Social, Emotional, and Cognitive Differences?" *Early Childhood Research Quarterly* 5 (1990): 555–72; Thomas J. Gamble and Edward Zigler, "Effects of Infant Day Care: Another Look at the Evidence," in *The Parental Leave Crisis,* ed. Edward F. Zigler and Meryl Frank (New Haven: Yale University Press, 1988), 77–99.

11. See, for example, Tiffany Field et al., "Quality Infant Day Care and Grade School Behavior and Performance," *Child Development* 62 (1991): 863–70.

12. NICHD Early Child Care Network Research, "Early Child Care and Children's Development Prior to School Entry," unpub. paper, 2001; Jay Belsky, "Type of Care and Children's Development at 54 Months," unpub. paper, April 2001; Belsky, "Further Explorations of the Detected Effects of Quantity of Early Child Care on Socioemotional Adjustment," unpub. paper, 2001.

13. NICHD Early Child Care Research Network, "The Effects of Infant Child Care on Infant-Mother Attachment Security," *Child Development* 68

(1997): 860–79; NICHD Early Child Care Research Network, "Early Child Care and Self-Control, Compliance, and Problem Behavior at Twenty-Four and Thirty-Six Months," *Child Development* 69 (1998): 1145–70; NICHD Early Child Care Research Network, "The Relation of Child Care to Cognitive and Language Development," *Child Development* 71 (2000): 960–80.

14. Michael E. Lamb, "Nonparental Child Care," in *Parenting and Child Development in "Nontraditional" Families*, ed. Michael E. Lamb (Mahwah, N.J.: Lawrence Erlbaum Associates, 1999), 48–49.

15. NICHD Early Child Care Research Network, "Child Outcomes When Child Care Center Classes Meet Recommended Standards for Quality," *American Journal of Public Health* 89 (1999): 1072–77.

16. NICHD Early Child Care Research Network, "The Effects of Infant Child Care on Infant-Mother Attachment Security," *Child Development* 68 (1997): 860–79.

17. Alison Clarke-Stewart, *Daycare*, rev. ed. (Cambridge: Harvard University Press, 1993), especially 61–75; Michael Rutter, "Social-Emotional Consequences of Day Care for Preschool Children," in *Day Care: Scientific and Social Policy Issues*, ed. Edward F. Zigler and Edmund W. Gordon (Boston: Auburn House, 1982), 3–32; Anders G. Broberg et al., "Effects of Day Care on the Development of Cognitive Abilities in 8-Year Olds: A Longitudinal Study," *Developmental Psychology* 33 (1997): 62–69; Bengt-Erik Andersson, "Effects of Day-Care on Cognitive and Socio-Emotional Competence on Thirteen-Year-Old Swedish Schoolchildren," *Child Development* 63 (1992): 20–36; Shahla S. Chehrazi, ed., *Psychosocial Issues in Day Care* (Washington, D.C.: American Psychiatric Press, 1990).

18. For some examples of this view, see Susan Moller Okin, *Justice, Gender, and the Family* (New York: Basic Books, 1989); Karla B. Hackstaff, *Marriage in a Culture of Divorce* (Philadelphia: Temple University Press, 1999); Diane Eyer, *Motherguilt: How Our Culture Blames Mothers for What's Wrong with Society* (New York: Times Books/Random House, 1996); Susan Chira, *A Mother's Place: Taking the Debate About Working Mothers Beyond Guilt and Blame* (New York: HarperCollins, 1998). Hackstaff adds a bold new dimension to this discussion by saying that "gender equality" has been produced by high divorce rates (p. 4) because both divorce and gender equality "challenge the power dynamics in marriage" (p. 47).

19. Judith A. Hall, *Nonverbal Sex Differences* (Baltimore: Johns Hopkins University Press, 1984), especially 142. See also the summary in Dianne Halles, *Just Like a Woman: How Gender Science Is Redefining What Makes Us Female* (New York: Bantam Books, 1999), 267.

20. Daniel Goleman, *Emotional Intelligence* (New York: Bantam, 1995), 140–41.

21. Ruben Gar et al., "Effects of Emotional Discrimination Tasks on Cerebral Blood Flow," *Brain and Cognition* 25 (1994): 271.

22. Quoted in Halles, 257.

23. Quoted in Halles, 244–45.

24. Michael E. Lamb et al., "Varying Degrees of Paternal Involvement in Infant Care: Attitudinal and Behavioral Correlates," in *Nontraditional Families: Parenting and Child Development*, ed. Michael E. Lamb (Hillsdale, N.J.: Lawrence Erlbaum, 1982), 117–37. The quotation is at page 135.

25. For a spirited defense of male-female differences in marriage, see Danielle Crittenden, *What Our Mothers Didn't Tell Us* (New York: Simon & Schuster, 1999).

26. Philip Blumstein and Pepper Schwartz, *American Couples* (New York: William Morrow, 1983), 52, 115, 118–25, 324.

27. *Washington Post/Kaiser* Family Foundation/Harvard University poll, September 7, 1997, as reported in *Public Perspective* (July/August 2000), 23.

28. A good, brief description of the Swedish system is Irwin Garfinkel and Annemette Sorenson, "Sweden's Child Support System: Lessons for the United States," *Social Work* (November 1982), 509–15.

29. David Popenoe, *Disturbing the Nest* (New York: Aldine de Gruyter, 1988), 290.

30. Elaine Sorenson and Chava Zibman, "A Look at Poor Dads Who Don't Pay Child Support," Assessing the New Federalism discussion paper 00–07 (Washington, D.C.: Urban Institute, 2000).

31. See the careful review of these efforts in Glenn C. Loury, "Preventing Subsequent Births to Welfare Recipients," in *Preventing Subsequent Births to Welfare Mothers*, ed. Douglas J. Besharov and Peter Germanis (College Park: University of Maryland School of Public Affairs, 2000), 13–28.

32. Robert Pear, "Changes in Welfare Bring Improvements to Families," *New York Times*, 1 June 2000, sec. A, p. 14.

33. Virginia Knox, Cynthia Miller, and Lisa A. Gennetian, *MFIP: Reforming Welfare and Rewarding Work* (New York: MDRC, 2000). For an account of how MFIP was created, see Michael O'Keefe, "Social Services: Minnesota as Innovator," *Daedalus* (summer 2000): 247–67. O'Keefe is the head of the Minnesota Department of Human Services.

34. Richard T. Gill and T. Grandon Gill, "A New Plan for the Family," *The Public Interest* (spring 1993): 86–94; Richard T. Gill, *Posterity Lost* (Lanham, Md: Rowman & Littlefield, 1997), 279–84.

35. Gill and Gill, 88.

36. This summary is from David L. Olds, *Prenatal and Infancy Home Visitation by Nurses, in Blueprints for Violence Prevention*, ed. Delbert S. Elliott (Boulder, Colo.: Center for the Study and Prevention of Violence at the University of Colorado, 1998). A complete list of Olds's scholarly reports on his work is included in the booklet.

37. Charles Siegel, *What's Wrong with Day Care?* (New York: Columbia University Teachers College, 2001), 48.

Chapter 9

1. Committee on Ways and Means, *2000 Green Book* (Washington, D.C.: U.S. Government Printing Office, 2000), table G–13.

2. Ibid., table G–1.

3. Isabel Sawhill, "Welfare Reform and Reducing Teen Pregnancy," *The Public Interest* (winter 2000), 49.

4. Ron Haskins, "Welfare Reform and Illegitimacy" (paper, Mathematica Policy Research, Inc., February 2000).

5. Suzanne Daley, "French Couples Take Plunge That Falls Short of Marriage," *New York Times*, 18 April 2000, sec. A, p. 1.

6. Dana Mack, *Hungry Hearts: Evaluating the New Curricula for Teens on Marriage and Relationships* (New York: Institute for American Values, 2000), 9.

7. Claudia Winkler, "Marriage 101: The Pitfalls of Teaching Matrimony in the Schools," *Weekly Standard*, 16 October 200, 16.

8. Professor Martha Fineman, Cornell Law School, as quoted in Tamar Lewin, "Is Social Stability Subverted If You Answer 'I Don't'?" *New York Times*, 4 November 2000, sec. A, p. 21.

9. Martha Fineman, *The Neutered Mother, the Sexual Family, and Other Twentieth Century Tragedies* (New York: Routledge, 1995).

10. Lewin, quoting Fineman, sec. A, p. 23.

11. Anthony Giddens, *The Transformation of Intimacy* (Stanford, Calif.: Stanford University Press, 1992), ch. 4.

12. Daniel Cere, "Courtship Today: The View From Academia," *The Public Interest* (spring 2001), 53–71.

13. Richard A. Posner, *Sex and Reason* (Cambridge: Harvard University Press, 1992), 161–73, 190–2, 441–2.

14. Hakan Stattin and David Magnusson, "Onset of Official Delinquency," *British Journal of Criminology*, 35 (1995): 417–49, esp. at 438–9. See also Eva Johanson, "Inmates of Youth Prisons Compared With Controls for Family Structure," *Acta Psychiatrica Scandinavica*, 44 (1963): 289–97.

15. Ibid., 191.

16. Duncan W. G. Timms, *Family Structure in Childhood and Mental Health in Adolescence*, research report 32 of project Metropolitan (Stockholm, Sweden: University of Stockholm, Department of Sociology, 1991), 74, 78.

17. Michael Gahler, *Life After Divorce: Economic, Social, and Psychological Well-Being Among Swedish Adults and Children Following Family Dissolution*. Swedish Institute for Social Research, Number 32 (Stockholm, 1998). See also Jan O. Jonsson and Michael Gahler, "Family Dissolution, Family Reconstitution, and Children's Educational Careers: Recent Evidence from Sweden," *Demography* 34 (1997): 277–93.

18. Peter Laslett, "Introduction: Comparing Illegitimacy Over Time and Between Cultures," in *Bastardy and Its Comparative History*, ed. Peter Laslett, Karla Oosterveen, and Richard M. Smith (Cambridge: Harvard University Press, 1980), 14–18.

19. Roger Lane, "Urban Police and Crime in Nineteenth-Century America," in *Crime and Justice*, vol. 2, ed. Norval Morris and Michael Tonry (Chicago: University of Chicago Press, 1980), 27; James F. Richardson, *The New York Police, Colonial Times to 1901* (New York: Oxford University Press, 1970), chap. 2; Paul E. Johnson, *A Shopkeeper's Millennium: Society and Revivals in Rochester, New York, 1815–1837* (New York: Hill and Wang, 1978), chap. 2.

20. Ted Robert Gurr, "Contemporary Crime in Historical Perspective," *Annals* 434 (1977): 114–16.

21. Lane, "Urban Police and Crime," 23–39; and Lane, *Violent Death in the City: Suicide, Accident, and Murder in Nineteenth-Century Philadelphia* (Cambridge: Harvard University Press, 1979), 71.

22. Eric Monkkonen quoted in Lane, "Urban Police and Crime," 35.

23. Ted Robert Gurr, "Historical Trends in Violent Crime," in *Crime and Justice*, vol. 3, ed. Michael Tonry and Norval Morris (Chicago: University of Chicago Press, 1981), 295–353. Eric H. Monkkonen, "A Disorderly People? Urban Order in the Nineteenth and Twentieth Centuries," *Journal of American History* 68 (1981): 536–59; see also Michael Katz et al., *The Social Organization of Early Industrial Capitalism* (Cambridge: Harvard University Press, 1982), 208–09.

24. Laslett, 18.

25. Lane, *Violent Death*, 152–53.

26. Theodore N. Ferdinand, "The Criminal Patterns of Boston Since 1846," *American Journal of Sociology* 73 (1967): 84–99.

27. Lane, *Violent Death*, chap. 6.

28. Monkkonen, "A Disorderly People?"; and Daniel Walker Howe, ed., *Victorian America* (Philadelphia: University of Pennsylvania Press, 1976), 6.

29. Kett, 107.

30. Gregory H. Singleton, "Protest Voluntary Organizations and the Shaping of Victorian America," in Howe, 49–50.

31. Boyer, *Urban Masses*, 43–49.

32. Ibid., 41.

33. Thomas W. Laqueur, *Religion and Respectability: Sunday Schools and Working-Class Children, 1780–1850* (New Haven: Yale University Press, 1976), 44.

34. Ibid., 219–27, 239–41.

35. Boyer, *Urban Masses*, 113.

36. Ibid., 119.

37. Ibid.

38. John Stuart Mill, *On Liberty*, ed. David Spitz (New York: W. W. Norton, 1975), 88. First published in 1859, eight years after Maine adopted prohibition.

39. Norman H. Clark, *Deliver Us from Evil: An Interpretation of American Prohibition* (New York: Norton, 1976), 20; William J. Rorabaugh, *The Alcoholic Republic* (New York: Oxford University Press, 1979), 233.

40. Nurith Zmora, *Orphanages Reconsidered* (Philadelphia: Temple University Press, 1994).

41. Hyman Bogen, *The Luckiest Orphans: A History of the Hebrew Orphan Asylum of New York* (Urbana: University of Illinois Press, 1992); David R. Contosta, *Philadelphia's Progressive Orphanage: The Carson Valley School* (University Park: Pennsylvania State University Press, 1997); Kenneth Cmiel, *A Home of Another Kind: One Chicago Orphanage and the Tangle of Child Welfare* (Chicago: University of Chicago Press, 1995).

42. Timothy A. Hacsi, *Second Home: Orphan Asylums and Poor Families in America* (Cambridge: Harvard University Press, 1997), 214–15.

43. Ibid., 219.

44. Richard B. McKenzie, "Orphanage Alumni: How They Have Done and How They Evaluate Their Experience," in *Rethinking Orphanages for the Twenty-First Century*, ed. Richard B. McKenzie (Thousand Oaks, Calif.: Sage Publications, 1999), 103–26.

45. Richard B. McKenzie, "Rethinking Orphanages for the 21st Century," in ibid., 295.

46. Clark, 13.

47. Martin J. Wiener, *Reconstructing the Criminal: Culture, Law, and Policy in England, 1830–1914* (Cambridge: Cambridge University Press, 1990), 38–48; F. M. L Thompson, *The Rise of Respectable Society* (London: Fontana, 1988), 260.

48. See Boyer, seriatim.

49. Boyer, chap. 9, 10.

50. Byron R. Johnson, David B. Larson, Spencer De Li, and Sung Joon Jang, "Escaping From the Crime of Inner Cities: Church Attendance and Religious Salience Among Disadvantaged Youth," *Justice Quarterly* 17 (2000): 377–91; and Richard B. Freeman, "Who Escapes? The Relation of Churchgoing and Other Background Factors to the Socioeconomic Performance of Black Male Youth From Inner-City Tracts," in *The Black Youth Employment Crisis*, ed. Richard B. Freeman and H. J. Holzer (Chicago: University of Chicago Press, 1986).

51. Byron R. Johnson, Sung Joon Jang, Spencer De Li, and David Larson, "The 'Invisible Institution' and Black Youth Crime," *Journal of Youth and Adolescence* 29 (2000): 479–98.

52. Bureau of the Census, *Historical Statistics of the United States* (Washington, D.C.: U.S. Government Printing Office, 1975), I, 379, 383; *Statistical Abstract of the United States, 1998* (Washington, D.C.: U.S. Government Printing Office, 1998), 167.

53. Norval D. Glenn, *Closed Hearts, Closed Minds: The Textbook Story of Marriage* (New York: Institute for American Values, 1997).

54. Frank F. Furstenberg, Jr., et al., *Managing to Make It: Urban Families and Adolescent Success* (Chicago: University of Chicago Press, 1999), 72–73, 82–83, 87–88, 216–17.

55. Richard J. Herrnstein and Charles Murray, *The Bell Curve* (New

York: Free Press, 1994), 172–75. In terms of intelligence, the very brightest people are half as likely to get divorced as are the remaining 80 percent of the population, but in this latter group IQ makes no difference.

56. New York: William Morrow, 1993.

57. John Witte, Jr., "An Apt and Cheerful Conversation on Marriage," in *A Nation Under God? Essays on the Future of Religion in American Public Life.*, edited by R. Bruce Douglass and Joshua Mitchell. (Lanham, MD: Rowman and Littlefield, 2000), 105–6.

58. Barbara Ehrenreich, participating in a debate with Lionel Tiger entitled "Who Needs Men" *Harper's*, June 1999, 46.

59. Richard B. McKenzie, "Rethinking Orphanages for the 21st Century," 295.

60. The evidence about the effects of family preservation programs on children do not permit a clear judgment as to their benefits and costs. See Peter H. Rossi, "Assessing Family Preservation Programs," *Children and Youth Services Review* 14 (1992): 77–92.

61. For an early but close look at the Massachusetts effort, see Kathleen Reich, *Improving Outcomes for Mother and Child: A Review of the Massachusetts Teen Living Program* (master's thesis, John F. Kennedy School of Government, Harvard University, 1996). For an overview of the program, see Kathleen Sylvester, *Seeking Supervision: Second-Chance Homes and the TANF Minor Teen Parent Living Arrangement Rule* (Washington, D.C.: Social Policy Action Network, 1999).

62. Gill, 284–88.

63. Data on the Muncie study supplied by Professor Theodore Caplow of the University of Virginia in a private communication.

64. Scott Walter, "Delinquents in Suburbia," *The American Enterprise* (June 2001), 22.

65. John Braithwaite, "Shame and Modernity," *British Journal of Criminology* 33 (1993): 1–18; Braithwaite, "Shame and Criminal Justice," *Canadian Journal of Criminology* 42 (2000): 281–300; Braithwaite, "Restorative Justice," in *Crime and Justice*, ed. Michael Tonry (Chicago: University of Chicago Press, 1999).

66. Larry Hugick, "Taking Credit Where It Is Due," *Public Perspective* (Oct./Nov. 1999): 10.

67. Hendrik Hartog, *Man & Wife in America: A History* (Cambridge: Harvard University Press, 2000), 311.

68. Arland Thornton, William G. Axinn, and Daniel H. Hill, "Reciprocal Effects of Religiosity, Cohabitation, and Marriage," *American Journal of Sociology*, 98 (1992): 628–51. This is a longitudinal study of white children growing up in the Detroit metropolitan area.

69. Steven Ozment, *Ancestors: The Loving Family in Old Europe* (Cambridge, Mass.: Harvard University Press, 2001), 111–2.

70. James Q. Wilson, *The Moral Sense* (New York: Free Press, 1993).

Index